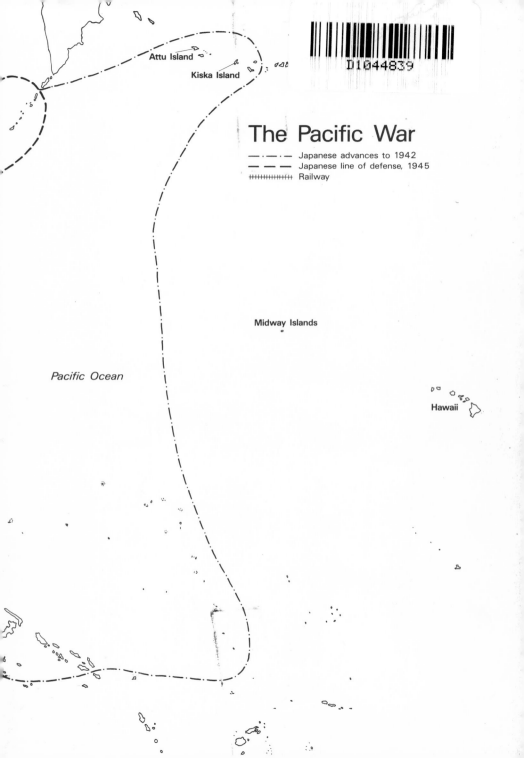

Attu Island

Kiska Island

The Pacific War

—·—·— Japanese advances to 1942
— — — Japanese line of defense, 1945
++++++++++++ Railway

Midway Islands

Pacific Ocean

Hawaii

THUNDER GODS

Hatsuho Naito

KODANSHA INTERNATIONAL
Tokyo and New York

THUNDER GODS

GODS

The Kamikaze Pilots Tell Their Story

FRONT Zero fighter diving toward the escort carrier USS *Sangamon* at Kerama, off Okinawa, May 4, 1945. The plane missed by about 25 feet. (U.S. Navy)

PAGE 1 Kadena Air Base, Okinawa, April 1945. One of the Ohka planes found by American forces after the fall of Okinawa. (U.S. Navy)

PAGES 2 & 3 Yontan Airfield (*left*), Okinawa, April 1945. Yontan fell to the U.S. on the first day of the invasion. Note the ships offshore. (U.S. Navy)

PAGES 4 & 5 The aircraft carrier USS *Enterprise* after being hit by a Zero fighter off Okinawa, May 13, 1945. (U.S. National Archives)

Thunder Gods was originally published in 1982 by Bungei Shunju under the title *Ohka hijo no tokko heiki.*

Distributed in the United States by Kodansha International/USA Ltd., 114 Fifth Avenue, New York, New York 10011. Published by Kodansha International Ltd., 2-2, Otowa 1-chome, Bunkyo-ku, Tokyo 112 and Kodansha International/USA Ltd., 114 Fifth Avenue, New York, New York 10011. Copyright © 1989 Kodansha International Ltd. All rights reserved. Printed in U.S.A.

Library of Congress Cataloging-in-Publication Data

Naitō, Hatsuho, 1921–
    Thunder gods.

    Translation of: Ōka.
    _1. World War, 1939–1945—Naval operations, Japanese.
2. Ōka (Airplane) 3. Kamikaze airplanes. I. Title.
D777 .N3413 1989   490.54′5952   88-81848
ISBN 0-87011-909-5 (U.S.)
ISBN 4-7700-1409-0 (in Japan)

First edition, 1989

Foreword

I read with growing fascination Hatsuho Naito's account of the kamikaze pilots who operated during the final stages of World War II in the Pacific. I was in the area when these first suicide planes began to strike our slow-moving ships, and know from battle reports the devastation they wreaked. Had the attacks come a year sooner or in greater numbers they might have played a decisive role in the war.

The background to the kamikaze concept of win-or-lose effort is well developed and one can sense the mixture of dread and exhilaration with which the young Japanese pilots approached this incredible assignment.

American military men who suffered the brunt of the kamikaze effort will be interested in what Naito has to say, because his careful research and unimpassioned writing makes many points clear. It was a unique approach to warfare and deserves an explanation, which he has given.

But one does not have to have been an American military man receiving the dreaded kamikaze attacks to appreciate the real contribution of this book. It explains how ordinary young Japanese, many of them farm boys, could be persuaded to accept missions that were openly admitted to be suicidal; the stories of their insane bravery are awesome.

Gripping is the account of the lowly young officer who spearheaded the kamikaze effort and who, at the moment of Japanese surrender, climbed into a small plane, bade his friends farewell and set out for a suicidal end to his life. Years later he turned up alive, cadging small gifts of money from his fellow survivors, and then disappeared once more, never to be heard from again.

Thunder Gods is a timely reminder of the humanity that exists within the inhumanity of war.

—James Michener

7

Key Military Bases in
the Ohka Program

HOKKAIDO

● Chitose

● Muroran

Tsugaru Strait

Kodomari ●
● Misawa
Aomori

TOHOKU

JAPAN

Japan Sea

Noto Peninsula

KANTO
● Konoike

● Komatsu
Tokyo

CHUBU
Atsugi ● ● Kisarazu
Yokosuka
● *Boso Peninsula*
● Nagoya
Tateyama

KINKI
Izu Peninsula

Kobe
● ● Osaka

CHUGOKU

Kikaigashima

Hiroshima ●
Kure ●
Koniya ● *Amami
Oshima*

Shimonoseki **SHIKOKU**
Kii Peninsula

Tokunoshima

*Amami
Islands*

Fukuoka ● Usa ●
Oita ●

Pacific Ocean

Sasebo ●
Kumamoto ●
Okinawa

Nagasaki ●
Kadena ● ●
Shuri

Kunisaki Peninsula

KYUSHU
● Tomitaka (Hyuga City)
Kerama Archipelago
Minami Daitojima

● Miyazaki

Kagoshima ● Kazanopara (Kasanohara)

Kanoya ●
Cape Toi
**Ryukyu (Okinawan)
Islands**

Satsuma Peninsula
Osumi Peninsula
Cape Sata

Tanegashima
Miyakojima

Yakushima
Ishigakijima

KEY OFFICERS WHO PROMOTED KAMIKAZE ATTACKS

Admiral Soemu Toyoda, commander-in-chief of the Combined Fleet.

Admiral Koshiro Oikawa, chief of the Naval General Staff.

Vice-Admiral Takijiro Onishi, zealous promoter of the kamikaze attacks; he also directed the first kamikaze attacks using fighter-bombers laden with 250-kilogram bombs in the Philippines.

Vice-Admiral Matome Ugaki, commander-in-chief of the Fifth Naval Aviation Fleet, who directed the kamikaze attacks against U.S. forces in Okinawa and carried out a suicide attack himself after the Emperor's declaration of surrender.

Vice-Admiral Ryunosuke Kusaka, the commander-in-chief of the Fifth Naval Aviation Fleet at the end of the war.

TECHNICAL OFFICERS INVOLVED IN DEVELOPING THE OHKA

Vice-Admiral Misao Wada, chief of the Naval Aeronautical Research Laboratory.

Technician Commander Masao Yamana, manager of the Design Division attached to the Aeroplane Section of the Naval Aeronautical Research Laboratory.

Lieutenant-Commander Iwao Nazuka, the senior officer in charge of producing the Ohka.

Technician Lieutenant-Commander Tadanao Miki, the chief designer of the Ohka under the supervision of Masao Yamana.

Flight Warrant Officer Kazutoshi Nagano, the test pilot for the Ohka.

Special Service Sub-Lieutenant Shoichi Ota, the man who dreamed up the manned bomb.

KEY MEMBERS OF THE THUNDER GODS CORPS

Captain Motoharu Okamura, the zealous promoter of the kamikaze attacks who became the commander of the Thunder Gods Corps.

Commander Shusei Igarashi, the first vice-commander of the Thunder Gods Corps.

Commander Kunihiro Iwaki, wing commander of the Thunder Gods; he was later appointed vice-commander, successor of Shusei Igarashi.

Lieutenant-Commander Goro Nonaka, leader of the 711th Betty Squadron attached to the Thunder Gods Corps; he was annihilated in the first Thunder Gods attack.

Lieutenant-Commander Jiro Adachi, leader of the 708th Betty Squadron attached to the Thunder Gods Corps.

Lieutenant Kiyoshi Yagita, division leader of the 708th Betty Squadron.

Lieutenant Tsutomu Kariya, division leader of an Ohka squadron, who died in the first training flight.

Lieutenant Akira Hirano, division leader of the Ohka squadron which was formed from the Tornado Corps.

Lieutenant Kentaro Mitsuhashi, division leader of an Ohka squadron, he died in the first Thunder Gods attack, with Nonaka's Betty Squadron.

Lieutenant Fujio Hayashi, division leader of an Ohka squadron.

Lieutenant Morimasa Yunokawa, division leader of an Ohka squadron.

Lieutenant Hiroshi Shinjo, division leader of an Ohka squadron.

Reserve Sub-Lieutenant Hachiro Hosokawa, senior reserve officer in an Ohka squadron.

Reserve Sub-Lieutenant Saburo Dohi, the only Ohka pilot to actually sink an American warship.

Reserve Sub-Lieutenant Kanae Okamoto, the Ohka pilot who commanded the last Thunder Gods attack by fighter-bombers laden with 500-kilogram bombs, from Kikaigashima Island.

Higher Flight Petty Officer Motoji Ichikawa, one of the ringleaders in the incident at the Konoike Air Base.

Higher Flight Petty Officer Bansaku Tamura, the best friend of Motoji Ichikawa; he was assigned to the Thunder Gods Corps as a training officer.

Higher Flight Petty Officer Masazo Okubo, an Ohka pilot; he tested the flying ability of fighter-bombers laden with 500-kilogram bombs.

Higher Flight Petty Officer Keisuke Yamamura, the Ohka pilot who returned alive three times: He survived the war.

Flight Petty Officer First Class Manabu Yamaguchi, court-martialed for taking part in the incident at Konoike Air Base.

CHRONOLOGY

1941

December

Japan attacks Pearl Harbor; Japanese land in Thailand, Malaya; take Hong Kong; begin attack on Philippines. U.S., Great Britain, and the Netherlands declare war on Japan

1942

January

Japanese invade Netherlands East Indies; continue invasion of Pacific areas

February

Singapore surrenders

April

U.S. forces in Philippines surrender. U.S. air raid on Tokyo

May

Battle of the Coral Sea

June

Battle of Midway Island

August 7

U.S. Marines land on Guadalcanal

1943

March

Battle of Bismarck Sea breaks Japanese power in Southwest Pacific

1944

Spring

Japanese working on production of body-crash weapons

June

Germans begin using V-1's in Europe

June 19

Captain Okamura asks authorization for aerial special attacks

June 27

Captain Okamura talks to Vice-Admiral Onishi about suicide attacks

July 18

Saipan falls to Allies

End of Tojo cabinet

July 20

American forces land on Guam

July 26

Operation Shogo announced

August 5

Japanese Supreme War Leadership Council tries to improve worsening situation

August 5

Plan for Ohka (manned bomb) plane presented to Naval General Staff

August 16

Order to begin trial production of Ohka planes; Aeronautical Research Laboratory briefed

Mid-August

Call for volunteers for suicide missions

Late August

Ohka model completed

Early September

First two Ohka planes off assembly line; Ohka goes into full production

Allies begin advance on the Philippines

September 15

Captain Okamura named to set up Ohka group

October 1

Ohka Special Attack Corps officially organized

October 5

Vice Admiral Onishi asks to use bomb-bearing fighter planes in suicide missions

October 12–14
America attacks Taiwan
October 17
Vice-Admiral Onishi arrives in Philippines at his new command
October 18
Americans begin invasion of Leyte
October 19
Vice-Admiral Onishi announces Special Attack (suicide) program
October 21
First special attack sortie
October 21–22
Battle of Leyte Gulf
October 23
Test of unmanned Ohka
October 31
Test of manned Ohka

November 1
First B-29s over Tokyo
November 8
Organization of Thunder Gods Corps
November 13
Fatal accident on the first day of pilot training
November 19
Naval General Staff agrees to send more planes to Philippines
November 19–22
Further test of Ohka plane
November 24
B-29s' first bombing attack on Tokyo
November 24
Ohkas to be shipped to Philippines and Taiwan
November 25
Thunder Gods Corps divided, ready to move to Philippines
November 29
Shinano, with Ohkas aboard, sunk by U.S.

December 1
Remaining Ohkas shipped to port en route to Philippines and Taiwan
December 1
Admiral Toyoda briefs Captain Okamura—says December 23 planned for Thunder Gods' Ohka attack in Leyte Gulf

December 6
Ohka maintenance group sent to Clark Field, Philippines
December 10
Thunder Gods' attack postponed to January 10
December 15
151 Ohka planes completed
December 19
Thunder Gods and T-Attack Corps merged
December 19
Unryu, with Ohka for Philippines, sunk
December 28
Decision to airlift some Ohkas to Philippines

1945

January 3, 4
American planes raid Taiwan and Okinawan Islands
January 6
American warships enter Lingayen Gulf in Philippines
January 8
American forces begin landing on Luzon
January 9
Riot by Thunder Gods at Konoike Air Base
January 10
Japanese First Naval Aviation Fleet leaves Philippines
January 20
Japanese Army and Navy begin first joint operation
January 20–25
Contingent of Thunder Gods sent to Kyushu
March 1
Americans begin Okinawa invasion
March 21
First Thunder Gods mission, led by Lieutenant-Commander Nonaka, a failure
March 23–31
U.S. air raids and naval bombardment of Okinawa. Thunder Gods reorganized—some to fly fighter-bomber suicide planes

March 26
Americans begin landing on island south of Okinawa

March 26
Japanese order for Operation Heaven No. 1

March 28, 29
Americans hit bases on southern Kyushu

Late March
Design work on Ohka Type-22 completed; also plans for Type-43B, catapult-launched plane

April 1
Thunder Gods' raid a failure; Americans begin landing in Okinawa

April 2, 3
Thunder Gods attack American fleet at Okinawa

April 3
Japanese begin series of ten Kikusui operations

April 4
Admiral Toyoda announces Japanese counterattack on Okinawa

April 5
Cabinet falls; Suzuki becomes prime minister

April 7
Americans sink Japanese battleship *Yamato*

April 8
Military Headquarters announces exaggerated U.S. losses

April 6–17
Japanese attacks sink several ships

April 17
Americans ask for aid against kamikaze attacks by Thunder Gods and special attack planes

April 17
U.S. B-29 squadron ordered to support invasion of Okinawa and bomb Japanese air bases

April 17
Some Japanese planes of Tenth Naval Aviation Fleet reassigned to Operation Ketsugo

April 18
Some redeployment of Tenth Naval Air Fleet; general redeployment and reassignment of Japanese naval air forces

April 26
Design of Type-43B Ohka completed

May 1
Newspapers carry story of unconditional surrender of Germany; Americans admit Japanese are using manned bombs

May 4
Thunder Gods again reorganized

May 8
V-E Day: End of war in Europe

May 12
Heaven Air Unit formed of remaining Thunder Gods planes

May 19
Vice-Admiral Onishi appointed vice-commander of Naval General Staff

May 28
Naval Ministry makes Thunder Gods' activities known

June 8
Heavy American air raids

June 11
Thunder Gods' final raid on Okinawa

June 12
Naval General Staff plans final defense of Japan—Operation Ketsugo

June 23
End of battle for Okinawa—Japanese commanders commit harakiri

June 26
Test of Ohka Type-22 catapult plane, death of test pilot

June 29
Model of Kikki jet plane completed

July 20
Unsuccessful tests on Ohka Type-22

July 27
Radio San Francisco announces Potsdam Declaration demanding unconditional surrender

July 28
Massive American air raids

August 5
Naval General Staff revises plans for Type-43B catapult sites

13

August 6
Atomic bomb dropped on Hiroshima
August 8
USSR declares war on Japan
August 9
Soviets cross into Manchuria
August 9
Atomic bomb dropped on Nagasaki
August 11
Naval General Staff orders attacks on American ships off Honshu and Okinawa
August 11
Radio San Francisco announces that Japan may not accept conditions for surrender
August 14
Vice-Admiral Ugaki gets orders to cease hostilites

August 14
Emperor decides to end war
August 15
Emperor's broadcast announcing end of war; Suzuki cabinet resigns.
Vice-Admiral Ugaki and his men attempt suicide attack
August 16
Vice-Admiral Onishi commits harakiri
August 18
Special Service Sub-Lieutenant Ota steals plane and flies away
August 21
Thunder Gods Corps disbanded; remaining members go home
September 2
Japanese sign surrender terms

Preface

by Hachiro Hosokawa

I was one of the members of Japan's World War II Thunder Gods Corps, the corps organized by the Japanese Imperial Navy for the specific purpose of carrying out aerial manned bomb attack missions against the American and Allied forces in 1944.

Of the 21 reserve officers of the original "special attack" unit, I am the only one who survived. The rest died either in the special attack weapons called Ohka (Exploding Cherry Blossoms) or in fighter bombers that were used as *kamikaze* planes. I survived partly because in addition to being a "kamikaze pilot" I served concurrently as a leader of a covering fighter squadron.

Following the end of the war, surviving members of the Thunder Gods Corps formed the Association of Former Thunder Gods Corps Members in memory of our fallen comrades. I am the permanent manager of this Thunder Gods association.

Hatsuho Naito, the author of this book, served in the Imperial Navy's Aeronautical Research Laboratory as technician lieutenant and was involved in the wind tunnel testing of the Ohka planes (which the American forces referred to as "baka bombs" or "crazy bombs").

In 1977 Naito contacted the Thunder Gods Association, informed them that he would like to compile an accurate record of the Thunder Gods Corps, and asked for our cooperation. The members of the association enthusiastically agreed to cooperate, despite the personal nature of the story and the fact that there were many conflicting views among the people involved.

Naito subsequently spent four years researching and writing the story of the founding and operation of the Thunder Gods Corps. His book was called *Ohka: The Merciless Special Attack Weapon*. It was published by Bungei Shunju, one of Japan's leading publishers. The Association of Former Thunder Gods Corps Members regards the book as the only accurate record of the corps and the most creditable of all the existing publications related to the Thunder Gods.

In 1965 I went to Washington, D.C., to visit the Smithsonian Institution, where an Ohka plane is on permanent display. As I stood before the exhibit my heart swelled with emotion.

I also visited Arlington National Cemetery to see the grave of former president John F. Kennedy. While there I happened to witness a funeral service, at which an honor guard fired the traditional mourning shots as the coffin, draped with the American flag, was lowered into the ground. I was horror-struck. I felt as if I had suddenly been transported back in time to the years of World War II. The scene was the very picture of the naval funeral services that were an everyday part of life in Japan during the last years of the fighting. The only difference was the flag.

In Japan, the defeated nation, the very memory of the war was falling into oblivion by 1965. In contrast, the United States, the victor, was fighting another war, leaving numerous soldiers dead and the bereaved in deep sorrow.

For a while, I could not move.

In war, whether you win or lose, the ordinary people on both sides suffer very much the same pain and anguish. Even knowing this, the human race continues to repeat the absurdity of war, over and over again.

When Japan was entangled in World War II, all the young people, myself included, were driven by the fear that if we did not do our best, if we did not make whatever sacrifice was necessary, our nation and our people would be destroyed forever. We eagerly volunteered to become pilots, knowing that our chances of survival were almost nonexistent. As the war situation deteriorated and death appeared inevitable under any circumstances, many of us just as eagerly volunteered to become Ohka pilots.

I do not believe this so-called suicide mentality is unique to the Japanese. The spirit of self-sacrifice exists in all countries among all people, particularly among the young, who are innocent and free of cynicism when they are in a wartime life-or-death situation. World history, in fact, is filled with similar examples.

What made the Thunder Gods Corps unique was that it was specifically organized as a one-way attack force, that the operation was continuous, and that the members of the corps literally lived in the face of death for a long period of time. At the same time, I must stress emphatically that even though members of the Thunder Gods Corps volunteered to give their lives for their country, they were not suicidal or unconcerned about their own lives.

In 1947 I received a call from Jiro Adachi, the former wing commander of the Thunder Gods Corps, who was then in charge of postwar management at the Demobilization Bureau. He said that personnel from General Douglas MacArthur's Supreme Commander for the Allied Powers (SCAP) headquarters in Tokyo wanted to interview surviving members of the Thunder Gods Corps, and asked me to participate in the interviews.

I went to the Imperial Hotel, which at that time was being used as a billet for ranking American military officers, and was introduced to Commander Hume, who was chief surgeon of the U.S. forces in Japan. The interpreter was Shiho Sakanishi, a member of the House of Councillors' Foreign Affairs Bureau.

Dr. Hume's questions focused on the motivation and sentiment involved in my volunteering for the Thunder Gods Corps, the organization of the corps and our training methods, and the emotional changes that occurred among the volunteers during the nearly one-year period in which we were working feverishly to prepare for our own deaths.

I told Dr. Hume that I had tried not to think about death, that it had been beyond my understanding.

Today I still recall with pride my young, innocent days when I was willing to sacrifice my life for my country and my people. Yet I have never wished that my children or grandchildren would follow the same path. I feel, in the utmost reaches of my heart, that we must make Japan a peaceful nation in which no one will ever again have to suffer the experience of my generation.

In this respect, Hatsuho Naito's book is not only a record of the Thunder Gods Corps, it is a symbol of the pain and sorrow of the people of a defeated nation.

This book was translated into English on the advice of an old American friend, William K. Nichoson, himself an ex-wartime pilot, in the hope that it would be read by many people in different parts of the world. I am very pleased to see this English-language edition of *Ohka*, and I add my heartfelt hope that the painful experience of the Thunder Gods will never be relived by anyone on earth.

Introduction

by Boye De Mente

The prewar beliefs and behavior that were typical of the Japanese up to and during World War II have by now undergone fundamental changes, but for anyone interested in Japan there are still important lessons to be learned from a review of the extent to which the Japanese went in the pursuit of their wartime goals. They fought the Pacific War with a ferocity and tenacity that shocked the world, finally resorting to the startling phenomenon of suicide attacks by pilots, submariners, and others.

When the tide of the war began to turn against the Japanese as early as 1943, ultranationalistic elements in the army and navy began to clamor for the use of "special attack" units to help stem the inexorable advance of the American and Allied forces. The term *special attack* was a typically Japanese euphemism for suicide missions. By 1943 it had become clear to many of Japan's military leaders—and especially to many lower-ranking officers who were in the front lines of battle—that not only was it *possible* for Japan to lose the war, but that the country was doomed to suffer the first defeat in its history unless some drastic measures were taken.

On an individual basis, a growing number of Japanese fighter pilots and other servicemen in the thick of battle began to resort to *kesshi* or "dare-to-die" tactics—meaning they would deliberately mount suicide attacks against enemy planes or ships in order to cause the maximum amount of damage possible.

The soon-to-be-famous term *Tokkotai* (Special Attack Corps) or suicide attack corps, was officially used as early as December 18, 1941, just days after the attack on Pearl Harbor. But well before the surprise attack on Pearl Harbor, there was open discussion of the principle that all Japanese should be prepared to die fighting for the Emperor and the Empire.

On January 3, 1941, General Hideki Tojo, then the minister of the army, ordered that an official code of ethics be published and distributed to every member of the armed forces. This code, known as *Senjin Kun* or *Ethics in Battle*, said: "A sublime sense of self-sacrifice must guide you throughout life and death. Do not think of death as you use up every ounce of your strength to fulfill your duties. Make it your joy to use every last bit of your physical and spiritual strength in what you do. Do not fear to die for the cause of everlasting justice. Do not stay alive in dishonor. Do not die in such a way as to leave a bad name behind you!"

Fighting to the death regardless of the odds or chances of success was a deeply embedded tradition in Japan. In fact, the greater the likelihood of defeat, the more certain it was that the Japanese would fight to the death in battle or kill themselves following defeat. To begin to understand the mentality that led Japan to make suicide attacks an official part of its war effort, one must know a great deal about her past.

Until 1868 Japan was a tightly knit, tightly closed feudal kingdom ruled by a military dictator (*shogun*), and an elite class of clan lords and professional, hereditary, sword-carrying warriors (*samurai*). The shogun and the clan lords (*daimyo*) had absolute power over the common people, who were permitted neither family names nor the right to travel.

This system had existed since the year A.D. 1192, when Minamoto Yoritomo, leader of the famous Genji clan, which had defeated the other clans in a war for military supremacy, prevailed upon the Emperor to appoint him *shogun* (generalissimo) and recognize his right to administer the affairs of the country in the name of the emperor. The professional warriors maintained by each of the clans and the shogun at that time were already an elite hereditary class, and soon came to be known as *samurai* which translates more or less as "guards."

The code of the samurai was a mixture of Shintoism, Buddhism, and Confucianism. Shintoism taught the warriors that they were descendants of divine beings and that upon death they, too, would become "gods." From Buddhism they learned to accept the transitory, fragile nature of life and to view death as crossing into another plane of existence. From Confucianism came the concept of absolute loyalty to their lord.

With the fall of the last shogunate dynasty in 1868 and the restoration of imperial authority for virtually the first time in 676 years, Shinto, the native religion on which the divinity of the imperial house was based, became the state religion. The people were taught to believe that the Emperor was a living god, and to treat him accordingly.

Yasukuni Shrine on Kudan Hill in Tokyo was established in 1868 as "The Patriots' Shrine" or "The Shrine of the Righteous Souls," where the souls of those killed in war were enshrined. It was considered the guardian shrine of the country, and next to the Emperor himself in importance.

Shortly after the Meiji Emperor's administration took over the country in 1868, a constitutional government was formed, with power invested in a prime minister, his cabinet, a House of Councillors, and a House of Representatives. Despite these intimations of democracy, but in keeping with deeply entrenched tradition, the military, primarily the army, began asserting itself, and by the early 1930's had total control of the government. General Hideki Tojo, who became prime minister in 1941, was a latter-day shogun. His highest henchmen were the new daimyo, and military officers were samurai—in khaki instead of kimono.

From early childhood, the Japanese were conditioned to believe that the Emperor was divine, and the spiritual head of the nation. They were also taught to accept the will of the Emperor (in reality, that of the ruling cliques) as both divine and absolute. Like the military fanatics of many countries, the ultranationalists among the Japanese believed they had a spiritual mandate to conquer and Japanize the rest of the world. Hence their wars against China, Russia, Southeast Asia, and eventually the United States were thought of as divine wars.

Very much like the Muslims of Iran in the 1970's and 1980's, Japanese servicemen were taught to believe that if they died in battle, especially if they died heroically, they would instantly become "gods", and join the guardian spirits of the nation at Yasukuni Shrine on Kudan Hill.

All during Japan's long feudal age (which actually did not end until 1945), to fail in battle or to be captured was not acceptable. In clan wars it was common for the losing side to be slaughtered to the last man— and often the women and children of the losing side as well. Enemies captured alive were routinely killed in painful and gruesome ways.

Suicide became the accepted way of expiating the disgrace of failure, and death by one's own hand or the hand of a trusted friend was eminently preferable to the double disgrace of being captured and made to suffer an ignoble death at the hands of a hated enemy.

As the 1941–45 war against the United States and its allies continued, the Japanese were constantly told that their primary purpose in life and the greatest glory they could achieve was to give their lives for the Emperor. They were also harangued with the warning that they should not allow themselves to be captured—that men would be tortured and killed, and women would be raped and then dispatched.

Eventually an edict was issued actually forbidding servicemen to allow themselves to be captured, making it, ironically enough, an offense punishable by death.

Nationalistic fever was also kept at a high pitch by the singing of the national anthem and popular war songs, and the repetitive recitation of the Imperial Rescript. Examples of heroic suicide exploits by servicemen during the preceding wars against China and Russia were held up as examples to be emulated.

The movement to make suicide attacks against the advancing American and Allied forces an official part of the country's military strategy was initiated by lower-ranking army and navy officers, mostly lieutenants and captains, some of whom were only in their early twenties.

One high-ranking advocate of suicide attacks was Rear Admiral Kameto Kuroshima, who asked the War Preparation Examination Conference in July 1943 to sanction the use of volunteer suicide attacks. He called his plan "Invincible War Preparation." At first the navy and army high commands refused to consider such a drastic step. They were proud and spirited men who still believed that they could defeat the Allied forces in regular combat. With the fall of Saipan in July of 1944, however, it became obvious even to the most obstinate nationalist that the vaunted Japanese spirit was no match for the growing superiority of the Allied forces.

As early as March 1944, Prime Minister Tojo himself ordered the Army Air Corps to begin making preparations for special suicide missions. The first officially planned suicide attack against an American ship occurred on May 27, 1944, when a plane crash-dived into the *Subchaser 699* off the coast of West New Guinea. In late June, Captain

Motoharu Okamura, a famous fighter pilot, then the commanding officer of the 341st Air Corps, asked for permission to lead "special attacks" against the enemy.

Captain Eichiro Jo, a highly respected officer who had served at the Japanese Embassy in Washington and as aide-de-camp to the Emperor, had often requested permission to set up a special suicide squadron using ordinary fighter planes, and later, specially built suicide planes.

As the American and Allied planes and ships battled their way closer and closer to the home islands of Japan, other advocates of using "sure-hit, sure-death" tactics against the American and Allied forces became more and more insistent. In effect, the Imperial Headquarters had already sanctioned suicide missions, called *tan* or "sincerity-loyalty" missions, by assigning pilots to attack targets that were well beyond their round-trip flying range. *Jibaku*, or "self-crashing" by pilots was becoming more common.

Little by little, the high commands of the army and navy gave in, and issued orders that preparations for all-out suicide attacks against the advancing Allied forces begin. Army leaders met on July 7, 1944, and ordered that a study be made on planes designed specifically for suicide missions.

By this time, the navy already had nearly a dozen unofficial "special (suicide) weapons" projects under way, including manned torpedoes and flying bombs. The human torpedoes were simplified midget submarines, designed in the early spring of 1943 by three naval officers who were still in their early twenties. They called the piloted torpedo *Kaiten* or "Heaven Shifter," the connotation being that with one single blow the torpedo could reverse an untenable situation. Other "sure-hit, sure-death" weapons in various stages of design or production were exploding boats and a self-propelled mine that was to be guided to its final destination by a human pilot.

A sub-lieutenant named Shohichi Ota, assigned to the 1081st Flying Corps, had worked out an idea for a rocket-propelled manned bomb called Ohka (Exploding Cherry Blossom) that would crash into a target at some 600 miles an hour, with devastating effect.

As the situation worsened for Japanese troops on the various islands of the Pacific, both servicemen and civilians were ordered to fight to the death, and to kill themselves if they were wounded and unable to fight. The *banzai* (literally "10,000 years"—a word expressing group resolution) charge by outnumbered and outfought Japanese troops became a dreadful commonplace. Mass suicides by civilians astounded the Americans. They did not know what to think of such an enemy. Nothing in their history, nothing in their experience, had prepared them to understand such behavior.

By 1944, the word *kamikaze*, literally divine wind, which originally referred to the winds that drove the Mongol hordes back from their intended invasion of Japan in the thirteenth century, became associated with the assumed divine protection of Japan. During the Pacific War, as sacrifice was increasingly demanded of Japanese forces, *kamikaze* came to be a general word referring to all pilots (and to a lesser extent submarine navigators) who crash-dived their planes into the enemy whether ordered to or not. All Japanese army flying corps pilots were routinely receiving instruction on how to ram attacking bombers. On August 20, 1944, during a bombing raid on the Yawata Iron and Steel Works by a squadron of B-29 bombers, two of the American planes were brought down by one Japanese suicide pilot. He rammed one plane, and the resulting explosion brought down the second plane.

Following the first official kamikaze attack against American ships on May 27, 1944, there was a gap of nearly five months while the Japanese Army and Navy worked feverishly to bring a whole series of special attack weapons on line to stop the advancing Allied forces. One of these was the Ohka manned bomb.

The next official suicide attack by fighter planes took place on October 13, and was followed by almost daily attacks for the rest of the month. On October 28, Radio Tokyo announced that Japan had discovered a secret weapon that guaranteed the defeat of the United States. At first, American military authorities in the Pacific tried to keep the "special attacks" secret. They were afraid the information would have a demoralizing effect on both the American armed forces and the American public. There was no effective defense against suicide attacks—kamikaze planes or manned rocket bombs. The death and destruction they were to rain upon the Allied fleets was considerable. In November there was a total of 9 Ohka attacks against American and Allied ships. In December there were 11. In January 1945, there were 12.

In mid-January 1945, the chiefs of the Japanese army and navy drew up a plan and submitted it to the Emperor, asking him to approve an order that would require *all* of the armed forces of the country to use suicide tactics. The Emperor was shocked, and began making discreet inquiries among his own staff about ending the war.

Japan's military leaders knew there was no way they could win the war. At this point their primary purpose was to inflict such heavy damage on the American forces that the U.S. would stop the war before invading the home islands, and would not insist on an unconditional surrender. Also by this time, the number of volunteers for suicide missions had dropped off dramatically, so much so that they had to be drafted. The remaining pilots knew the war was lost, and began wondering why they should die for nothing. There was at least one instance of a pilot, forced to take off on a suicide mission, strafing his own command post in a parting gesture of anger and frustration.

In February 1945 there were only two suicide missions against the American forces. The U.S. began its long-expected campaign to take Okinawa on March 26. There were six suicide missions before the end of the month, and in April 21 waves of suicide planes and Ohkas were launched against the invading forces. The kamikaze planes and Ohkas managed to sink 15 American ships, and damage 59 others during the Okinawa campaign. A total of 12,300 American servicemen were killed and another 36,400 were wounded in the suicide attacks.

Massive suicide assaults by both fighter planes and the Ohkas continued, with 16 in May. Then they dropped off dramatically as the Japanese began running out of both planes and men to pilot them. There were only nine kamikaze attacks in June; three in July and two in August—the last one on August 13, just two days before Emperor Hirohito announced Japan's surrender. The last American ship to be sunk by a kamikaze pilot went down on July 29.

Altogether, 3,913 Japanese kamikaze pilots died in the "special attack" missions against U.S. and Allied forces during the war. Of these, 2,525 were navy men, most of whom were between the ages of 18 and 20. Some of them were 17. The remaining 1,388 were army pilots, most of them aged between 18 and 24. There are no accurate records of how many Japanese servicemen died in individual, spontaneous suicide attacks during the war, but the number was apparently significant.

Japanese servicemen who died in official suicide attacks were given posthumous promotions, from two to four grades, depending on their former rank and unit of service.

The most coordinated and ambitious of Japan's special suicide attack forces was the one involving the specially made Ohka or "Exploding Cherry Blossom" manned rocket bombs—the brainchild of Sub-Lieutenant Ota. By the end of 1944 there were many, especially in the navy, who pinned their final hopes, if not for victory then at least for the survival of Japan as a nation, on the success of the tiny, fragile Ohka craft and the indomitable spirit of their pilots, who came to be known as "Thunder Gods."

The story of the Thunder Gods, told here by men who helped set up and administer the program, reveals much about Japan—much that is still applicable today in any attempt to understand the country and its people.

Chapter 1

O n that August day of 1944, the very runway seemed to quiver in the heat waves rising from the airfield on the plains of Aonogahara near the center of the Harima Plateau. The water in a pond adjoining the airfield was still and as smooth as glass. In contrast, the Kako River, flowing along the eastern flank of the plains, sparkled in the blistering sun as it rushed across the plateau on its way to the Inland Sea. The sky, a brilliant blue, was broken only here and there by puffs of cumulus clouds drifting in the same direction, and only lately disturbed by planes returning as if for an afternoon siesta.

The Himeji Naval Flying Corps was in training at Aonogahara. Flights had ended early, while the sun was still overhead, but it was fuel shortage, not heat, that brought the flyers and their instructors home early. Nor were they alone, for shortage of fuel had been severely limiting all Japanese military aviation training programs for some time. On the field, the roar of the engines of the Type-97 and the Tenzan carrier attack bombers, nicknamed Kate and Jill by the Americans, had ceased, and the parked aircraft looked lonely and fragile.

"Well, another day over," sighed Higher Flight Petty Officer Motoji Ichikawa as he removed his heavy flying suit.

One of the leaders of the petty officers' flight instructor group, Ichikawa was well aware of the urgency of training new aircrew members. Nevertheless, he was unhappy with his own current assignment, so far from the front lines. He knew no one equalled his combat experience, even among the officer corps, but this did not lessen his feelings of dissatisfaction with being out of the real action of the war. He missed the intense excitement of the great battle Japan was fighting. He had never known fear, even during his closest encounters with death in aerial combat over the Coral Sea.

That great sea battle of May 1942 had been fought exclusively by the air forces on both sides. Not only had it been a high point in the career of Higher Flight Petty Officer Ichikawa, but it marked the high point of the great Japanese push through the Pacific. In the two years that followed, the tide of the war had turned against Japan. Through 1943 and 1944, the American forces had advanced island by island toward the Japanese home islands. On the eighteenth of July, news came that every man on the island of Saipan, noncombatants as well as combatants, had died in the American onslaught on the island. A few days later, the Tojo cabinet fell and was replaced by a coalition cabinet with Kuniaki Koiso as both prime minister and minister of the army, and Mitsumasa Yonai as minister of the navy. The new cabinet convened a special Supreme War Leadership Council on August 5, in an effort to improve the rapidly worsening situation. From deep inside China, waves of U.S. B-29 bombers, known as Flying Superfortresses, were raining bombs on the western and southern areas of the island of Kyushu—that is, on Japan itself.

Ichikawa began putting on his civilian clothes, intending to go into the nearby town of Hojo for a few drinks and perhaps a little entertainment. Suddenly the voice of the officer of the day broke through the perpetual static of the barracks' public address system.

"All pilots are restricted to quarters! I repeat, all pilots are restricted to quarters!" the voice crackled.

In carrier-based attack bombers, the pilots, navigators, and radiomen (who also served as gunners) always flew in teams. Pilot Instructor Ichikawa thought it was strange that only pilots were being restricted to the base. He waited for the rest of the announcement.

"All pilots line up in front of headquarters! All pilots line up in front of headquarters!" the OD added.

Still wearing a sweat-stained flying jacket, Ichikawa left the barracks and walked rapidly up the narrow clay road leading to the headquarters building on top of a pine-clad hill. There he joined the other officer pilot instructors, petty-officer pilot instructors, and assistant instructors as they closed ranks, mumbling in perplexed voices about what was going on. The sun's rays were beginning to bend slightly, but it was precisely the time of day when the infamous summer heat of the Inland Sea made it difficult to breathe.

As soon as they were in formation, the wing commander emerged from the headquarters building, mounted the command platform in front of the men, and turned to face them with an unnatural, frozen expression on his face.

Without preamble, he shouted harshly, "All those men who have single parents or are only children, raise your hands!"

A number of arms rose hesitantly into the air.

"You men leave the formation and return to your quarters!" the wing commander barked.

Puzzled, these men left the formation and began walking back along the clay road to the barracks.

"First sons also, break ranks and return to your quarters!" the commander yelled.

Three more men filed out of the group.

The wing commander stared at the men in front of him. "Form a circle in front of me!" he ordered.

After the remaining men had regrouped, the wing commander began to speak in a grave voice.

"The war news is very bad. The enemy is advancing in the Marianas. Our men on the front lines are doing their best, but we are seriously outnumbered. If the present situation continues, the enemy will soon be in the Philippines, Taiwan, and Okinawa. Even the home islands will be in danger of invasion by the enemy forces. We must therefore somehow mount an offensive that will bring excruciating pain and damage to the enemy. We must do this to gain time—to forestall an attack on Japan itself!"

The wing commander stopped for a few seconds, steeled himself, and then continued.

"Without taking extreme measures against the enemy, we will not be able to go on. We must do something that is unique in the annals of military history. Otherwise we will be ground down and destroyed as a nation.

"To achieve this, we have developed a new and very special instrument of certain death. I am not at liberty to give you the details yet, but it is absolutely certain that if you hit even the largest enemy aircraft carrier with this new weapon, it will sink for sure!"

The wing commander again stopped talking. There was a strained look on his face that the men had never seen before.

He began again, slowly, deliberately, "But in order for this kind of special attack to succeed, the weapon has been designed as a one-way trip. There is no way the pilot can return alive."

Ichikawa had been listening intently to the words of the wing commander. Now he felt the blood drain from his face. His legs were suddenly weak. He had been face-to-face with death in combat many times, and knew the smell of it. Now the feeling returned with a rush, but this time it felt cold and clammy.

The wing commander spoke again. "You are absolutely free to decide on an individual basis if you want to volunteer for this drastic measure, but I appeal to the best in you as navy pilots."

The men in the circle were stunned. In the heat of battle, each one of them would have instantly given his life for his country. But this was different. They were being asked to volunteer to die. The men looked at each other, but no one spoke.

"You all have varying circumstances, so please think about your decision very carefully," the wing commander said. Then he added ominously, "But you are prohibited from discussing your situation or your choice with your fellow pilots, or contacting your relatives. You must make your own choice!"

Again the commander stopped for several seconds to let his words sink in. "You all have identification cards," he said. "After you have made your decision, mark the cards with either 'Yes' or 'No.' All officers are to bring their cards to my room and put them in a special box that will be provided for that purpose. All petty officers take your cards to your squad leaders' quarters, where similar boxes will be provided."

The wing commander paused, then said earnestly, "This is not an order, but I appeal to your best instincts as navy men." He then quickly left the podium and walked briskly back into the headquarters building.

The pilots, still in a tight circle, were silent, each one caught up in his own thoughts. Then, still silent, and almost cautiously, the circle began to break up, as each man moved off alone and walked back toward the barracks.

Ichikawa was well aware that navy combat flight crews were basically expendable, and he had long ago become resigned to the idea that he would die in the performance of his duty. But he was acutely aware of the difference between facing death as a risk in combat, and being compelled to embrace it.

"This is like suicide," he said to himself, and then he thought, "No, it is not like suicide, because in suicide there is some measure of free will with respect to how and when! In this case, you are simply sent on a mission to die!"

Ichikawa was totally sincere in his strong desire to get back into a combat unit and join his comrades fighting at the front, but he did not have a death wish. He wanted to live. His first inclination was to write "No" on his ID card, but he knew he could not. He knew he would be condemned as unmilitary, as unmanly, if he were to refuse. And besides, because of the rigid training and discipline within the Imperial Navy, he was not accustomed to making decisions on his own.

As soon as Ichikawa entered his quarters, he was besieged by several of the young assistant instructors who were among those asked to volunteer for the special attack force.

"Sir," one of them said earnestly, "if we simply write 'Yes' on our cards, we may not be among the first ones selected to fly these missions! We want to make sure we are chosen by marking our cards in blood! Do you think that would help?"

Ichikawa understood and appreciated the eagerness of the young men to die for Japan in one glorious explosion that would wreak havoc upon the enemy, but he could not help but be disturbed. "Yes," he said quietly, "that would surely help demonstrate your sincerity." He was not able to work up the highly emotional spirit that consumed these bright young men.

Later, when he was alone, Ichikawa wrote the "Yes" in small characters on his ID card, and dropped it into the box that had been delivered from headquarters.

On that same day at the same hour, from the northernmost Japanese island of Hokkaido, to occupied Taiwan in the distant south, all navy flight instructors and pilots of single-engine aircraft, including fighter planes, reconnaissance planes, carrier-based attack planes and dive bombers, were presented with the same choice—whether to go on record officially as willing to make the supreme sacrifice for Japan.

Most of the pilots were very young—many of them in their teens. But they were the best the Navy had, because the majority of its veteran pilots were already dead—killed in combat against the enemy. The young pilots were, therefore, of inestimable value to Navy and country, and Ichikawa knew that the decision to ask them to sacrifice their young lives had not been made lightly.

What Ichikawa could not know was that he was experiencing the ripple effect of events that had begun far from where he stood, but had for some time been spreading toward him. Some two weeks before the wave reached Ichikawa, it had touched and chilled Technician Lieutenant-Commander Tadanao Miki in the Design Division of the Naval Aeronautical Research Laboratory's Aeroplane Section on the Miura Peninsula.

Many of Japan's primary naval installations were located along the shores of this peninsula, which forms the western coast of Tokyo Bay, and were centered around the great Yokosuka Naval Base. Among these facilities was the Naval Aeronautical Research Laboratory (NARL), made up of the main laboratory at Oppama and a branch laboratory in Kanazawa–Hakkei.

The combined facilities of the Aeronautical Research Laboratory employed some 2,000 researchers and 32,000 workers, and was one of the world's most advanced aerial technology development centers.

The laboratory's mission was to conduct inspections and tests of trial planes built by private firms under the supervision of the Naval Aeronautical Department of the Navy Ministry, and to engage in research and development activities of its own in an ongoing effort to improve the performance of Japan's warplanes.

The Design Division of the Aeroplane Section, under Navy Technician Commander Masao Yamana, was regarded as the core of the laboratory. This division was divided into three groups. Group One was in charge of aircraft developed by private firms. Group Two was in charge of planes developed at the laboratory. Group Three was in charge of what was called "Aircraft of the Future"—planes of advanced design that were expected to play a leading role in air combat in the future. The head of Group Three was Technician Lieutenant-Commander Tadanao Miki.

Miki was highly regarded by his superiors and the Naval General Staff (NGS). Earlier, when he had been asked by the NGS to provide plans for a warplane that was capable of horizontal bombing, nose-dive bombing, as well as serving as a torpedo plane, he and his group produced the very successful land-based Ginga bomber, known to the American forces as "Frances."

Some two weeks prior to the nationwide recruitment of Ichikawa and other volunteer suicide pilots for crash-dive bombing missions, Miki received a call from Vice-Admiral Misao Wada, chief of the laboratory.

"There's a man here who has a plan for a glider-bomber. Could you and your division manager please come up and take a look at it?" Wada said.

Miki hung up the phone, displeased by the call. He was getting tired of so-called new weapons. The laboratory was always receiving requests from naval operation units to improve on already existing planes, but few of the new models already approved were in mass production, because of the growing shortage of materials and a serious deterioration of manufacturing skills.

Development of the advanced carrier fighter plane called Reppu (Sam) that was to replace the famous Zero (Mitsubishi Type-0 Carrier Fighter) had stopped completely because of a problem with the engines. Also, production of the four-engine Renzan (Rita) attack bomber had just been suspended because of lack of construction materials.

Part of the problem at the laboratory was caused by a rush program to produce jet- and rocket-propelled aircraft based on specifications brought in from Germany by a Japanese submarine.

Hardly a day went by when someone from the outside did not appear at the laboratory with plans for some kind of new weapon. There had been a significant increase in the number of plans for different types of winged bombs, most of them inspired by the V-1 winged bombs introduced by Germany in Europe about the time the battle for Saipan started in the Pacific. Because the V-1 could not be guided after it was launched, all of the adaptations brought to the laboratory featured some kind of guiding mechanism.

Miki grimaced as he and his manager made their way to Vice-Admiral Wada's office. It was these guiding mechanisms that had made all of the plans he had seen so far impractical or worthless. Some plans proposed radio guidance systems. One suggested the use of a heat-seeking system, while another proposed the use of a tunnel of light that the bomb would follow. Miki was sure he was going to be subjected to some other harebrained scheme that would probably never materialize.

In Wada's office, a broad-shouldered man wearing a full beard was sitting in front of the boyish-looking chief. He stood up and exchanged name cards with Miki. On his card was printed: *Special Service Sub-Lieutenant (Second Class) Shoichi Ota, Attached to the 1081st Naval Flying Corps.*

"You were talking about a sure-hit bomb. . . ." Wada said to Ota, gesturing for him to continue.

Ota took a rather sloppy brush drawing from his briefcase and handed it to Miki. At first glance it appeared to be a small high-speed aircraft of some kind, but had no propeller and no landing gear. A line drawn from the nose of the plane was labeled "Explosives." A line drawn from the tail of the plane was labeled "Rocket." In one of the upper corners of the sketch was an equally rough drawing of the Mitsubishi Type-1 Attack Bomber (Betty) showing the small, propeller-less plane suspended beneath it, indicating that it was to be dropped from the bomber.

Ota explained that the rocket to be used in the plane was the "rogo-type" propellant in which condensed hydrogen peroxide reacted with hydrated hydrogen, which had been developed by Mitsubishi Heavy Industries and was being tested by the army as the energy source for guided bombs. When the navy learned that the German Comet rocket used the same kind of liquid propellant, it became interested in the rogo-propellant system.

Miki was not impressed. "This man must be a fool," he thought. "Is what he calls a new weapon? He's probably thinking about using the latest guidance system theory, just like everybody else."

"What about the guidance system?" he asked, already sure he knew the answer.

Ota did not reply immediately, and looked a little uncomfortable.

Miki repeated the question, adding, "I mean the device to make sure it hits the target."

Ota nodded, and replied steadily, "A man would be on board."

Miki couldn't believe what he had heard. "What!" he yelled, staring at Ota in disbelief mixed with anger.

Obviously trying not to be intimidated by Miki's loud reaction and angry glare, Ota continued, "It will be carried by a Betty until it is in the vicinity of the target. Then a pilot will enter it from the mother plane. At the proper time, it will be dropped by the mother plane. The pilot will then set the course for impact against the enemy target. There will be just enough propellant in the plane for it to dodge enemy aircraft and smash into the target. So it will be sure-hitting."

Miki was shocked at the suggestion. "Sure-hitting! You idiot! We will not produce such a thing!" he shouted.

Ota's face was red, but he held his ground. "Japan will be pushed further and further into a corner if we don't take some drastic action. The enemy now has command of the air. We can no longer stop the invasion forces of the enemy by conventional means. My plan is to destroy the enemy's aircraft carriers with this system of crash-diving into them, and reverse the situation. It is vital to the survival of our country. We must produce it!"

Miki knew that the military situation was indeed very serious and getting worse. He also knew that the technical sector was partly to blame for the decline in Japan's ability to wage the war effectively. Ota's idea could be viewed by the technical sector as a way of bringing pressure upon itself to remedy the situation. But he could not agree to the plan, even if the results could be guaranteed. The thought of treating human beings as if they were machines struck him as profaning technology. He kept shaking his head and saying "No!"

Beside him, Division Manager Yamana remained silent, with a grim look on his face. To break the tension, Wada spoke up.

"Miki, how about giving some technical advice?"

Miki's reply was blunt. "From a technical point of view, this couldn't possibly be called a weapon. Besides, there is still considerable doubt about whether or not it could successfully crash-dive into a moving target. With that thing suspended beneath it, the speed of the Betty will be drastically reduced, and it is already lacking in protective firepower. The chances are too great that both of the planes would be destroyed before they could reach the target area."

"You're right. It would be necessary to have a number of fighters to provide protection. . . ."

"Wait a minute!" Miki said, visibly agitated. "I'm not saying that the idea is good or that it would work if there were covering fighter planes!"

All the men were silent for several seconds. Wada appeared disappointed at Miki's reaction, and Miki suspected that the vice-admiral had already made up his mind to recommend the idea to higher authorities for consideration.

Miki had known that various other "body-crash" weapons were already being developed for water surface and underwater use, and that it was probably just a matter of time before aerial body-crash weapons were developed. But the difference was that in such surface weapons the crew would have a chance to survive.

Finally, Miki turned to the determined Ota and asked the question that had been on his mind from the beginning of the conversation.

"Sub-Lieutenant Ota, you are suggesting that this weapon be crash-dived into its targets, but who is going to pilot it?"

"I will, of course," Ota said instantly.

Miki caught his breath. Even if prompted by a sincere desire to reverse the desperate war situation, Ota's willingness to sacrifice his own life in such a way was a surprise. The earnestness and dedication of this common sailor impressed him, and Miki was silent again. Maybe Ota was right after all. Given the circumstances of the war, it might be that such crash-diving tactics were the only thing left to Japan. And even though he did not like the idea, it would still be Miki's responsibility to produce the human bombs if the higher authorities accepted the idea. Miki was embarrassed by the thought that he could after all rationalize a concept that transcended logic and rationality. Miki and Yamana were in low spirits when they left the laboratory chief's office.

"Before this is over, we, too, will have to take a dive on that plane," Yamana muttered.

Two main events had separately started the waves whose ripples reached first Miki and later Ichikawa. The first arose from the influence of the worsening military situation and the loss and weakening of much of Japan's naval power. The second, of course, was Ota's idea for a new and devastating weapon.

In addition to having fewer aircraft than the Americans, the slow training process for new pilots was a major factor in the defeats the Japanese forces were suffering. The forward bases of the Combined Fleet on Rabaul, the Truk Islands, and Palau were at a considerable disadvantage because of the growing scarcity of trained and combat-hardened pilots. The whole structure of the Western Pacific Defense Zone had been weakened and made more susceptible to enemy attacks.

Frustrated and angry at not being able to hold back the advancing American forces, soldiers on the front lines were starting to resort to suicide attacks. Sometimes suicide squads or larger groups would hurl their bodies or their planes at the enemy in what came to be described as "kamikaze" attacks, designed to inflict as much damage as possible on the enemy by deliberately sacrificing their lives.

Among the higher authorities in Tokyo, an increasing number of staff officers began to favor the systematic use of suicide attacks against the enemy. But tactical experts were reluctant to endorse the idea officially. They reasoned that the basic principle of military strategy was to destroy the enemy while preserving one's own life, and that large-scale suicide attacks would undermine the foundation of the Supreme Command.

Still, they could not devise an alternative to such a drastic measure, and the entire headquarters staff became pessimistic and desperate.

In the spring of 1944, the tactical authorities at Naval General Staff did decide to go ahead with the production of various types of manned body-crash weapons. Aerial body-crash weapons were not included in these plans, however, as there would be no chance for the crew to survive such attacks.

Immediately after Japan suffered a crushing defeat in the South Pacific front, however, Captain Motoharu Okamura, one of the front's flying corps' commanders, began asserting the need for the use of special attacks against the enemy. On June 19, when Vice-Admiral Shigeru Fukutome, commander-in-chief of the Second Naval Aviation Fleet, visited the corps on an inspection trip, Okamura appealed to him to authorize the use of aerial special attacks.

Following his return to Tokyo a few days later, Vice-Admiral Fukutome reported the proposal to the vice-chief of the Naval General Staff, Seiichi Itoh. Itoh's response was that the time was not yet right for such desperate measures, but promised that he would take the suggestion to the chief of the Naval General Staff, Shigetaro Shimada, and that studies would be conducted on the feasibility of staging large-scale special attacks.

Okamura did not stop with his appeal to Fukutome. He began an intensive effort to persuade other individuals in the chain of command to support the idea. One of the men he approached was Commander Minoru Genda, air staff officer of the Naval General Staff. Genda had assisted Vice-Admiral Takijiro Onishi in planning the Pearl Harbor surprise attack operation, and since then had been regarded as the top authority on aerial operations. Genda had considerable respect for Okamura, who was his senior by two years, and was strongly attracted by Okamura's special aerial attack plan.

On June 27, Okamura called on Onishi at the Munitions Ministry, where Onishi was then the director of general affairs in the Aerial Munitions Bureau. Okamura laid out his entire plan and asked Onishi to order the development of a special plane that could be used for suicide missions.

Lieutenant General Saburo Endo, chief of the Aerial Munitions Bureau, was present when Okamura made his proposal to Onishi. That evening Lieutenant General Endo wrote in his diary, "A divine godly soldier has appeared. I am very much impressed."

Opposition to the idea of using squads of suicide planes in the war was still strong, however, and no action could be taken.

In July, American troops landed on Saipan, annihilating the Japanese forces in the Marianas. The main islands of Japan then came under almost daily attack by B-29s based on Saipan.

The officers favoring the use of aerial suicide attacks against American warships began to gain ground. Most active among this group was Captain Motoharu Okamura, commander of the 341st Flying Corps at Tateyama Base in Chiba Prefecture. Okamura was a veteran fighter pilot, and his corps had previously earned the nickname "Okamura's Circus" because of earlier exploits against enemy forces.

When Saipan fell, Onishi tried to appeal directly to Emperor Hirohito to get his approval and backing for an attempt to retake the island. His move was blocked, and Onishi realized that unless he became vice-chief of the Naval General Staff, he would no longer be able to carry out any kind of operation.

Twelve days after the fall of Saipan, the government of Hideki Tojo collapsed. A few days later, Onishi went to the huge Yomiuri newspaper company with the story of the plan to produce body-crash weapons. The *Yomiuri* carried the story on July 19. It said in part:

> We have weapons called aircraft. If one is willing to crash a plane into the enemy, we need not fear the enemy's mobile units, and B-29 bombers would not be able to intrude into the mainland of Japan. If an enemy aircraft carrier came into sight we would be able to destroy it with a crash-dive attack. If B-29s came into sight we would be able to hit them with our body-crash attacks. Once we make the decision to use body-crash attacks, we are sure to win the war. Numerical inferiority will disappear before the body-crash operation. And those who would make body-crash attacks without heed for their lives deserve the name of godlike soldiers.

On July 21, Shimada presented a new set of operational plans to Soemu Toyoda, commander-in-chief of the Combined Fleet. He called the plans "Combined Fleet Provisional Operations."

Having lost its main aircraft carriers in the sea battle for the Marianas, the navy could no longer expect to stage any large-scale operations against the enemy. The new plan combined both land-based aircraft and carrier-based planes, and called for the introduction of water-surface and underwater special attack weapons. There was also tacit approval for the use of aerial special attacks.

On the following day, a coalition government headed by Kuniaki

Koiso and Mitsumasa Yonai was formed. Onishi called on Yonai at his home. There he ceremoniously took out a brush and a roll of paper, and inscribed in large characters, RESTORATION OF THE NAVY!

He presented the paper to Yonai and said, "The time has come for the Navy to wake up!" He then detailed a plan to stage a decisive air battle against the American forces rapidly closing in on Japan, and recommended that he be appointed vice-chief of the Naval General Staff.

There were already rumors that Onishi might be appointed vice-chief of the NGS, but Yonai had other ideas. He appointed him commander-in-chief of the First Naval Aviation Fleet, which was stationed in the Philippines. This post, he explained to Onishi, was a far more suitable base for implementing special attack plans for suicide aerial missions against the enemy.

On July 26, the "Provisional Operations" plan was given the name of Operation Shogo (Swift Victory). Operation Shogo was divided into four subdivisional operations: Division One was to cover the area around the Philippines. Division Two was responsible for the island of Taiwan, the southwestern islands (including Okinawa) and southern Kyushu. Division Three covered northern Kyushu, Shikoku, and the main island of Honshu. The last division covered the northernmost island of Hokkaido. The most critical area at that time was the Philippines, because it was known that General Douglas MacArthur was preparing to invade the islands from his base in Australia.

While the commanders were struggling with the question of whether or not to authorize aerial special attacks, Special Service Sub-Lieutenant Ota had begun his search for the weapon to be used, and finally developed the idea of the "human-guided missile."

Ota had joined the Naval Barracks in 1928 as a navigator. In the U.S.–Japan conflict he had fought on the southern front for a year, during which time he had witnessed many hard-fought aerial battles between Japanese and American forces. In the spring of 1944, Ota was transferred to the 1081st Flying Corps (Aerial Transportation Corps) at Atsugi Air Base, west of Yokohama. Aware both of the shortage of new pilots and of the special attacks on the ground and in the sea, he gradually realized that a similar tactic from the air could be used against the superior American naval forces. He knew that such tactics would not require skilled fighter or bomber pilots, that someone who could just barely fly a plane would be able to make a significant strike against the enemy.

While the special attack program was being incorporated in the overall naval program at headquarters in Tokyo, Sub-Lieutenant Ota was stationed at Atsugi Air Base, where he used all of his spare time working on ways to use "human missiles" to the best possible advantage.

Ota had learned that in all of the planning, everyone had been assuming that the aircraft to be used in the crash-diving missions would be ordinary planes loaded with high explosives. This meant that, unlike bombs that accelerated after they were dropped from the plane, the final impact of the bomb-laden plane would be no faster than its regular flying or diving speed. Furthermore, Ota reasoned, because the nose and the cockpit of the plane would impact first, the speed at which the explosives struck the enemy target would be considerably lessened.

Ota then heard that the Army was developing a guided, winged bomb that could be dropped from a mother plane. He obtained an introduction to someone at Mitsubishi's Nagoya Engine Factory, which was producing the bomb, and obtained an outline of the design. He also learned that the bomb was to be propelled by a rocket using rogo-propellant and that its flight would be controlled by radio from the mother plane.

The speed that could be achieved by the guided bomb was substantially greater than the flying speed of a bomb-laden plane and would therefore have the desired effect upon impact with the target. But there were problems with the accuracy of the guidance system, and Ota was told it would be some time before these problems could be overcome. There was, however, no guarantee that the problems could be solved, so Ota concluded that the only way the plan could be put into effect in time to save Japan from defeat was to substitute human pilots for the guidance device.

With this in mind, and using the same introduction, Ota went to the Aerial Research Department attached to the Engineering School at Tokyo Imperial University, and asked Professor Taichiro Ogawa to help in designing a small, rocket-propelled craft that could be used as a pilot-guided missile.

Hidemasa Kimura at the Research Department undertook the design, giving special attention to the shape of the hull and the airfoil. A model was quickly constructed and tested in a wind tunnel. The tests were conducted by Professor Ichiro Tani and then given, along with a rough drawing, to Ota. Ota concealed the fact that he had consulted with civilians outside of the military system.

With the test results and the drawing, Ota asked his commander, Captain Hideo Sugawara, to make arrangements to submit the plan to the highest military authorities. Sugawara did not ask where the plans came from, but he was cautious, and felt it was necessary to first consult the Navy's technical division. He told Ota to take the plans to the NARL, and to make the appointment with Wada at which Miki was present.

Wada reported Ota's proposal to the Naval Aeronautical Department, which immediately assigned Commander Sukemitsu Ito, who was in charge of coordinating the development of new planes in the Technical Division of the Administrative Section, to meet with Ota and find out more about the proposal.

Commander Ito was then coordinating the production of German-designed jet and rocket planes, but he knew they would be too little and too late to have a decisive impact on the outcome of the war, and he was eagerly looking for some kind of super weapon that could make the needed difference.

Ito was attracted to Ota's concept, and consulted Captain Chihaya Takahashi, manager of the General Affairs Division. Takahashi sat with his eyes closed while Ito explained the plan to him. He then suggested that Ito contact the Naval General Staff, and thus Air Staff Officer Minoru Genda came into the picture.

Top naval leaders of the Naval General Staff were immediately interested in the potential of Ota's special attack plan because of the value it could be to their own Operation Shogo, scheduled for implementation in the next few weeks. The outline of the special attack plan was presented at a meeting of the Naval General Staff on August 5. Genda vigorously promoted the plan, and obtained permission from Admiral Koshiro Oikawa, newly appointed chief of the NGS, to begin development of the small rocket plane immediately. When Vice-Admiral Onishi, who was still at the Munitions Ministry, heard that the NGS had decided to adopt the plan, he added his unofficial approval.

On August 16, the Naval Aeronautical Research Laboratory received an order from the Naval Aeronautical Department to begin trial production of the manned bomb. It was given the code name *Maru Dai.* "Maru," meaning circle, indicates a code name, and the "Dai," which can also be read "O," was a gesture toward its founder, Ota.

Wada called Rear Admiral Jiro Saba, director of the Aeroplane Section, Technician Commander Masao Yamana of the Design Division, and Technician Lieutenant-Commander Tadanao Miki, chief of Group Three in the Design Division, and informed them that the laboratory was to begin the development of the plane immediately. It was decided that 100 of the planes would be built by the end of October.

Miki was still shocked when the order came down from the Naval Aeronautical Department to produce the human bomb, although he had been expecting it for some time. When he was ordered to take the initiative in the development of the missile, he again rationalized by telling himself that it was the business of technicians to produce things without asking how they were to be used. It was a fate he had to accept as a military technician.

The trial production team was made up of Miki as the chief designer, Lieutenant-Commander Rokuro Hattori in charge of structural design, Lieutenant Kyuichiro Washizu in charge of performance calculation, and some ten others. The project was given the production number MXY-7.

To make sure the project was kept secret, the team was confined to the third floor of the central laboratory building, with one room for the designing work and another to be used as a dormitory. Both rooms were strictly off-limits to all other personnel. On August 18, Ota was sent to the laboratory to brief the team members on the way the planes were to be used.

Section Director Saba went to the Munitions Ministry to discuss production arrangements for the plane, expecting to have some of the work done by outside industry. He was sharply rebuffed by Lieutenant-Commander Yokei Matsuura, the man who had been assigned to oversee the production.

"There is no way we could assign this project to private firms. Besides the security problem, they would think the Navy had gone crazy. Production must be done inside the laboratory, in secret," Matsuura said.

Matsuura then admitted to Saba that he did not approve of the plan. "As a technician, I find it extremely difficult to accept the idea of producing a plane that assures the death of the crew, even if it is an order," he said. "I believe we should produce only conventional airplanes and leave it up to the tactical sector to decide how they are to be used.

In that case we technicians could escape from giving direct help in suicide missions, and if that were the case, I wouldn't feel as badly as I do now."

Matsuura's remark, indirectly criticizing the Tactical Sector, was depressing, and Saba returned to his quarters in very low spirits.

The next day Saba consulted with Lieutenant-Commander Iwao Nazuka, senior officer in charge of the production shops, about producing the suicide plane. Nazuka was skeptical and insisted on confirming the production order before he would take any action.

"A sure-death aerial weapon like this will have a grave impact on military discipline," he said. The iron rule in producing last-ditch weapons of this sort, ever since the Lushun Port Blockading Squadron in the Russo-Japanese War, had been to leave some chance for the user to escape with his life and return. He felt that they should try to find a way the pilot could eject once the plane was set on its course. But Nazuka knew he was only going through the motions. He knew there was no way a pilot could parachute from such a plane with any chance of surviving, given the expected altitude and the velocity of the craft at the moment of bailout.

The success or failure of the plane itself depended on the results of the research and the trial production. But all those who were involved were more concerned about whether or not it would be possible to get enough volunteers to fly the planes to their death. It was important that the commanders know as early as possible if they were going to have enough volunteer pilots to form a unit.

The classified request from the Navy Ministry's Personnel and Education bureaus, asking all flight instructors in small-size aircraft training units to volunteer for the program, went out simultaneously with the order to begin research and development on the planes.

The memorandum specified that not even the name of the plane, much less its nature, be revealed to the potential volunteers, and that only those who were least tied to their families should be accepted.

As soon as flight instructors throughout the country had turned in their ID cards signifying whether or not they volunteered for the project, each air corps classified the volunteers into four groups according to the degree of their zeal. These four groups were designated as *VERY EAGER, EAGER, EARNEST* (those who submitted their acceptance written in blood), and *COMPLIANT.*

Each volunteer was then evaluated on his comprehension, judgment, and decision-making ability, and was rated excellent, good, or fair. All the records pertaining to each volunteer were then sent to the Personnel Bureau of the Navy Ministry.

The fears of the navy brass that not enough people would volunteer for the project were quickly dismissed. There were more than enough to form a unit, and the Personnel Bureau went to work, further sorting out the volunteers.

The heat of the late summer was still intense. In the secret designing room, where all the windows were covered by curtains, Ota's original plan for a human-guided bomb was being reexamined and refined by experts. The "Trial Production Program Request" submitted by the Naval Aeronautical Department was different from anything they had ever used in the production of conventional aircraft. The specifications were that:

1. The warhead should account for 80 percent of the fully loaded weight of the aircraft.
2. The warhead should be the armor-piercing type, and should have a fail-safe fuse.
3. The craft should be extremely fast, so that it would be able to dodge enemy fighter planes and reach the target.
4. The craft's cruising range should be only a little more than enough for a one-way trip.
5. The plane's stability and operational performance should suffice for aiming it at the target.
6. The craft should be as small as possible and easy to dismantle and assemble, so that several of them could be transported and housed in cramped quarters.
7. The materials used in the plane should not be valuable light alloys, but should be wood, and other materials easy to obtain.

The materials and parts required for the production of the Ohka planes were far less complicated than the designers usually faced in developing a new plane. Yamana saw immediately that it was more a winged bomb than a true aircraft. He sketched out in pencil the parts that would be needed. Sweat dropped from his forehead onto the rough paper. When he was done with the drawings, he took them to Miki for his approval.

The plane had to be small enough to be suspended between the landing gears of the Betty mother plane. This meant that its wings were more like fins. A twin-tail system was adopted, with two end plates, so that the tail fins could project up on each side of the hull of the mother plane. The men worked around the clock to prepare the necessary blueprints.

While work on the design was still going on, it was learned that the rogo rocket engine, which was to be used to power the plane, was so unstable that several of them had exploded during test runs. A jet engine being developed by the Mortar Section was Miki's second choice for the plane, but he was told that it would be several months before it would be ready for practical use.

This meant that the only rocket system available for use in the plane was the gunpowder type, which had a burn time of only ten seconds, virtually eliminating any self-propelling or maneuvering ability. Once dropped from the mother plane, all the little plane could do would be to dive toward its target.

Miki and the design team met with Technician Commander Sozaburo Chiba, who was in charge of gunpowder rockets in the Catapult Section, and discussed the alternatives. It was finally decided to equip each of the small human-bomb planes with a total of five rockets with a combined thrust of 3,200 kilograms. Three 800-kilogram rockets would be attached to the rear part of the body, and two 400-kilogram rockets were to be suspended beneath the wings.

The front half of the plane was to be filled with explosives. The designers knew that the more blasting powder they could pack into that area, the more effective it would be. They also knew that they would have to achieve a balance between the weight of the explosives and the desired cruising range and gliding ability of the plane. It was finally decided that the optimum weight of the warhead would be 1,200 kilograms. Lieutenant-Commander Hitoshi Hayakawa, in the Bombing Section of the laboratory, was asked to provide a detailed design for the explosive.

Hayakawa designed a bomb that would carry approximately 500 kilograms of blasting powder, with fuses at both the nose of the bomb and at the base. A setscrew on the top fuse would start spinning as soon as the plane was dropped from the mother plane, arming the bomb. The pin in the head fuse would penetrate the blasting powder the instant the bomb impacted with the target.

Four other fuses, placed in the tail end of the bomb, would also be detonated by the impact, so there was virtually no way the bomb could fail to explode. A time lag was built into each fuse, so that the primary explosion would occur after the armor-piercing bomb had penetrated the hull of the enemy ship.

The hull design of the manned flying bomb was kept as simple as possible, to conform to the shape of the bomb in its nose as well as to simplify the manufacturing process. Yamana repeatedly emphasized to Miki that the wings, too, should be as simple as possible.

"It's not expected to engage in delicate operations. The only things we have to keep in mind are that the plane must detach successfully from the mother plane, and then glide to its target," he said.

The crucial element in the wing design was adjusting the lift of the wings, so that the plane would not rise after being detached and crash into the mother plane. If there was too much lift suppression, however, the degree of descent would be increased and the range of the missile shortened. Working out the most practical relationship for the wing lift was one of the most difficult jobs the designers faced.

Lieutenant-Commander Hattori, who was in charge of the structural design of the craft, had his problems too. The Naval Aeronautical Department had ordered that the planes be constructed out of wood instead of scarce metals. Hattori found that it was impossible to construct a wooden hull strong enough to support the heavy bomb in the nose of the plane and to withstand the high temperatures created by the rocket blast at the rear.

He was finally forced to use a light metal alloy for the hull and make only the wings and tail out of wood. Birch veneer was selected for making the wings, which were to be of the box type for increased strength. Hattori had been told that the wings had to be strong enough to withstand a critical airspeed of 550 knots without fluttering.

Hattori and his team had to make several test-model planes and repeatedly revise their calculations before they succeeded in producing a successful model.

Designing the cockpit was not difficult. Bulletproof steel plates were installed in the front and back of the pilot's seat to protect him if he came under attack before he reached his target. The only instruments in the cockpit were an airspeed indicator, an altimeter, fore and aft indicators for the pilot to use in lining up on his target, and a speaking tube for the pilot to communicate with the mother plane before he was dropped. There was also a rocket ignition button on the control bar for the pilot to depress after he was detached from the mother plane. The little plane was to be attached to the mother plane by a metallic ring fixed to the front of the cockpit. The aircraft was to be detached from the mother plane by an explosion detonated from the mother plane. The pilot in the mother plane was provided with a manual wire release to pull in case the explosion failed to break the connection between the two planes.

The designing of the suicide plane took exactly one week. The hull of the plane was 6.07 meters long, it was 1.16 meters in height, and the wingspan was 5.12 meters. The wing rockets weighed 140 kilograms. The fuselage rockets weighed 360 kilograms. The bomb weighed 1,200 kilograms. The plane itself weighed 440 kilograms. Fully equipped and loaded, it weighed a total of 2,140 kilograms.

Three different views of the craft were drawn—a lateral view, a front view, and a plain figure. The hull of the plane resembled a long-nosed shark. The lateral view of the craft showed the silhouette of a pilot wedged into a tiny compartment between the bomb and the rockets, his hands on the control bar.

The three drawings of the craft, along with separate drawings of the airfoil, wings, and hull, were sent to the laboratory's Scientific Section for analysis. Miki asked that Takio Kitano, civil engineer, be put in charge of the Scientific Section's testing team, because he was well known for his expertise.

On August 25, ten days after the designing of the plane began, Kitano completed a model of the craft and began testing it for lift, drag, rolling, and other functions. Workmen assigned to the project were not told of the nature of the weapon they were working on. The wind tunnel was off-limits to all unauthorized personnel during the tests, and the entrance to the building was guarded by naval guards dispatched from Yokosuka Naval Station. All offices and work areas in the vicinity of the testing tunnel were evacuated.

The huge wind fan in the testing area, and the voices of the testing team shouting out commands, could be heard from outside the building well into the night. A few days after the completion of the wind tunnel tests on the plane itself, tests began on the process of detaching the craft from the mother plane. High-speed photography was used to help determine the optimum posture, angle of elevation, and wind speed for the best launching conditions. Rumors passed among the workers that the photographs being taken of the testing procedures were to be presented to Emperor Hirohito.

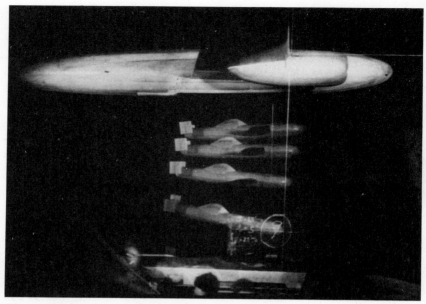

The angle at which the Ohka dropped away from the Betty was calculated to ensure that it did not rise slightly and collide with the Betty or dive too steeply. Here the angle is tested in various wind speeds. Photo of Ohka Type-11 test taken by strobe camera in the NARL wind tunnel. (Courtesy of Tadanao Miki)

The fragile-looking little craft passed all of the critical tests, much to Miki's relief. Technician Lieutenant Kyuichiro Washizu, responsible for calculating the performance capabilities of the craft, reported that its glide speed would be 250 knots, and that, with the firing of one fuselage rocket or both wing rockets, the craft would achieve a speed of 350 knots—just fast enough to outrun the Americans' Grumman F6F fighter planes, which had a maximum speed of 340 knots.

The main problem was the cruise range. Even if the wing and fuselage rockets were fired one at a time, the Maru Dai could not fly more than ten times its altitude at the time of the drop from the mother plane. The ceiling for the Betty bomber, with the Maru Dai attached to its belly, was estimated to be 6,000 meters. This meant that the cruise range of the Maru Dai was around 60 kilometers at best. It was known that American airplanes flying protective cover over U.S. ships generally covered an area of some 90 kilometers-plus in radius. It was therefore obvious that both the mother ships and the Maru Dai flying bombs could come under attack while still attached to each other.

Since the rockets barely provided the craft with straight-flight propulsion power, any course corrections or escape maneuvers would drastically reduce their practical cruise range. The average cruise range of the Maru Dai was set at about half of its actual potential, or just five times its altitude at the time of detachment. There was no choice. If the Maru Dai were to be used, the mother planes would have to carry them to within 25 or 30 kilometers of their targets.

The results of the performance calculations were sent to the Naval General Staff via the Naval Aeronautical Department. There they were subjected to intense study. The NARL chief submitted a strongly worded request to the Navy General Staff that it assign fighter planes to cover the mother planes and the suicide pilots until they were separated and the mother planes had left the danger area.

The original plan had called for the construction of 100 Maru Dai planes by the end of October. After receiving the report that the design work on the Maru Dai had been completed, the Naval Aeronautical Department cancelled the tentative schedule and made the formal decision to produce 100 planes by the end of November. The NARL was ordered to start mass production immediately.

Motozo Nishimoto, an Aeroplane Section civil engineer, was appointed chief of production. The production of the alloy hulls was assigned to the First Shop. Production of the wings, tails, and assembly was assigned to the Second Shop. Both shops immediately prepared standard jigs and began work.

As soon as the hulls, wings, and tails were assembled, the few instruments installed, and the front and back of the cockpit lined with steel plates, the rockets were attached. The bombs were fixed with detachable covers so that the explosives and fuses could be inserted just prior to takeoff.

All work on the planes took place behind locked doors and curtained windows. Huge ventilators were kept going at all times to help keep the workers from being felled by heat exhaustion. They still did not know they were producing human missiles, and some commented repeatedly that they were embarrassed to be working on planes that looked like toys.

In early September the first two planes came off the assembly line, and were designated trial planes. It was officially decided to name the tiny planes Ohka, or "Exploding Cherry Blossoms." Five cherry blossom petals were painted in pink on each side of the craft's nose.

Chapter 2

In September—the same month that the Ohka went into full production—the Allied forces began their advance on the Philippines and captured several of the southernmost islands. The Japanese Naval General Staff knew that the decisive battle for the whole area was imminent. But neither the Japanese First Naval Aviation Fleet stationed in the Philippines, nor the Second Naval Aviation Fleet in Taiwan, was capable of mounting an effective defense against the overwhelming might of the U.S.

In desperation, the Second Naval Aviation Fleet in Taiwan organized the so-called T-Attack Corps and began carrying out surprise raids at night during rainstorms. The "T" was taken from the word "typhoon," because typhoons had destroyed the Mongol fleets of Kublai Khan that attacked Japan in 1281 and 1284, and had been named *kamikaze* (Divine Winds) by the grateful Japanese.

As the situation on all fronts continued to worsen rapidly, even the T-Attack Corps were not enough, and the navy's leaders began to pin more and more of their hopes on the success of the Ohka suicide planes. The Naval General Staff sent an urgent request to the Naval Aeronautical Department of the Navy Ministry to speed up the formation of an Ohka squadron.

The Yokosuka Flying Corps, located next to the Naval Aeronautical Research Laboratory, was assigned to work with the Aeroplane Testing Section of the laboratory to test-fly the Ohka, and to cooperate in its production. On September 15, Captain Motoharu Okamura, long one of the strongest advocates of using special aerial suicide attack missions, was appointed chairman of a preparatory committee charged with the responsibility of setting up the Ohka group, and was dispatched to the Yokosuka Flying Corps.

One of the first officers assigned to the proposed group was the already well-seasoned and tough-minded Lieutenant-Commander Kunihiro Iwaki, wing commander of the 341st Flying Corps. Iwaki was getting ready to leave for Taiwan when he received orders from the Personnel Bureau to report to the Yokosuka Flying Corps. He tried to contact Okamura, his commanding officer, to find out why he was being transferred to Yokosuka instead of Taiwan, but he could not locate the captain, and no one on the base would talk about him.

Completely mystified, Iwaki packed up and left for Yokosuka. Formerly assigned to fly the reconnaissance seaplanes, Iwaki had participated in the aerial attacks of Nanyu (Nanxiong) Base in China on February 24, 1938. During the battle, his plane was attacked by ten enemy fighters. Iwaki was hit in the leg and the navigator sitting behind him was killed. His plane went into a spin. Sure that he was going to die in the crash, Iwaki drew his legs up in the formal cross-legged position and composed himself for his last few seconds of life. Suddenly, the plane came out of the dive by itself, and the wounded Iwaki managed to fly it back to his base. After he landed, the plane was found to have been hit 138 times by the attacking aircraft. The recovery of the plane was so miraculous that it was displayed for inspection by the Emperor, and then taken to the Edajima Naval College to be used as a teaching exhibit.

This experience reinforced Iwaki's strong belief that spirit could overcome all obstacles, and he became increasingly impatient with people who were less dedicated, and whose attention to duty waned. When such individuals were his subordinates, Iwaki demonstrated his anger and disapproval by slapping them. Petty officers who had received their share of slaps from Iwaki had nicknamed him "One of the Three Bastards in the Navy."

When Iwaki reported in at the headquarters building of the Yokosuka Flying Corps, he found Captain Okamura waiting for him. He then learned for the first time that a special suicide attack squadron was to be formed and that he was appointed vice-chairman of the preparatory committee. He also learned for the first time that Okamura had been secretly pushing for special aerial attacks for several months.

Iwaki was given an official arm band imprinted with the characters for Maru Dai, to show that he was a figure of importance, and escorted to a covered trench at the edge of the air base runway, where one of the Ohka planes was displayed for instructional purposes. He was shocked.

The Ohka's small size, obvious fragility, and other limitations gave him grave doubts about the value of the project.

He was especially concerned about the effect the sight of the tiny plane would have on the pilots chosen to fly it. He knew there would be serious discipline problems and wondered if he could play the role he had been ordered to assume. He told Okamura that it might be too much for a man who had been labeled a bastard by his own subordinates. Okamura laughed and said that his reputation would turn out to be an asset. At this, Iwaki resolved to play the role of disciplinarian with his accustomed dedication.

While Okamura concentrated on rounding up the rest of the staff that would be needed to organize and operate the special Ohka squadron, Iwaki, with the help of officers from the Yokosuka Flying Corps, began studying tactics for the coming Ohka attacks. He also ordered Flight Warrant Officer Kazutoshi Nagano, who was to be in charge of feasibility experiments on the project, to organize a training program for the pilots who were to make the one-way missions.

Since the Ohka planes were to fly into their targets following a gradual descent, Nagano developed a training program based on using Zero fighter planes to make repeated diving runs on simulated targets. The volunteer pilots would thus learn the crucial tactic required of the Ohka.

The first trial flight of the Betty bomber with an Ohka plane hanging on to its belly brought several unwelcome revelations. The Betty had to taxi from 500 to 600 meters farther than usual when fully loaded with bombs. Consequently the fuel load of the Betty had to be reduced to compensate for the extra weight of the Ohka, even though the Betty's fuel consumption went up drastically. Also, its maximum range of 4,700 kilometers (at an altitude of 3,000 meters and an airspeed of 170 knots) was reduced by some 30 percent. Its cruising speed of 170 knots was reduced by about 10 percent because of the additional air resistance from the suspended plane.

These new realities spread a blanket of gloom over the whole program. It was obvious that both the Betty and Ohka would have to have substantial fighter protection if the special suicide attacks were to succeed to any substantial degree. Iwaki held repeated discussions with related officials of the Yokosuka Flying Corps to determine the minimum number of covering fighters needed.

Two ways of providing protection for the missions were discussed—

one direct and the other indirect. In the indirect method, covering fighters would go in first and draw the enemy planes away from the targets and destroy them if possible. In the direct method, the covering fighters would stay with the Bettys and attempt to drive off any approaching enemy aircraft.

Iwaki wanted to use both methods simultaneously, but he was aware that the number of fighter planes available for such coverage was seriously limited and getting worse. According to his calculations, four fighter planes would be needed for each Betty in the formation. Since it had been decided to send out 18 Betty–Ohka combinations on each mission, that would mean 72 fighter planes.

Iwaki took his conclusions to Commander Minoru Genda, chief of staff at the Naval General Staff Office. Genda approved, and promised Iwaki the planes he wanted. Even with this number of fighter planes flying protective cover, it was calculated that the Betty–Ohka squadrons would suffer serious losses during each attack. Okamura was therefore determined that the mission commander should be the most experienced pilot available, especially one who had been through numerous aerial dogfights with enemy planes. He contacted the Personnel Bureau of the Navy Ministry and detailed the kind of man he was looking for.

The Personnel Bureau selected Lieutenant-Commander Goro Nonaka for the post. Goro was the younger brother of Shiro Nonaka, who had shot himself to death after participating in the infamous February 26 Incident in 1936, when a group of insurgent officers tried to take over the government in a bloody coup. Goro Nonaka had been involved in more than 350 aerial attacks in battles against the Americans in the South Pacific, including the attack on Port Darwin, the Kupang Operation, the New Guinea Attack, the South Sea Battle, and the Gilbert Aerial Attack.

One of the most unusual characters in the Japanese Navy, Nonaka was tolerated by the navy brass only because he and his squadron were so successful in combat. Goro and his men almost totally disregarded rank and the accompanying strict formalities that were characteristic of all branches of Japan's military. He gave his orders in colorful language, and his men responded in kind.

After especially difficult missions, Nonaka would hold a tea ceremony for his men, during which he would regale them with stories of his previous war experiences. He kept numerous publications in his room, with jackets that had such titles as *Working Rules of Night Raids* and *SOP of Air Defense*. In reality, all of the publications were popular magazines, especially the kind featuring traditional sword-fighting serials. It was from these magazines that Nonaka's military vocabulary was derived.

On October 1, 1944, the Thunder Gods Special Attack Corps was organized officially, and designated the 721st Naval Flying Corps. Captain Okamura was named commander of the corps; Lieutenant-Commander Iwaki, wing commander; and Lieutenant-Commander Nonaka, Betty squadron leader. The special attack corps, as part of the Yokosuka Naval Station, was ordered to do its training at the Hyakurigahara Base, in Ibaragi Prefecture, until an exclusive training area could be found.

Coded messages began going out to all training commands in the country, ordering the "dead-sure attack" volunteers to report to Hyakurigahara.

At the Himeji Flying Corps base, Higher Flight Chief Petty Officer Motoji Ichikawa, who had written *Yes* in small letters on his ID card when asked to volunteer for the special mission, was envious when his best friend, Higher Flight Petty Officer Bansaku Tamura, received orders transferring him to the 721st.

"Don't worry. Yours will come in soon," Tamura said confidently. "By the way," he added, "do you have any idea what '721' stands for? It's weird to be transferred to an air corps with a 721 number."

Ichikawa shook his head and agreed that the number was strange. In 1917 the Japanese Navy had changed the names of all operational air corps from location names to names made up of three or four numerals. Each one of the numerals stood for a different type of operation.

The 100's digit indicated the type of aircraft. The numeral 1 stood for reconnaissance planes; 2 and 3 for fighter planes; 4 for reconnaissance seaplanes; 5 for carrier dive bombers or attack bombers; 6 for carrier-based planes; 7 for land-based attack bombers; 8 for flying boats; 9 for patrol aircraft; and 10 for air transport planes.

The 10's digit indicated the naval station. Zero, 1 and 2 stood for Yokosuka Naval Station; 3 and 4 for the Kure Naval Station; 5, 6, and 7 for the Sasebo Naval Station; and 8 and 9 for the Maizuru Naval Station. The numeral at the far right indicated the nature of the corps. Even numbers were for special corps; odd numbers for regular corps.

Thus the 721st Naval Flying Corps meant "Land-based attack bomber, Yokosuka Naval Station, Regular Corps." It didn't make any sense to Ichikawa and Tamura that they were to be transferred to such a corps, because they were carrier attack-bomber pilots.

"Since they say it's sure death, I've suspected all along that we were to crash-dive our planes into targets, but I don't understand why they would assign ship-borne plane pilots to large-sized land-based planes," Ichikawa said.

Tamura nodded in agreement. "That's the point. I've been thinking that I'd be put on one of the V-1's we've been hearing rumors about."

Ichikawa asked him to send a postcard when he got to the new base. "As soon as you're sure it's going to be a crash-dive attack, just write 'bump' or something like that somewhere on the card."

While other special attack volunteers were receiving their orders and wondering about their new assignment, transfer orders were also being delivered to Betty bomber crews, as well as to maintenance, communications, and medical personnel, along with paymasters.

None of these people thought anything was unusual about the new assignment. Betty crews in particular saw nothing odd in being assigned to the 721st, and were totally ignorant of the circumstances that were soon to make them play a key role in a bizarre twist in the war.

In the meantime, Special Service Sub-Lieutenant Shoichi Ota, who had come up with the idea for the special suicide attack bomb, was also assigned to the 721st Naval Flying Corps. Because he was not a pilot, he was not qualified to volunteer for the program. He had been a navigator and therefore was qualified to join the crew of one of the Betty bombers, but instead was given the task of confirming the results of the suicide attacks.

On the day that the 721st Corps was inaugurated, Technician Lieutenant-Commander Miki, at the Naval Aeronautical Research Laboratory, compiled a one-and-a-half-month practical test-flight program. Although it was called a practical exercise, it was impossible to test the final efficiency of the design with a pilot aboard, since the plane was designed to crash at the end of its first flight.

The plane had no landing gear and no flaps for reducing speed, and even if it had had flaps and wheels, they would not have assured a safe landing because the weight of the plane was much larger than the lift.

Some other means had to be contrived to substitute for a test with a live pilot aboard. The task gave Miki more trouble than designing the plane, but after considerable trial and error he worked out an alternative plan.

The detaching and gliding capabilities of the plane were simple enough to check. A non-operational plane could be loaded with sandbags to substitute for the weight of the bomb, rockets, pilot, and accessories. Of course, the plane would destroy itself in the crash landing. The real problem was presented by the need for an operational performance and stability test, which meant that a test pilot actually had to fly the plane.

There were several facets to the dilemma. The landing speed had to be reduced to ensure a safe landing. One possibility was to reduce the weight of the plane. But if this were done, it would defeat the purpose of the test, which was to examine the operational performance of the plane when it was in flight and fully loaded. The only way was to reduce the weight of the plane while it was in flight.

At first, Miki thought of using sand or lead as ballast, which would be dropped after the performance test was complete. But there were too many problems in using such materials, and he finally settled on water. He would put water tanks in the bomb and rocket cavities. He solved the problem of landing gear by fixing sled runners to the fuselage and outfitting it with a simple flap. Because the wooden wings and tail would not hold up under the impact of a landing, even without the water ballast, Miki had the wings and tail of the test plane changed to ones made of a light metal alloy.

To check the performance of the plane during glide at the maximum speed of 350 knots and the critical speed of 550 knots, Miki decided to use a sandbag-laden dummy plane equipped with three tail rockets. The rockets would ignite automatically when the plane was dropped from the mother plane, and it would then glide to a crash landing while being photographed with high-speed cameras for later analysis.

Five hundred and fifty knots was Mach 0.85, and as there had been no test flights at that speed, there were no guidelines of any kind. Something might happen that was beyond the understanding of the designers. Miki was especially concerned about the possibility that the plane would begin to vibrate and shake itself apart, even though the wind-tunnel tests had indicated that it would not flutter at that speed.

Miki finally proposed a three-stage test program. The first, to test detaching and glide performance, would be with an unmanned dummy plane loaded with solid ballast and propelled by three rockets. The second test would be with a manned plane carrying water ballast, which would be jettisoned after the pilot tested the plan's handling characteristics and stability. The plane would then land on sled runners. The third test would be a fully equipped, unmanned Ohka with its rockets set to go off seconds after it was dropped from the mother plane, to see how it would react at maximum and critical speed. A number of ground tests were also devised, including a series to determine the reliability of the rockets and to examine the explosive power of the bombs that had been designed for the plane.

Miki called his testing program "The Maru Dai Weapon Exercise Implementation Draft" (Naval Aeronautical Research Laboratory Classified Document No. 9269), and had the master copy signed by Misao Wada, chief of the NARL; Fusazo Murakami, chief of the Second Naval Explosives Factory; Tadao Kato, commander of the Yokosuka Flying Corps; and Motoharu Okamura, commander of the 721st Naval Flying Corps, and then sent copies to all of the key officers concerned with the project.

The Aeroplane Section of the NARL began hurriedly preparing for the tests, while Miki went over the draft again and again to make sure that the testing procedures would accomplish their purpose. He was especially anxious about the manned glide test using water as ballast.

While all this work on the Ohka was going on, the idea began to grow among the higher-ranking officers of both the navy and army that "body-crash" attacks by bomb-laden fighter planes already available would make it possible for Operation Shogo No. 1 to stem the advance of the American forces, if not turn the tide of the war itself.

The man who was most enthusiastic about the potential positive effects that body-crash tactics could have on the progress of the war was Vice-Admiral Onishi, commander-in-chief designate of the First Naval Aviation Fleet in the Philippines. On October 5, four days after the inauguration of the 721st Naval Flying Corps, Onishi called on the chief of the Naval General Staff to get his official approval to carry out special attacks using bomb-bearing fighter planes. Onishi felt that the situation had become so desperate that the navy could not wait for the completion of the Ohka planes.

Admiral Koshiro Oikawa was reluctant to give the order, but finally said, "Considering the current situation of the war, I cannot help but repress my tears and approve the plan. But you must promise me that you will respect the free will of the plane crews. They must not be forced, under any circumstances." Onishi agreed that suicide missions using fighter planes would be entirely voluntary. With the admiral's approval, Onishi next went to Minoru Genda, NGS's air staff officer, to get his help in planning how such suicide attacks should be carried out. At the meeting it was decided to call the new corps the Kamikaze Special Attack Corps, but not to make the plan public until a more propitious time.

On October 9, Onishi started for the Philippines to take up his appointment as commander-in-chief of the First Naval Aviation Fleet. Already, Japanese bases on Taiwan, and in Kyushu, Japan's southernmost main island, were put on the highest alert for the appearance of an American task force, because more and more of the Japanese patrol planes dispatched toward the islands of the southwest were not returning to their bases.

On October 10, while Onishi was still at Kanoya Base in Kyushu, en route to the Philippines, the U.S. forces launched a massive air attack against the Ryukyu Islands two weeks before it was expected. Onishi was forced to detour through Shanghai to reach Taiwan.

The U.S. air attack against Taiwan and the islands between Taiwan and Kyushu continued for three days. All of the Japanese air corps stationed in the area, including the T-Attack Corps, were involved in a counterattack against the American forces.

The Taiwan air battle was reported to Tokyo as a great victory for the Japanese. The navy department of the military headquarters, and the headquarters of the Combined Fleet, were excited about the good news after such a long interval of discouraging reports. Front-page newspaper stories credited the Japanese forces in Taiwan with sinking eleven American aircraft carriers, two battleships, three cruisers, and one other vessel.

In reality, the T-Attack Corps had succeeded in sinking two large cruisers. The Frances dive bombers, attacking under cover of darkness, were not able to find their targets and were confused by flares dropped by Allied planes. In the flashing lights of the flares, the American ships seemed to disappear, while one after another of the planes were shot down or missed their targets and crashed into the sea.

Former American fighter pilot James Sweeney said the high miss rate of the suicide planes was caused by the inexperience of the Japanese pilots. According to him, the pilots "dived directly at

American ships at full throttle, without compensating for the lift factor, which more often than not raised them up over their targets." They would have been more successful if they had shut their engines off and gone into a negative G. The overall effect of the counterattack was to virtually destroy the Japanese air forces in the area.

Japan's air corps was no match for the invading forces. The First Aviation Fleet had only about 40 planes that were still operational. The air force in the Philippines, including the Army, had fewer than 100 aircraft. The Second Aviation Fleet in Taiwan was down to approximately 300. The Japanese were both outnumbered and outfought. On October 17, during a rainstorm with winds of up to 30 meters per second, American forces seized the island of Suluan at the mouth of Leyte Gulf, and began massing ships in the gulf for an attack on the main island of Luzon. It was on this day that Vice-Admiral Onishi arrived in Manila from Taiwan. As soon as he was told of the number of aircraft available in the Philippines, he decided to begin using the remaining fighter planes for crash-dive attack missions immediately.

The American invasion of Leyte began the following day.

The Japanese Combined Fleet Headquarters ordered the implementation of Operation Shogo No. 1. The main fleet, at an anchorage south of Singapore, and the detached fleet, at Amami Oshima Island, were ordered to head for Leyte at top speed. A task force waiting in the Inland Sea was ordered to lure American warships in the Philippine area to the north, away from Leyte.

In the early morning of October 19, Onishi called Mabalacat Base, north of Manila, and ordered Captain Sakae Yamamoto, Commander of the 201st Flying Corps, to report to him in Manila. Yamamoto was in the midst of directing the counterattack against the American forces in Leyte, and did not leave the base until around two o'clock in the afternoon.

In the meantime, Onishi grew impatient and started to Mabalacat by car. When he arrived there he found that Yamamoto had left for Manila. He nevertheless immediately issued an order for an assembly of all the executive officers of the corps.

When Yamamoto arrived in Manila and found that he had missed Onishi, he boarded a Zero fighter piloted by Lieutenant-Commander Tadashi Nakajima, wing commander of the 201st Flying Corps, to fly back to the base. Immediately after takeoff, the plane's engine went out and they had to make a forced landing. One of Yamamoto's legs was broken in the landing and he was hospitalized. Nakajima suffered only a minor face injury, but he had to wait until the following morning to return to the base.

With both Yamamoto and the wing commander absent, the 201st Flying Corps' Vice-Commander Asaichi Tamai assembled the other leaders of the corps as Onishi had directed. It was already dark when the men gathered on the balcony of the second floor of the headquarters building. The only light was provided by a beer-bottle lamp burning coconut oil. The men sat in a semicircle facing the vice-admiral.

"If Operation Shogo should fail," Onishi began slowly, "the results will be so grave, there will be no chance for us to recover. It is therefore imperative that our counterattack be successful. In order to make absolutely sure that it is successful, we must inflict enough damage to the decks of the American aircraft carriers that they cannot be used for at least a week.

"Our naval troops can successfully enter Leyte Gulf only if we render the enemy aircraft carriers useless. Our battleships *Yamato* and *Musashi* will then crush the enemy invasion forces."

Onishi paused for several seconds, then continued, choosing his words carefully. "I believe that the only way we can successfully destroy the usefulness of the enemy aircraft carriers is to crash-dive Zeros loaded with 250-kilogram bombs onto their decks."

The night air was oppressive. The only sound was the flickering flame of the lamp. Onishi was silent, staring at the men, waiting for them to respond. Finally, Vice-Commander Tamai broke the silence. "We will have to wait until Commander Yamamoto returns, to find out what he wants to do," he said.

"I've already discussed this with Yamamoto in Manila," Onishi lied. "He said to tell you that he was giving you the authority to make the decision."

Tamai motioned for the senior squadron leader to follow him into an adjoining room for a private discussion. A few minutes later they returned to the balcony with strained faces.

"We agree with your assessment of the situation," Tamai said. "I respectfully request that the formation of this special attack corps be left up to the Air Corps," he added.

A great weight seemed to have been lifted from the vice-admiral's shoulders. He stood up. The officers jumped to their feet. Onishi bowed to the men, showing his deep respect for them. He then left for Commander Yamamoto's private quarters.

Tamai ordered the flight petty officers in the corps to meet him in the orderly room. All 23 of them quickly assembled.

After informing them of the meeting that had just taken place, Tamai asked for volunteers for the sure-death mission that the admiral had proposed. All 23 of the men raised their hands. Tears came into Tamai's eyes. He could only thank the men for their spirit and dedication.

Because of the nature of the mission, it was important that the commander of the squadron be a Naval College graduate. Tamai appointed Lieutenant Yukio Seki, who had been transferred from Taiwan to the Philippines just a month earlier. The group was named the Kamikaze Special Attack Corps, and divided into four units—Shikishima, Yamato, Asahi, and Yamazakura.

At 10 o'clock the following morning, the 23 pilots and Lieutenant Seki lined up in the courtyard of the headquarters building for a greeting by Vice-Admiral Onishi. As soon as the men were in formation, Onishi emerged from the building and walked slowly but deliberately to the box-podium in front of the group. He stepped up on the box and then turned to face the young men. There were tears in his eyes, and he had to struggle to maintain his composure. He was pale and quivering.

Finally he spoke. "The crisis facing us is not one that can be solved by the navy minister, the chief of Naval General Staff, or an admiral. It is only you innocent and energetic young men who can do that!

"You are already gods! Being gods, you must be beyond all desires. The only thing you may regret is that you will not know if your attack was successful or not. Do not worry. A confirming plane will report the results, and I will personally report the results to your souls, and to the Emperor as well. So feel confident, and go!"

Onishi was silent for several seconds, struggling to maintain control of his emotions. "Be brave!" he shouted loudly. He then descended from the box and grasped the hands of each of the pilots in farewell.

At eleven o'clock that morning, American forces in Leyte Gulf began landing at Tacloban on the east coast of Leyte Island. Wing Commander Nakajima, who had returned from Manila earlier in the day, led the Yamato unit of the Thunder Gods Corps to Cebu Island to the west of Leyte, and Vice-Admiral Onishi, returning to the Manila head-quarters of the First Naval Aviation Fleet, officially took over from Kinpei Teraoka as the new commander.

The following day, October 21, all four of the sure-death units—the Yamato in Cebu, the Shikishima, Asahi, and Yamazakura at Mabalacat—staged their first sortie in search of enemy aircraft carriers. The weather was so bad, however, that no targets were found, and the units all returned to base. On the twenty-fourth, the Second Naval Aviation Fleet from Taiwan made a sortie from Clark Field, north of Manila, and discovered a large number of American aircraft carriers. That night more than 300 conventional planes of the Second Naval Aviation Fleet carried out repeated raids against the American fleet. The loss of planes was heavy, and the results minimal. The Japanese succeeded in sinking one aircraft carrier, two cruisers, and three destroyers.

Meanwhile, American submarines and carrier-based fighters had met the Japanese fleet rushing toward Leyte, and virtually destroyed them, including the great battleship *Musashi*, which had never once fired its massive guns in combat. The plan to protect Leyte from the American invasion forces was a total failure and was abandoned.

Immediately after this devastating defeat, nine members of the kamikaze units—five from Mabalacat, two from Cebu, and two more from an additional unit that had been formed at Davao Base on Mindanao Island—succeeded in sinking two American aircraft carriers and seriously damaging four others. This minor victory had no effect on slowing the American invasion of Leyte, but it was the most successful action the Japanese Naval Air Corps had waged in many months. Onishi received the report of the kamikaze attacks with tears in his eyes.

"It was worth it," he mumbled brokenly. "Now we've found a way. . . ."

With this success in the Philippines, Vice-Admiral Shigeru Fukutome, commander-in-chief of the Second Naval Aviation Fleet in Taiwan, who had not yet been convinced of the value of the suicide attacks, changed his position and informed Onishi of his decision. At a meeting held at the Manila headquarters of the First Naval Aviation Fleet, the First and Second Naval Aviation fleets were combined. Under the seniority system, Fukutome became the commander, with Onishi as his assistant.

Onishi then drove to the Naval Aviation Base at Clark Field for a meeting with key officers from all air corps units. The majority of the officers at the meeting were from the Second Naval Aviation Fleet. Onishi was determined to get his way about the special attacks program and began the meeting on an aggressive note.

"As you all know," he said, "the results of the most recent kamikaze attacks against the enemy naval forces were remarkable, and we will continue this operation—every corps in both the First and Second Naval Aviation fleets. It is my conviction that this is the only way Japan can win the war. No criticism will be allowed. No objections will be tolerated!"

When Onishi first decided on the desperate measure of kamikaze attacks, his aims were relatively modest: to neutralize enemy aircraft carriers. But the spectacular results of the most recent attacks had revived his hopes that Japan might still succeed in stopping the Allied advance. He had convinced himself that by incorporating the kamikaze attacks into the command system instead of leaving them up to volunteers, Japan could win the war.

On October 26, the chief of the Naval General Staff reported the results of the kamikaze attacks to Emperor Hirohito. Two days later he submitted a "Detailed Explanation" of the attacks to the Emperor's aide-de-camp. The explanation said in part: "The Kamikaze Special Attack Corps differs from conventional attacks in that the planes deliberately dive into enemy ships, so there is no possibility of their return. In the beginning, this tactic was used only by fighter planes attached to the First Naval Aviation Fleet. Now all air corps and all types of planes are to be included."

Nevertheless, the number of fighter-bombers that could be used for suicide missions was rapidly decreasing. The situation was critical. On November 19, the NGS agreed to a request from Vice-Admiral Onishi to augment the forces in the Philippines by dispatching training units to the area. The plan was risky, because mobilizing instructors and aircraft from the training units would have a profoundly negative effect on the navy's whole training program. The NGS decided, however, that the circumstances made the risk worth taking. The rationale was that the move would be a temporary measure to help shore up the defense of the Philippine region until the Thunder Gods Corps was ready and could go into action there.

Admiral Oikawa, chief of the NGS, went to the Imperial Palace to explain the move to Emperor Hirohito. The message he delivered to the

Emperor read in part: "The special attack unit made up of the nation-resuscitating weapon Ohka will be ready for use in the Philippines by mid-December. So, as a temporary measure, approximately 150 aircraft from various training units in Taiwan and the mainland will be dispatched to the Philippines."

At dawn on October 23, when the situation in Leyte was at its most critical point, the chief designer of the Ohka suicide planes, Miki, headed for the airfield at Kisarazu Air Base in Chiba Prefecture to test the plans. There he met Lieutenant-Commander Nazuka, who was in charge of assembling and rigging the tiny planes, and Technician Lieutenant Washizu, who was responsible for calculations.

"The test plane is already attached to the Betty," Nazuka said. Miki nodded.

At the edge of the runway, three Bettys were lined up. Miki could see the Ohka, filled with sandbags, suspended from one of them. The two extra planes were to fly observation to film the detaching and gliding performance of the Ohka.

Miki and Washizu boarded the mother plane. Nazuka boarded one of the observation planes. The first test of the "Exploding Cherry Blossom" was about to start.

After taxiing nearly to the end of the runway, the mother plane laboriously climbed into the air. Flying in wide circles, the plane managed to reach its maximum altitude, then took off to the south with the observation planes on either side. Passing over Oshima Island, the planes flew on for another 15 minutes to the testing area over the Pacific.

The observation planes took up their positions. The crew on the mother plane opened a floor hatch, revealing the cockpit of the Ohka. Cold air hissed through the opening.

"You can watch it from here," one of the crewmen yelled to Miki. He lay down on his stomach and stuck his head through the floor hatch.

The pilot of the mother plane then counted down and pressed the detach button that had been rigged up to release the Ohka. The tiny, shark-shaped plane dropped away from the mother plane smoothly, causing the Betty to rise suddenly.

Miki poked his head farther through the hatch to get a better look at the Ohka as it began its curving dive toward the ocean. Washizu, in the rear seat, twisted around and, trying to get a better look out, bumped into Miki. "Stop moving!" Miki yelled.

The Ohka dropped smoothly away from the mother plane, reflecting the morning sun on its orange body. It took the precise course that Washizu had calculated, and gave no sign of any design problem as it dived into the ocean, throwing up a column of white water. The film taken by the two observation planes corroborated Miki's visual report. The Ohka had passed its first test.

In the meantime, the 721st Naval Flying Corps at Hyakurigahara Air Base was welcoming Lieutenant Tsutomu Kariya and Sub-Lieutenants Kentaro Mitsuhashi and Fujio Hayashi from the Naval College. The three young college graduates had been assigned to help Commander Okamura and Wing Commander Iwaki in forming the Ohka Squadron. Betty Squadron Leader Nonaka greeted them with his usual flippant vulgarity.

"All right, you little gods. You've had the balls to come this far, now we'll see if you can go all the way! Me, I'm just an ordinary guy! If you've brought your name cards, you might as well donate them to the war effort, because you're not going to need them! And if you're still virgins, you better go out and get laid right away!"

The three young men were stunned by Nonaka's unmilitary-like behavior and stared at him, speechless.

Immediately thereafter, the men who were to make up the Thunder Gods Corps began arriving—reserve officers and petty officers. Higher Flight Petty Officer Masazo Okubo was the first noncommissioned officer to arrive. He had previously belonged to Commander Okamura's fighter squadron in the south and had fought with him there. He had heard about the suicide squadron while attached to a training division in Konoike in Ibaragi Prefecture, north of Tokyo.

Frustrated because he was no longer able to participate in the war directly, and angry at the inability of the Japanese forces to defeat the enemy, Okubo had long ago accepted the fact that fighter planes were no match for aircraft carriers and battleships. He resolved that it was better to crash-dive into the enemy and die like a man, and had volunteered for the 721st.

Soon after arriving at the base, Okubo made a courtesy call on Okamura, his former commander. Okamura greeted him enthusiastically.

"I'm glad you came," he said. "This time your task is to make a body-crash in an Ohka. One of the training planes is in the hangar. I suggest you go take a look at it."

In the hangar was a toy-like plane that reminded Okubo of a winged torpedo. He immediately recognized it as a manned bomb, and for the first time understood why the corps name began with a "7". He then recalled that when he had been in the Celebes with Okamura and things were going badly, Okamura had suggested that suicide missions against the enemy seemed to be the only choice they had. "So this is what it has come to," he thought.

Okubo tapped the wooden wing of the Ohka. The strange sound made him uneasy, and suddenly he missed the sleek metal fighter planes he had flown so often. For a moment he wondered if there was any way he could avoid making his last flight in such a fragile, insignificant craft.

The pilots assigned to the 721st Flying Corps began making practice runs in Zeros. They were ordered to dive repeatedly at designated targets in an effort to get the "feel" of actually crash-diving into an enemy ship. This brought home the seriousness of the training and kept their emotions high.

Then came the news of the kamikaze special attacks in the Philippines. The members of the Ohka Squadron were shocked, and their spirits plummeted. They had so far been sustained by the belief that their own glorious sacrifice would be remembered forever as a major element in the defense of Japan.

There was considerable grumbling among the men as they tried to overcome their disappointment and regain their spirit. "It's all right. We'll do a better job with the Ohka!" they said over and over.

On October 31, the top officers of the Naval General Staff, Aeronautical Department, and the Naval Aeronautical Research Laboratory gathered at Hyakurigahara Air Base to observe the second stage of the Ohka test, in which the plane was loaded with water ballast and a test pilot, Nagano, was on board. All of the pilots in training for the one-way missions were also lining the airfield.

Miki was too agitated to sit down. He kept pacing back and forth in front of the exercise commanding officer. Washizu suggested that he sit down. He did, but got up almost immediately and began pacing again. For the last several nights he had been suffering from recurring nightmares that the plane would fall apart in the air or crash and kill the test pilot.

Miki had complete faith in Nagano, the test pilot. It was the plane he did not trust. Would the ballast upset the balance of the plane and make it impossible to steer? Would Nagano be able to jettison the water? Nagano had been instructed to remove the cockpit cover and parachute out if the plane began to fail in midair, but would he be able to get out quickly enough?

The two Bettys participating in the test had taken off from Yokosuka a few minutes earlier. Miki could hear the roar of their engines as they approached the field at an altitude of 3,500 meters. He could just make out the Ohka suspended from the belly of one of the planes. This time Nazuka was aboard the second Betty as an observer.

Iwaki's Zero training plane took off from the base to observe the experiment. The Betty carrying the Ohka circled the field for several minutes, then dropped a flare indicating that the Ohka would be released in exactly five minutes. Miki followed the passing of the five minutes on his stopwatch, alternately staring at the circling plane in the sky.

Aboard the observation Betty, Nazuka noticed that water leaking from the Ohka's ballast tank had frozen into ice. He himself suddenly felt as though the blood in his veins had frozen. If the ice around the outlet failed to melt, the ballast water could not be jettisoned, which meant that the test plane would crash into the ground fully loaded.

They had been flying at 3,500 meters. The ballast water was to be jettisoned at an altitude of 3,000 meters. Nazuka closed his eyes and prayed that the warmer temperature at that altitude would melt the ice.

The countdown was under way—three . . . two . . . one . . .

The Ohka parted from the mother plane smoothly, dropped almost vertically, and then went into a glide. The wing rockets fired and then dropped off—it seemed at almost the same time. Two black objects appeared by the Ohka, leaving trails of smoke behind them.

"The rockets dropped too early!" Nazuka screamed, fear coursing through his body.

But the test plane was still flying beautifully, rapidly pulling away from Iwaki's Zero, which had been following close behind it.

On the ground, Washizu began yelling, "It's flying! It's flying!"

As the officers and men on the ground strained their eyes, the orange dot in the air grew bigger and bigger. Suddenly it began emitting white vapor. It was a second before Miki realized that Nagano was discharging the water ballast.

The Ohka continued to emit a vapor trail as it twice circled the base, making a slight metallic sound as it passed over the assembled crowd and lined up with the runway. Nagano guided the little plane to a smooth landing. The Ohka on its runners slid to a stop near the end of the tarmac. The pilot emerged from the craft in a cloud of dust.

Miki jumped on a truck, raced to the Ohka, and congratulated Nagano profusely. The other members of the team surrounded them, congratulating each other. After the officials had left, the team gathered around a table to discuss the flight.

"Why did you drop the wing rockets earlier than had been scheduled?" Miki asked.

"The horizontal wave was so intense it interfered with the steering, so I decided to drop them," Nagano replied.

Miki knew immediately this meant that the thrust of the two rockets was not synchronized. That was a point that had been overlooked during the emission test on the ground. If it had resulted in a failure, the technicians would have been blamed.

"That was the only problem," Nagano added. "Stability and function of the controls were perfect. The speed can match that of fighters."

"How did it feel when you were dropped from the mother plane?" someone asked.

"It felt like I was being pushed vertically away from the plane, but I had lift effect as soon as I began to glide."

"What happened when you began to discharge the water?"

"The plane lifted up a little, but the stability and operational performance remained virtually the same."

"And the landing?"

"Much easier than I expected."

There had been no damage to the makeshift landing gear.

"Do you think it can be used for training?"

"Absolutely. But it might be better to take the wing rockets off on training flights."

The test had taken place almost exactly two months after work had begun on the design of Ohka, and it had worked perfectly. In his excitement over the success of the test, Miki forgot for a moment the purpose of the deadly weapon he had helped build.

With these tests of the Ohka complete, the commitment of the 721st Naval Flying Corps to the battle was assured.

On November 1, the first American B-29 reconnaissance plane from the captured air base on Saipan appeared over Tokyo as an ominous warning of what was to come. On the same day, officers at the Department of Naval Aeronautics met to consider a series of requests from the 721st Naval Flying Corps. The request presumed that the corps would immediately be transferred to Konoike Air Base, and that all training would be completed by December 20. The requests were:

1. That 20 training Ohkas and 30 Bettys capable of transporting the smaller planes, along with 20 training Zeros, be assembled at Konoike as quickly as possible.
2. That the number of maintenance personnel, including communications and paymasters, be 70 percent above what a combatant corps would have, and that reserve crews be guaranteed.
3. That the pilots who were to crew the Ohka planes be classified into A, B, C, and D groups. Those in the A Group were to be the ones who were ready to go at any time. Those classified as B were the ones who could be considered ready, depending on the circumstances. Those in the C class were those ready in some cases, and the D group were those needing additional training and should be used only on special occasions.

All of the 721st's requests were granted, and it was unanimously agreed that the 721st should be given priority for whatever it needed.

The Naval General Staff concluded that the Ohka Squadron could be dispatched to the Philippines by the end of December. They decided that out of the 100 Ohka planes scheduled for completion by the end of November, 30 should be sent to the Philippines and the remaining 70 to Taiwan. At the same time, the Naval General Staff ordered the Aeronautical Department to increase the number of Ohka planes to be completed from 100 to 150.

Ground testing of the Ohka's fuselage rockets was completed on November 6, and the Naval Aeronautical Research Laboratory immediately went into mass production of the planes. It soon became obvious, however, that the laboratory could not meet the demand for 150 planes by the end of November, primarily because of the time it took to produce the wooden wings and tail. It was decided, therefore, to subcontract the production of the wings and tails to several private firms, despite the strong feeling that the manufacture of the Ohka should be a strictly military matter.

The manufacturers of the Betty bombers were also ordered to speed up their production schedules. The Second Naval Aeronautical Arsenal at Kisarazu, in Chiba Prefecture, and the 22nd Naval Aeronautical Arsenal in Kanoya, Kagoshima Prefecture, were engaged in converting conventional Bettys over to mother planes to carry the Ohkas. The Mitsubishi Nagoya Aircraft Company, the manufacturer of the Bettys, was ordered to increase the protective armament of the planes, even though it meant sacrificing some of its performance capabilities.

The Betty bombers often had one fatal weakness: Fuel tanks were built into the wings, and when the wings were struck by enemy fire, they often burst into flames. As the Americans increased the pace and volume of their attacks against the Japanese forces, more and more of the Bettys were lost because of this problem.

One countermeasure that the manufacturer took was to coat the wings with rubber to help prevent fuel from leaking out when the tanks were hit. This method had a serious drawback of its own, however, as it changed the airfoil, increased wing drag, and reduced the bombers' cruising speed by 10 knots.

Mitsubishi also designed a fuel tank that had an automatic fire extinguisher filled with carbonic acid. If a fire broke out, the acid was released. Steel plates were installed around the fuel tanks inside the hull, and also behind the pilot's seat. These protective measures further increased the weight of the planes, reducing their speed even more. Even so, the danger from fire was far from solved.

The 721st moved from Hyakurigahara to Konoike Air Base on November 8. Two sign plates were then attached to the front of the main gate at Konoike. One of them read: 721ST NAVAL FLYING CORPS. The other one read: *KAIGUN JINRAI BUTAI* (Navy Thunder Gods Corps). Okamura was the godfather of the corps.

When the independent-minded Lieutenant-Commander Nonaka arrived at the new base, he brought with him two large banners and a war drum that was to be used for the call to formation. The banners read: *HI-RI-HO-KEN-TEN* and *NAMU-HACHIMAN-DAI-BOSATSU*, both favorite sayings of the famous general Kusunoki Masashige, who, in the mid-fourteenth century attempted to help the Emperor regain power from the ruling shogun, and killed himself when he failed.

HI-RI-HO-KEN-TEN was an acronym for: Irrationality can never match reason—Reason can never match law—Law can never match power—Power can never match Heaven. The inscription on the second banner was a popular Buddhist prayer.

North of the airfield, across the Horiwari River, was a sandy area that had been used for bombing practice. The sands were graded to turn the area into a practice field for Ohka training planes.

By this time, all the key personnel assigned to the 721st had arrived at Konoike. Among the lower-ranking personnel who arrived at this time were Commander Shusei Igarashi and Lieutenant Morimasa Yunokawa. Most of the reserve officers assigned to the corps were from the thirteenth graduating class of the cadet school. Igarashi was appointed vice-commander of the corps.

Higher Flight Petty Officer Ichikawa was among the new arrivals. He immediately went to see his friend Tamura.

"Why didn't you send me a postcard?" he asked. "What happened to the 'bump'?"

" 'Bump' is not the word," Tamura replied. "Come on. I'll show you." He led Ichikawa to a hangar and pointed to one of the Ohka trainers.

"That's gonna be your coffin," he said.

Ichikawa's small conviction diminished further as Tamura explained that the Ohka would be carried aloft under a Betty and dropped in the vicinity of its target. "Don't be so disappointed," he said to his friend. "If you crash-dived in an attack bomber, no one would be watching you die. In this thing, you'll be diving in front of the entire crew of the mother plane."

That night, before going to sleep, Ichikawa opened his notebook and wrote on the back of the cover: "After some 20 years I have nothing to leave behind except this little notebook, which I dedicate to my parents, who have always enfolded me in love."

In mid-November, large packing crates containing disassembled Ohka trainers began arriving at the air base. Reserve Lieutenant Kazuyoshi Nakao and his Ohka Maintenance Division immediately began assembling the planes.

On November 13, Vice-Admiral Michitaro Totsuka, chief of the Aeronautical Department, visited Konoike to watch the first Ohka descent exercises to be staged at the new location. Lieutenant Tsutomu Kariya, a graduate of the Naval College, was chosen to make the first trial flight in one of the Ohka trainers.

The mother plane with the Ohka suspended beneath it took off, circled the field, and dropped the Ohka at the scheduled 3,000-meter level. The first portion of the Ohka's flight went as expected. But immediately after Kariya jettisoned the water ballast, the plane's nose went up; it lost speed and then began a steep dive toward the ground.

Everyone watching from the ground jumped up. As the plane approached the ground, they were visualizing Kariya's struggle as he tried to bring the nose of the plane up. The plane plunged into the sand and flipped end-over-end. A rescue team rushed to the crumpled plane and dragged Kariya out. There were no conspicuous external injuries, but his face was ashen and he was groaning with pain.

Within a few minutes after being taken to the dispensary on the base, Kariya lapsed into unconsciousness. Two hours later, paralysis caused by total body contusion set in. His arms and legs became cold, his pulse waned, and he died. It was later learned that the accident was caused by a mistake in jettisoning the water ballast. The night before the test, Nakao, leader of the Maintenance Division, had gathered all of the Ohka pilots and given them a detailed explanation of why the water in the tail tanks should be discharged first. Kariya had discharged the water in the nose of the plane first.

There was nothing that could be done. It was a pilot error. There was no time to mourn Kariya's death, but the Thunder Gods Corps held an extraordinary meeting and decided to exclude the water ballast from future training exercises. The following day, immediately after a brief funeral ceremony for Kariya, the training flights were resumed.

The real cause of Kariya's death was covered up by the Aeronautical Department. In the official record it was noted: "It is suspected that water leaked into the nose cavity when the ballast was being loaded, and got into the cabin during the glide, obscuring the pilot's view."

Chapter 3

It was a chilly, windy day in November and the Thunder Gods were in the final stages of their training at Konoike Air Base. Lieutenant-Commander Goro Nonaka's *HI-RI-HO-KEN-TEN* banner fluttered in the breeze in front of the formation area. His war-drum beat over the PA system announced to the crews of the Ohka and Betty bombers to fall in.

"Ohka Squadron ready!"

"Betty Squadron ready!"

On the commanding platform, Nonaka responded to the salute of the squadron leaders in his usual way—more of a wave than a salute. "It's a goddam beautiful day!" he shouted. "Betty Squadron, drop 'em when you think the time is right! Ohka Squadron, keep your eyes open! Peel and dive! Go for it!"

Three Bettys took off, the shark-shaped Ohkas attached to their bellies looking like minnows. Once they had reached 3,000 meters, two of the planes moved away and began circling. The third headed for the drop zone.

The floor hatch of the third Betty was opened and cold wind gushed into the plane. A crew member, fighting the force of the wind, reached down through the hatch and used an L-shaped pole to unlatch the cockpit cover of the Ohka. The Ohka pilot climbed down into the cramped cockpit space, closed the cover, and released the belts that held the control bar and foot levers steady. He then hooked a band from the dashboard over the control bar, so that it would not move in the drop from the Betty. Then he fastened his seat belt and tapped out a "Ready" signal on the intercom hookup with the mother plane.

As the Betty approached the drop zone, the Ohka pilot watched a red light on his control panel. There were three short flashes and a buzzing sound. This was followed by one long flash and a short one, at which instant the Ohka dropped from the mother craft like a stone.

The pilot saw dust rising around him in the cockpit and he suddenly felt utterly weightless. He released the band from the control bar and gripped it, watching the ground appear below. The plane fell for nearly 300 meters before it began to glide at 250 miles per hour. Banking to the left, the pilot had a fleeting glimpse of the Pacific Ocean. He lowered the flaps and began lining up on the makeshift airport.

He braced himself for the impact as, altitude decreasing rapidly, he approached the sandy runway at a hundred miles per hour. The runners bit into the sand. The plane bounced and slid for several hundred yards before stopping in a cloud of dust. The pilot was unhurt, but wet with sweat. He had been involuntarily holding his breath during the two minutes after being dropped from the Betty, and it rushed out in a deep sigh now. He was glad it was over, thinking that his death dive would be easier than the practice one.

The practice dives continued. The Ohkas were picked up from the landing runway and returned to the main runway by truck and aboard a small steam locomotive on a temporary track laid by Reserve Lieutenant Iwao Tsuji, a group sub-leader of the Maintenance Division. Before each of the Ohka pilots climbed into the planes for his practice dive, Iwaki would shout several times: "Hit the carrier with your forehead! Hit the carrier with your forehead!" The men named him "Toad" because of his big mouth. When each of the Ohka pilots had completed the diving exercise, his classification was upgraded to an "A".

On November 15, two days after the training began, the Thunder Gods Corps was officially attached to the Combined Fleet on the Pacific War front. Lieutenant-Commander Hachiro Yanagisawa was appointed flight squadron leader of the Ohka Squadron, and Lieutenant Akira Hirano was assigned to replace Lieutenant Kariya, who had been killed in the first test. The Betty Squadron was named the 711th Attack Squadron, and Lieutenant-Commander Nonaka was officially confirmed as its leader. The fighters assigned to cover the Betty bombers and their precious cargoes were designated the 306th Fighter Squadron, with Lieutenant Kunio Kanzaki as its leader.

It was unprecedented for one corps to possess three different flight squadrons—the Ohkas, the Bettys, and the Zero fighters—and this was an indication of the magnitude of the operation.

As the days passed, some of the resolve of the Ohka pilots began to waver. Those who had been pilots of fighter planes, especially, missed the aircraft they were familiar with. Higher Flight Petty Officer Masazo Okubo was one of these. His colleagues Goro Tsuda and Kojiro Murakami, both of whom had transferred to the Thunder Gods Corps from the 306th Fighter Squadron, urged him to reconsider, saying he should stay with the fighter planes a bit longer. Okubo agreed, but was not sure if he could get released from the program. Tsuda and Murakami submitted a petition to Squadron Leader Kanzaki, asking that Okubo be transferred, but Kanzaki rejected the request. The names of the Ohka crews had already been submitted to Emperor Hirohito, and it was therefore too late for anyone to change his mind.

The training flights of the Ohka continued, but there was a great deal of grumbling about the plane. Lieutenant-Commander Nonaka, leader of the mother-plane squadron, made no attempt to disguise his contempt for the plane. In a reference to the Navy principle that it would fight to the death with whatever weapons were available, even spears, Nonaka quipped, "This spear is hard to use!"

In the privacy of his room, Nonaka expressed his anguish to his colleagues, saying, "I always talk big, using vulgar language. But I'm a timid man, afraid of dying. I swear to divert my mind, to put myself in a position where I can't chicken out at the last minute. But I don't want to kill myself, especially with this cheap spear! I wish I could go back to night raids and blitz as much as I want to!"

Nonaka's comments and complaints came to the attention of Special Service Sub-Lieutenant Ota, who had originated the plan for the special suicide plane. He did not criticize Nonaka directly, agreeing instead that the Ohka planes should have been equipped with rogo rockets as originally planned.

Ota's point was that rogo rockets would have increased the range and capabilities of the Ohka planes, thereby reducing the burden placed on the mother planes. But the war would not wait for the perfection of the rogo rockets, and the Naval General Staff did not share Ota's misgivings about the powder rockets. The ranking officers of the NGS had convinced themselves that with sufficient fighter protection, the Ohka planes could be turned into "fail-safe killing spears."

On November 23, Admiral Oikawa, chief of the Naval General Staff, visited the Thunder Gods Corps to check on its progress. One of the officers in the unit suggested that a special event be staged for the admiral—a dive performed by one of the pilots who had done an especially good job on a previous test. Reserve Sub-Lieutenant Hachiro Hosokawa was selected for the honor.

Hosokawa did not consider it an honor, however, and complained to his commanding officer, Lieutenant-Commander Yanagisawa. "I don't want to put on a show just for the admiral! Why don't they let a scheduled trainee make the dive?" he said. "I'm ready to go on a real mission in the Ohka, but why should I risk my life now just for show?"

Yanagisawa agreed with Hosokawa. "There is no need for us to go out of our way to please the admiral. We'll go ahead with the regular training schedule."

On the following day, just before the training was to get under way, there was an air-raid warning and the exercise was called off. Ninety-three B-29 bombers based in the Mariana Islands came in over the Izu Peninsula, bombed the Nakajima Aircraft Company's Musashino factory, and passed over the Kujukuri Coast toward the Pacific Ocean following the attack. Helpless, members of the Thunder Gods Corps watched the condensation trails of the huge bombers as they headed back toward their base.

On November 25, Corps Commander Okamura divided the Thunder Gods Corps into four units in preparation for the move to the Philippines. Each unit comprised 53 members—7 reserve officers and 46 petty officers. Each unit was under the direct command of a graduate of the Naval College.

After the divisions had been formed, Flight Squadron Leader Yanagisawa got into an argument with Okamura over the nature of his assignment. Yanagisawa had been transferred to the 721st as a regular staff officer, not as an Ohka pilot. But he had taken it for granted that he would share the fate of his men.

"It is a Navy tradition that a commander leads his men. As the flight squadron leader I should make the first attack!" he shouted.

"I didn't bring you here with the intention of putting you on an Ohka!" Okamura replied in an equally loud voice. "Your job is to maintain the morale of the men until they are sent out, and then recruit other pilots to take their place!"

"You mean I have to stay right out of the battle!" Yanagisawa yelled.

"All right! All right!" Okamura said. "You can go in the end, but not before that!"

Okamura knew that once a mission began, there was no need for a flight commander. The Ohka pilot was just a passenger aboard a Betty until the target was within range, and after he entered the Ohka he was nothing more than a bomb. Actual command in the attacks would be in the hands of the leader of the Betty Squadron. He explained this to Yanagisawa as patiently as possible.

"The morale of a squadron is usually built up doing formation flight training and in preparations for group attacks, but there is no need for such training with the Ohka. It is, therefore, very important that you concentrate on keeping the morale of the men up," he added.

"In that case," Yanagisawa retorted, "it makes more sense for the leader to dive first to set an example!"

The argument continued for several minutes. Finally Yanagisawa said, "I will not accept a role in which I can't fight along with my own men. I'd rather have some older person assume this task. Please send me back to conventional fighters!"

Okamura realized he had reached an impasse with Yanagisawa, and since he could not force him to accept an assignment requiring extraordinary sensitivity and commitment, he gave in and subsequently put Wing Commander Iwaki in charge of the Thunder Gods Corps, and gave him the responsibility of maintaining morale and recruiting new Ohka pilots.

This move caused considerable gossip among the Thunder Gods pilots, and rumors began to fly. "This means the Ohka Squadron is nothing more than an arsenal, and Yanagisawa has refused to act as its watchdog," the men complained.

As the gossiping and the rumors continued, it became more and more obvious to the Ohka pilots that they were really on their own; there was no way the many staff officers involved with the project could feel as they felt, or share their fate.

Reacting to and trying to cope with their extraordinary position, the petty officers who had been chosen as Ohka pilots began to manifest strong anti-organizational behavior. They started slacking off on the strict military discipline required of all members of Japan's armed forces. Their salutes were sloppy, if they bothered to salute at all. They wore their mufflers when they were not on duty, saying they were cold. Some began letting their hair grow long, despite the regulation that only officers could grow their hair. Complaints about the food became commonplace.

The worst offenders belonged to the Hayashi Division of the Thunder Gods, but Lieutenant Hayashi ignored their behavior, saying that rules meant nothing to men who were going to certain death in battle.

Finally, the behavior of one of the petty officer pilots got to Wing Commander Iwaki. He called the four division leaders in, dressed them down, and ordered them to see that the heads of all the offenders in their divisions were shaved.

Division Leader Mitsuhashi, who also had long hair, had his head shaved first as an example to his men. Lieutenant Hayashi disagreed with the order, but finally gave in and persuaded his men to follow suit. Iwaki himself shaved the head of the man who was considered the worst offender in the squadron. He left one tuft of hair on top of the man's head, and said brusquely, "You can send it to your parents as 'Hair of the Departed'!"

Two serious accidents at the air base further exacerbated the growing tension among the Thunder Gods pilots. One pilot was killed during a training exercise in a Zero fighter plane. Another was gravely injured when he failed to land his Ohka plane correctly. Still, the training continued.

In the meantime, the performance tests on the Ohka had reached their final stages. On November 19, the wing rockets were retested on the ground at the Naval Aeronautical Research Laboratory. It soon became clear there was no sure way of equalizing the thrust of the rockets, so it was decided to dispense with them.

The next day, the bomb warhead was tested. An Ohka loaded with the bomb was dropped into the Pacific Ocean. It exploded on impact, sending up a column of water more than 50 meters high, and causing white impulse waves to rise to the surface for several seconds after the explosion.

Then came the first speed test, to check the stability and operational efficiency of the plane at 350 knots. Although the initial plan had been to use an unmanned plane, Flight Warrant Officer Nagano flew the Ohka because he felt it could be landed safely with just one fuselage rocket. In the test, the Ohka was dropped at an altitude of 4,000 meters. As soon as it began to glide, Nagano ignited the single fuselage rocket. The speedometer jumped to the calculated speed of 350 knots. The plane performed as expected, and Nagano landed safely.

This left only one test: to see whether the plane would perform equally well at a critical speed of 550 knots. Three tail rockets were to be attached to the Ohka, which was to be taken aloft and dropped, but without a pilot.

The rockets were equipped with automatic ignition devices. The plan was to fire the first rocket when the plane reached 200 knots, then fire the second and third rockets when it reached 500 knots. It was estimated that the plane would be traveling at 550 knots when it impacted with the target. The drop was to be filmed by high-speed photography for analysis.

Chief Designer Miki began making the final preparations for the speed test. He was both excited and relieved that the project had reached the final stage. The previous months had been the most intense and trying of his life.

However, on the night of November 24, American forces launched their first great saturation-bombing air raid on Tokyo. The damage and the shock to the nation were indescribable. Reverberations quickly affected the Ohka test program.

The morning before the scheduled speed test, Nazuka rushed to the design room to find Miki. "Can the critical-speed test be postponed?" he asked. "We don't have a test plane ready," he added.

"What do you mean?" Miki said in surprise. "They are supposed to have 150 planes done by the end of the month. I understood that 30 of them were already completed, and we made arrangements to get one of them days ago!"

"The Naval General Staff has ordered that 100 planes be ready by the twenty-seventh, and they are refusing to release even one before then," Nazuka answered.

Miki was dumbfounded. "What do they want them for?" he asked.

"They're going to put them on board the *Shinano* in Yokosuka." The *Shinano* was a *Yamato*-type battleship that had been converted to an aircraft carrier and had just completed its trial run.

Nazuka continued, "The enemy air raids on Tokyo indicate that there will be raids on Yokosuka any day. So the NGS has decided to move the *Shinano* to the Inland Sea. It's supposed to leave on the twenty-eighth. They've decided to ship the Ohkas to Kure now to get them out of danger and then send them to Taiwan and the Philippines."

Miki knew that the Yokosuka Flying Corps was frantic with fear that the enemy would begin bombing the base at any moment. "All right," he said. "I'll postpone the test until the next group of planes are completed, but we have to make that test," he added, with emphasis.

The various subcontractors, including Nippon Aircraft Company's Ofuna factory and the Chigasaki Company factory, responsible for making the wooden wings, were ordered to speed up their production schedules to complete the 100 planes in the next three days. The hold-up was actually in the Aeroplane Section's own Second Shop, which was responsible for the assembly and rigging of the planes. The shop was put on a 72-hour-a-week schedule.

Workers were divided into three eight-hour shifts, so work went on around the clock. Nazuka simply stopped going to bed and kept watch over all of the shifts. The noise and the movement of cranes and parts were incessant.

There was no place inside the shop to store completed planes. As they came off the assembly lines they were trucked to a hangar belonging to the Yokosuka Flying Corps. Nazuka went to the hangar to check the performance of the control bar and foot pedals of each plane. After the checkup, the planes were packed in large wooden boxes and sent directly to the *Shinano* in the harbor.

By the morning of the twenty-seventh, the third day of the marathon effort to complete the 100 planes, Nazuka was exhausted. He had been taking stimulants to stay awake. His feet began to swell, and he could no longer feel or fully control his own body. His working speed slowed drastically. At noon on that day, B-29s raided Tokyo again.

A Navy officer marched up to Nazuka where he was working in the hangar. "I'm the wing commander of the Thunder Gods Corps. Are you the person in charge here? Why aren't all the planes completed? What the hell is wrong with this place?" he shouted aggressively.

Nazuka was shocked and offended. "We're doing the best we can," he answered. "Mind your own goddam business!"

"What do you mean by that crack?" the officer yelled. "If you don't get the job done on time, we'll bomb this damn place ourselves!"

"Do it!" Nazuka shouted in reply.

Late that evening the last of the 100 Ohkas was delivered to the packing crews. Nazuka returned to the Second Shop, thanked the workers for their superhuman efforts, then lay down on a cot in the shop and went to sleep for the first time in nearly four days.

November 28 dawned cloudy and chilly. The shop went back to its normal schedule and continued working on the remaining order of 50 planes. At four-thirty in the afternoon, the *Shinano*, escorted by two destroyers, passed along the coast in sight of the laboratory. Many of the men responsible for its cargo of Ohka planes watched the great ship steam by, but they felt dejected and angry. Nazuka had been informed earlier that, due to the hectic situation, only 50 of the planes were aboard the *Shinano*. Feeling helpless and still out of touch with his body, Nazuka slowly waved his cap to the 50 Ohkas on the ship.

The next day an officer from the Yokosuka Flying Corps came up to Nazuka looking pale and distraught.

"What is it?" Nazuka asked.

The man could not look Nazuka in the face. He was obviously suffering from shock. Finally, he managed to whisper, "The *Shinano*'s done!"

"Done? What do you mean 'Done'?" Nazuka said in growing alarm.

"Gone," said the man. "It was sunk this morning by an American submarine."

Nazuka felt as though he were going to faint. He was stunned. His mind went blank.

The *Shinano* had waited in Kaneda Bay near the tip of the Miura Peninsula until nightfall and then had begun cruising southward along the Izu Islands. As she approached Mikura Island, she was spotted by the U.S. submarine *Archerfish*, which was in the area to rescue any B-29 crews who had to ditch their aircraft in the nearby waters. The *Archerfish* quickly ran down the *Shinano*, launching six torpedoes in rapid succession. Four of them struck the ship, all on the starboard side. The ship had not been given a full-scale water-pressure test, and its crew was not sufficiently trained in damage control. Seven hours after it was struck, the *Shinano* rolled over and sank, 55 miles off the Cape of Shio, Wakayama Prefecture. The personnel on the *Shinano* were 1,800 crew members and 700 workers who were aboard putting the final touches to the ship's rigging. Nearly half of them were lost.

On December 1, a total of 88 Ohkas, including the 50 not on board the *Shinano*, were shipped overland to the Kure Naval Port. From there, 30 were to go to Clark Field in the Philippines, and 58 to Taiwan. The Aeronautical Department ordered the Naval Aeronautical Research Laboratory to add an additional 50 to the original order to make up for the ones lost in the sinking.

The day the 88 Ohkas began their overland journey to Kure along the Inland Sea, Admiral Soemu Toyoda, the commander-in-chief of the Combined Fleet, came to Konoike to see Okamura and brief him on the current plans for the operation.

"On December 22 the 721st Flying Corps will advance on Clark Field from Taiwan. The Ohkas will begin their first attack with a large-scale assault on enemy ships in Leyte Gulf on the twenty-third," he revealed.

Toyoda presented each Ohka pilot with a short sword and a white headband. On each headband Toyoda had inscribed in large red characters the words THUNDER GODS. The division leaders, Mitsuhashi, Yunokawa, and Hayashi, were promoted to lieutenant. Hosokawa and other sub-lieutenants were promoted to first class reserve sub-lieutenant.

After inspecting the Thunder Gods Corps, Toyoda and his entourage joined the corps' executive officers for dinner. The countdown had begun. There were 22 more days before the first "Exploding Cherry Blossoms" and their pilots were scheduled to blow themselves to bits against the warships of the enemy. Many toasts were drunk to the upcoming event, each man consumed by his own thoughts.

A little drunk from the toasts, the maverick Goro Nonaka felt totally alien and did not participate in the attempts to keep the mood up. In an effort to bolster Nonaka's mood, Admiral Toyoda leaned over and asked him, "How is your family doing?"

Nonaka stared at the admiral disdainfully and replied, "Well, sir, old ladies would never bitch if their kids were home!"

The admiral gave up the attempt to make small talk with the notorious fighter pilot.

As the group became more and more intoxicated, the talk became louder and wilder. The men began to brag about totally destroying the enemy ships in Leyte Gulf and making it possible for the Japanese forces to recover the island. The bragging disgusted Nonaka, but he did not dare leave the table.

Finally, Okamura stood up, declared that the dinner was over, and recommended that the admiral and his staff take advantage of their presence at the base to go duck hunting the following morning.

"Konoike is famous for its wild ducks," he said. "I myself enjoy casting nets occasionally, and just the other day I caught a whole truckload of ducks. That requires a little skill, but I'm sure you'll be able to bag as many ducks as you want with your pistols."

The visitors swallowed Okamura's story, and the following morning got up before daybreak to go hunting. When it was light enough to see, there were only a few ducks on the famous pond, and no more showed up. The admiral's staff took random shots at the straggling ducks, without any success at all. The Thunder Gods smiled and joked about the incident.

On December 3, Navy Minister Yonai also visited the Thunder Gods Corps. This was the first time that any Japanese flight group had ever been visited by the three top navy leaders—the chief of Naval General Staff, the commander-in-chief of the Combined Fleet, and the navy minister.

A few days later, Fleet Admiral Osami Nagano also appeared at the base. Following his inspection of the Thunder Gods, a sumo wrestling match was staged for the benefit of the pilots, who expected to be dead before the next regularly scheduled sumo tournament. A group of the pilots added to the festive atmosphere by singing a humorous sortie song written by Nonaka to the tune of a popular melody.

On December 6, as plans went ahead for the move to the Philippines, Reserve Sub-Lieutenant Iwao Tsuji and 11 petty officers were picked from the Ohka Maintenance Division and dispatched to Clark Field on Luzon, from where the first Ohka attack would be launched. A communications team was to follow. The packing of equipment began. Marcotte Airfield, located at the southern tip of Clark Field, was selected as the base for the Thunder Gods Corps. Several tunnels were hurriedly dug into the low hills on the southwest side of the field to house the Ohkas.

On December 10 the Combined Fleet headquarters set December 20 as the date for the Thunder Gods Corps to move, and informed Clark Field headquarters of the decision. The date for the first Thunder Gods attack against the American forces in Leyte, originally set for December 23, was postponed to January 10.

On December 13, a meeting was held to discuss the best way of shipping the Ohkas from Kure to the front lines in the Philippines and Taiwan. It was decided that the 30 planes destined for Clark Field should be put aboard the aircraft carrier *Unryu*, which was to leave port on the sixteenth. The 58 planes slated for Taiwan would leave Kure a week later on board the carrier *Ryuho*.

The Naval Aeronautical Research Laboratory reported on December 15 that it had completed 151 planes—150 for combat use, and the extra one for the final critical-speed test. The laboratory then suspended work on the Ohkas and began producing training planes. Production of the Ohkas was transferred to the First Naval Aeronautical Arsenal in

Ibaragi, which had already begun making preparations for large-scale production of the human-missile planes. Altogether, 600 Ohkas were scheduled for completion by the end of March 1945.

Nazuka was reassigned to supervise the production of wooden dive bombers at the Matsushita Aircraft Company in Osaka. The original Val-class carrier-based bombers had been designed to be made of metal.

On the same day, American forces landed on the island of Mindanao, between Leyte and Luzon, blocking the Japanese supply route and threatening the plan to stage a last-ditch battle on Luzon to stop the American advance.

The aircraft carriers *Unryu* and *Ryuho* were ordered to speed up their departure for the Philippines and Taiwan. The *Unryu* left Sasebo Naval Port on December 17.

On December 19, the navy department of the military headquarters merged the Thunder Gods Corps and the T-Attack Corps, originally formed in Taiwan, into the 11th Aviation Group. At the same time the 708th Attack Squadron, which had belonged to the T-Attack Corps, was transferred to the Thunder Gods Corps to reinforce the number of mother planes.

Lieutenant-Commander Jiro Adachi, leader of the 708th Attack Squadron, had been a classmate of Nonaka's at the Naval College and had had similar battle experiences, but he was the opposite of Nonaka as far as battle tactics were concerned. He preferred "nonchalant" sorties.

Adachi and his group were moved to Miyazaki Air Base in Kyushu and ordered to commute to Konoike for training, acting as mother planes for the Ohka Squadron. It was also decided that 27 Bettys from Adachi's squadron and 27 from Nonaka's group would be transferred to the Philippines, along with 60 Zeros from the 306th Fighter Squadron, to act as cover for the Bettys and Ohkas.

Three of the four Ohka units were to be sent to the Philippines. The fourth group was to remain at Konoike to help with the training of the new pilots. Iwaki had a difficult time trying to decide which of the four groups should be left behind. Mitsuhashi, Yunokawa, and Hayashi had all graduated from the Naval College the same year. He knew there would be a problem if he chose one of them to stay behind. He finally chose Lieutenant Akira Hirano, who was senior to the other three by two years, to remain.

Hirano refused to accept the order and started a loud dispute with

Iwaki. Exasperated, Iwaki finally shouted, "If you want to go that much, find somebody who will stay here in your place!"

Most of the members of Lieutenant Hirano's group were also unhappy about the decision. They knew they were going to die, and the waiting often seemed worse than death. Besides, they were all anxious to be the first Thunder Gods heroes to die. "The first attack will make national headlines, but the second one will be buried somewhere on the inside," they said.

Having been treated as live heroes, the men did not want to be forgotten so quickly and easily when they died. Higher Flight Petty Officer Ichikawa led a group to Hirano's room to complain. Hirano understood the men but explained there was nothing he could do. "Someone has to stay. Please do it for my sake," he said.

Ichikawa lost control and began to drink heavily. He quarrelled and fought with everybody he met. The thought of his best friend Higher Flight Petty Officer Tamura being included in the first Ohka attack especially galled him.

The Ohka Squadron pilots in the three groups which were to be in the first assault against the enemy began their final preparations. Those who were to fly the 30 Ohkas then on board the carrier *Unryu*, destined for Clark Field, would be the first to receive their final orders.

At 4 P.M. on the same day (December 19) word came that the *Unryu* was under attack by an American submarine (the *Redfish*). It had been hit by two torpedoes and suffered an explosion in one of its munitions rooms. The ship went under in 30 minutes.

This disaster finally made navy headquarters aware of the danger in trying to get ships through to the Philippines and Taiwan. The *Ryuho* had a better chance of making it to Taiwan simply because of the shorter distance. But having the Ohkas in Taiwan instead of at Clark Field presented another problem. The distance from Taiwan to Leyte Gulf was beyond the range of the fighters which were to protect the Bettys and the Ohkas.

The distance between Takao (Gaoxiong) Air Base in Taiwan and Leyte Gulf was 1,400 kilometers. The Bettys, burdened by the extra weight and drag of the Ohkas, would barely be able to make the round trip, and there was no way the fighter planes could travel that distance. The only solution was to send the fighter squadron on to Clark Field in advance, then have the fighters rendezvous with the Bettys somewhere over the Philippines.

The Combined Fleet Headquarters dispatched Vice-Admiral Ryunosuke Kusaka and his support staff to Clark Field to work out strategy for the Thunder Gods attack. The war front staff severely criticized this decision, saying it would be impossible to successfully carry out such a plan in airspace totally controlled by the enemy. The first meeting between Kusaka and the staff at the war front headquarters was anything but harmonious.

On December 28 the Naval Aeronautical Department examined the idea of ferrying the Ohkas directly to Clark Field on Luzon by air, in order to stage the Thunder Gods attacks from there. It was determined that a Betty would be able to reach the Clark Field area from Japan only if the 1,200-kilogram bomb in the nose of the Ohka were removed.

The decision was then made to airlift 30 of the empty Ohkas to Clark Field, and to send the warheads by transport ship. Ten other fully equipped Ohkas were scheduled to be shipped to Manila by sea convoy in early January.

Since the first Thunder Gods assault could not be made until the Ohkas arrived in the Philippines, the transfer of the pilots from Konoike to Taiwan was once again postponed, this time until January 10, the day scheduled for the first Thunder Gods attack if everything had gone according to plan. The tenseness that had been growing among the members of the Ohka Squadron lessened considerably with this news. Several of the petty officers decided to talk to Iwaki. They went to his room.

"Aren't you afraid of dying?" one of the pilots asked him.

"Of course, now that I can stand on my own feet, I find the thought of dying difficult to accept," he replied.

"Then why do we have to make the special attacks?" another of the petty officers demanded.

Iwaki got angry. "Because we volunteered! That's why!"

The petty officers were not satisfied with his response, and started to protest further.

"It doesn't make any difference what you say. We're going to do it, and that's final!" Iwaki said with cold determination.

The petty officers continued staring at him. They didn't know what else to do. Finally one of them said sourly, "All right! At least we're gonna die together!" Then they left his room.

Concerned that the morale of the group would fall even lower, Iwaki summoned the reserve officers in the Thunder Gods Corps, gave them a pep talk, and ordered them to take immediate steps to reverse the situation.

Several of the stricter reserve officers began putting the petty officers in their groups through the same kind of hard physical training that they themselves had received. This included repeatedly forcing the men to fall out in formation in the cold weather and go through other basic routines. One of the petty officers began limping, saying he had injured his leg. The group leader slapped him sharply and yelled, "How dare you complain, a mere petty officer!"

The petty-officer pilots believed there should be no class or rank discrimination between them and the reserve officers in this corps, particularly as many of the reserve had been their former students. They were willing to acknowledge the superior authority of the division leaders because they were career officers who had graduated from the Naval College. But they were not going to accept abuse from the reserve officers, who had received all their training in a special 90-day speeded-up wartime course.

The most disliked reserve officer was Sub-Lieutenant Katsuhei Terashita, who was especially zealous in performing what he regarded as his sacred responsibility.

Flight Petty Officer First Class Manabu Yamaguchi repeatedly went to Senior Reserve Officer Hosokawa and told him there was a serious morale problem in the Ohka Squadron. Hosokawa did nothing about the warnings. He was too inexperienced to perceive the real problem behind the complaints of the other petty officers.

In early January, 150 of the U.S. warships that had massed in Leyte Gulf began moving northward toward Luzon, the main island of the Philippines. The few suicide attacks on the ships by fighter planes had no effect. Virtually all of the planes were shot down before they could reach any target.

The site of any decisive battle to come was thus moved from Leyte to Luzon, which meant, however, that the enemy ships would soon be within range of the fighters assigned to protect mother planes bringing the Thunder Gods in from Taiwan.

On January 3 and 4, American ships and planes carried out containing raids on Taiwan and the Ryukyu Islands, then moved off to the east. The Japanese aircraft carrier *Ryuho* took advantage of this opening and moved across the East China Sea, arriving in Taiwan on January 7. The 58 Ohkas were housed in a shelter prepared at Takao

Air Base. The Combined Fleet Headquarters announced that the Thunder Gods Corps and the T-Attack Corps would be moved to southern Kyushu in late January, in preparation for their transfer to Taiwan.

At the Ohka Squadron base in Konoike, the three divisions that were to ship out first took turns going to Tokyo to pay their final visits to the Imperial Palace and to Meiji, Togo, and Yasukuni shrines to pray for victory. Sub-Lieutenant Hiroshi Shinjo joined Lieutenant Hirano's group of Ohka pilots as his assistant.

On January 6, American warships entered Lingayen Gulf, midway up the island of Luzon, and began bombarding Japanese installations ashore. The Thunder Gods Corps was informed of this new development by Military Headquarters. The men were sure their time was drawing near. But more and more of the pilots began to have doubts about their resolve to deliberately blow themselves to bits against American warships. The wait had been so long, and had been postponed so many times, and the consequent suffering they were experiencing had become increasingly intense.

While plans were being made and unmade about transfer of the original Thunder Gods to the battle areas, a large number of newcomers were sent to the Thunder Gods Corps as supplementary forces. Some of them had just graduated from the reserve officer training programs. Others were from the Naval Training School. They had finished only the most basic level of flight training and were barely able to maintain horizontal flight. All of them received a "D" classification when they joined the elite Thunder Gods Corps.

As a result of this influx of untrained men, there were 190 pilots with an "A" classification, 6 with a "B" classification, and 215 with a "D" ranking—a totally ridiculous proportion in the minds of the old-timers. The A and B pilots, who had been there from the start felt that this was humiliating. Friction between the newcomers and the staff officers of the corps grew steadily. What the old-timers did not know was that Okamura had planned from the start to use D-ranked pilots in the program as a means of saving the better-trained pilots for other duties.

On January 8, two days after the pilots had visited the leading shrines in Tokyo, a troupe of entertainers from the Toho Entertainment Company was brought to the base as a consolation for the Thunder Gods. The show seemed to relax the men somewhat, but tension remained high. After the show, when the pilots started returning to their barracks, one of the petty officers walked on a lawn that was off-limits. He was struck by Sub-Lieutenant Terashita, the reserve officer who was especially strict. The petty officers were incensed and began talking about getting revenge on the reserve officers.

All of the Thunder Gods Corps officers above the rank of group leader left the base with the members of the entertainment company to go to a restaurant in the nearby town of Itako. A short while later, to help relieve the tension, the petty officers were given permission to leave the base, but only a few actually left. Most of them gathered in the petty officers' barracks. Feelings were running high.

Ichikawa stood up and said, "We've had enough of the way some of the reserve officers treat us. Let's have it out with them tonight. Depending on what happens, we may lose a service stripe, so anybody who is not ready for that, better go on to bed!"

Someone brought bottles of beer and saké into the room, and the men began to drink. The drinking bout itself was not unusual, but this time the men were especially agitated and became louder and more passionate in their condemnation of the reserve officers.

To avoid having trouble with the other officers in the corps, Ichikawa, accompanied by his friend Yamaguchi, went to the senior sentry corporal's office and told the corporal that the men were drinking and there might be a little more noise than usual, but that it was nothing to worry about.

Surprised and pleased by the civil attitude of the Ohka pilots, usually so rude and arrogant, the corporal said, "I understand. Just don't get too wild."

He then offered the two a toast of saké.

When Ichikawa and Yamaguchi returned to the petty officers' lounge, the men were still drinking; they had their swords out, and were talking about taking revenge on the reserve officers.

The yard between the reserve officers' billets and the barracks of the petty officers was lit up by a bright moon. When some of the newly arrived reserve officers came out into the yard and began admiring the moon, it was the last straw for the inflamed petty officers. They rushed outside and started abusing the reserve officers. Other petty officers who were less drunk finally managed to drag their excited comrades back into the barracks, reminding them that the newcomers had nothing to do with their problem. The more belligerent of the petty officers were not satisfied, and were determined to vent their frustration.

"Somebody go get Terashita and bring him here!" they began shouting. "Ichikawa, you go get him. If he won't come we'll raid his room and drag him here!"

Ichikawa agreed to go. He marched out the door, yelling at the others to arm themselves and get ready.

"I'll help you drag him here!" Yamaguchi declared, following Ichikawa outside.

Ichikawa entered the reserve officers' billets but, not being familiar with them, began wandering around, looking for Terashita's room.

Several reserve officers caught sight of Ichikawa and challenged him.

"Hey! What are you doing in here?"

"I'm calling on Terashita," Ichikawa replied.

"What for?" they wanted to know.

"Because I have something to tell him."

"You can do that right here," a reserve officer said.

The other reserve officers began to shout abuse at Ichikawa. Yamaguchi, still waiting outside, heard the uproar, ran back into the petty officers' barracks, and shouted, "Ichikawa's caught!"

The petty officers stormed out of the building, some of them through the windows. From the opposite side of the yard, a group of reserve officers, pushing Ichikawa ahead of them, also spilled out into the yard. Ichikawa staggered toward his own group. Someone handed him a saber.

The petty officers and the reserve officers stared at each other for several seconds. Ichikawa raised his saber high in the air and yelled, "Attack!"

The two groups surged forward and began grappling, punching, and mauling each other. The officer of the day, called by someone not involved in the melee, tried to stop the fighting. He was knocked down and his glasses were broken. Several reserve officers and petty officers who had not been involved in the drinking bout with Ichikawa and the others also tried to stop the fighting but failed. A few minutes later, Hosokawa, the ranking reserve officer, and Hiroshi Takano, the senior petty officer in the corps, arrived, but there was nothing they could do to separate the men. The riot had been going on for nearly an hour before the fighting began to slacken off.

Suddenly someone standing on a podium in the center of the yard cried out: "Petty officers, withdraw!"

The voice belonged to Special Service Sub-Lieutenant Ota, the man who had originated the Ohka plan, a man who had worked his way up from fourth-class seaman and was greatly respected by all of the petty officers.

With both their frustrations and their energies spent, the petty officers obeyed Ota and returned slowly to their barracks. Many of them were nursing painful bruises and other wounds.

Hosokawa waited until all of the men were in the room and had settled down, watching him silently. There were tears streaming down his face.

"How dare you do such a thing!" he said. "It will destroy the whole military system!"

Yamaguchi, one of the leaders in the riot, spoke up quickly. "Sir, that's why I've been telling you there was a problem in the corps. Crying now doesn't do any good. It's too late."

Hosokawa didn't know what else to say. Finally he said: "All of you go to bed now. We'll talk about it tomorrow."

The next day the ranking officers who had been in Itako, enjoying themselves with the Toho entertainers, were shocked to hear the story of the riot. Nonaka was furious. "The ringleaders should be shot!" he said vehemently.

It was the general consensus that the incident was a premeditated criminal act by the leaders of the riot who had taken advantage of the officers' being off post. Training was suspended and a curfew was imposed. A legal officer was dispatched to the base from the Judicial Center to set up court-martial proceedings.

The petty officers remained defiant. Mitsuhashi begged Yamaguchi to apologize. "Please," he said, with tears in his eyes, "just say you were wrong, and we may be able to avoid more serious repercussions!"

Yamaguchi refused. "I don't think I did anything wrong," he insisted. "Why should a man be punished if he is crippled and cannot attend a formation? Even dogs and cats are given sympathy when they are injured!" He was referring to the injured petty officer who had been slapped by the reserve officer for missing a formation.

When questioned by the judicial officer, Ichikawa replied, "The Imperial Rescript for Servicemen states that one should respect one's seniors. But when those seniors fail to respect their juniors, they are equally to blame." He continued to deny responsibility for the riot.

Nonaka was as angry with the reserve officers as he was with the petty officers. He called the officers together and lectured them in the harshest terms possible.

"You are 90-day wonders!" he said. "You still have the mentality of students! The petty officers look down on you and make fun of you!"

Later Hosokawa also met with the reserve officers. "It's true that we only did a 90-day course before active duty," he said, "but unlike graduates of the Naval College, we didn't join the navy to become fleet admirals. We joined the navy because we believed our sacrifices would help save this country. No matter what people say about us, we are proud of that spirit."

Hosokawa blamed himself for some of the problem. He admitted to the men that if he had taken Yamaguchi's warnings more seriously, he might have recognized the arrogance of some of the reserve officers and advised them to change their attitudes and behavior. He said he preferred to interpret the incident as something that happened on the spur of the moment, because the men were under such extraordinary pressure.

After examining the report submitted by the judicial officer, the commanding officer of the corps refused to cover up the incident, saying that such a direct confrontation between petty officers and reserve officers in public could not be condoned. Both Yamaguchi and Takano, a ranking petty officer, remained defiant, refusing to apologize. The corps commander decided to turn them over to Yokosuka Naval Station for trial.

There was some sympathy for Takano, who was being held responsible primarily because of the military system. There was also some sympathy for Yamaguchi among those who felt he was being used as a scapegoat to settle the incident. Both were scheduled to be in the first Ohka suicide attack.

The decision to hold the two men for courts-martial was kept confidential from the command. It was announced that they would be dismissed from the Ohka Squadron and assigned elsewhere.

As soon as the preliminary hearing was over, Wing Commander Iwaki ordered all of the Ohka pilots to run in double-quick time from the base to Kashima Shrine and back, a distance of 16 kilometers. He made the run with them.

The members of the Thunder Gods Corps thought this was the end of the incident, but a month after the corps was transferred to southern Kyushu on the first leg of its journey to the front, Takano and Yamaguchi were sent to the brig at Yokosuka Flying Corps to await trial. Takano was acquitted, and assigned to duty at the Yokosuka Air Base.

After he had been released, Takano visited the judicial officer in charge of prosecuting Yamaguchi and made a strong appeal for his innocence. But the attempt failed. Yamaguchi was found guilty and sentenced to a prison term. He was in jail in Yokosuka when the war ended.

Chapter 4

The new year, 1945, began with a month that was no more auspicious than December had been. In the Philippines, the Navy was running out of airplanes to use in special suicide attacks. On January 9, the day the riot took place at Konoike Air Base, U.S. forces began landing on Luzon from Lingayen Gulf. Before the day ended they had completed a solid bridgehead on the island.

At Japanese-held Clark Field, some 1,000 kilometers south of Lingayen, the remaining forces of the Second Naval Aviation Fleet, including Fukutome, its commanding officer, had begun withdrawing from Luzon to Taiwan three days before the Allied attack began. The staff of the First Naval Aviation Fleet, including Onishi, also flew to Taiwan in the early morning of January 10.

After the evacuation of the leaders and staff of both the First and Second Naval Aviation fleets, the remaining officers formed themselves and the enlisted men into several brigades and moved into mountain camps to the west, determined to make their last stand there.

The Ohka Maintenance Squadron, led by Reserve Sub-Lieutenant Iwao Tsuji, who had been dispatched from Konoike Air Base to the Clark Field command to await the arrival of the Ohkas, was incorporated into one of the brigades and charged with transporting goods and ammunition. The secret tunnels that had been dug into the slopes southwest of Marcotte Airfield for Ohka planes were turned into ammunition storage dumps.

The only recourse left to the Japanese was to launch a counterattack against the American forces from Taiwan. This necessitated still another change in the plans for the Ohka Corps.

As soon as the riot incident at Konoike was closed, the whole Thunder Gods operation was reexamined, and it was determined that the best use of the Ohka planes would be to mount a Taiwan-based attack against American ships in the Lingayen Gulf. The major concern remained the ability of the covering squadron of fighters to protect the mother ships and the Ohka before and during the launching of the Thunder Gods.

Arrangements had been made for support from other units, but with each passing day the number of planes and trained pilots decreased dramatically. Combined Fleet Headquarters was unable to find enough planes to form a second squadron of fighters.

Since many of the petty officers who were first selected to become Thunder Gods were trained fighter pilots, 21 of them—nine from Mitsuhashi's group and 12 from Hayashi's division—were chosen to form the Ohka Special Fighter Squadron as a reserve cover force. This did not mean these members were removed from the list of those who were to mount the first Ohka attack against the enemy. In fact, there were no available fighter planes for them to fly, so they ended up being placed under dual chains of command, on call from both. Higher Flight Petty Officer Okubo, who had failed earlier to be transferred to the 306th Fighter Squadron, was one of the men chosen for this dual role. He was happy with the idea that he might be able to make at least one more flight in a fighter before making his final dive.

The reaction of Higher Flight Petty Officer Keisuke Yamamura was exactly the opposite. He refused repeated orders to join the new squadron, saying "I have no intention of joining such a weird group. I'm never going to be a fighter pilot again. Those who leave the Ohka Squadron are cowards!"

The high command began looking for someone to take charge of the new reserve fighter squadron, and decided on Senior Reserve Officer Hosokawa. But Hosokawa also rejected the nomination, pointing out that he did not have the experience to direct and control 21 veteran career petty officers.

Igarashi, the man who had nominated Hosokawa for the position, refused to take *no* for an answer. "I'll take care of them in the air. You just take care of them on the ground," he said.

Hosokawa knew there was a possibility that the fighter pilots would return from an Ohka mission. Those who were not ex-fighter pilots and therefore could not be reassigned from the Ohka planes to the fighters might take it as discrimination and cause their commanding officer a lot of trouble. He also suspected that the ranking officers did not want to place any graduates of the Naval College who had avoided getting involved in the recent riot in such a sensitive position. He knew he was being ordered to play the role of shock absorber.

Lieutenant Kiyoshi Yagita was division leader of the 708th Attack Squadron stationed at Miyazaki Air Base, but had not yet seen the Ohka planes, so he decided to visit Konoike and inspect the Ohkas. Earlier, he had flown with Nonaka.

Yagita was not impressed with the planes and, following his inspection, thanked Nonaka heartily for undertaking the difficult task of the training of his men, who had been sent to Konoike to practice carrying the Ohka beneath their planes.

The two men had not seen each other since fighting together at Rabaul, and while reminiscing about their experiences on the front, Nonaka invited Yagita to his quarters for a private tea ceremony.

After the ceremony, Nonaka suddenly said, "You can call me a traitor if you want, but I wish Headquarters would cancel this damn Ohka operation! I'm not afraid of dying, but do you really think it is possible for the Bettys to get near the enemy fleets? Do you believe the fighters can actually protect us? I just can't stand the idea of leading my men on attacks that won't do any good.

"Let's suppose that we were lucky enough to reach the enemy. According to the plan, after the Bettys drop the Ohkas they will return to base to prepare for another flight. Do you think we can do such a thing? Our men, the ones we have been living with, are being escorted to their deaths in the bloodiest and most cold-hearted way possible. Do you think we can leave them and return again and again? On my first mission I'm going to crash-dive myself. There is no other way," he said.

Nonaka had decided to die on his first mission as a way of protesting the suicide missions. He had long been haunted by the memory of his brother, Shiro, who had been forced to kill himself following the ill-fated uprising against the government in 1936, and whose picture he always carried. He had already sent his personal belongings, including his favorite tea-ceremony kit, back to his wife.

The curfew imposed after the riot was still in effect, but several of the veteran petty officers ignored the order and continued to sneak into town to drink and carouse, rationalizing that, since they were to die soon, the rules did not apply to them. The reserve officers, who took their new rank and duties more seriously, stayed on base.

However, one of the reserve officers, Sub-Lieutenant Mitsutaka

Nishio, had fallen in love with a *ryokan* (inn) maid, Taeko, in the nearby town of Sawara. Nishio's friends as well as his division leader, Hayashi, were aware that he had been smitten by the girl and felt sorry for him. Even though he knew he was going to die, Nishio made up his mind that he wanted to become engaged to Taeko.

After he went off duty on a cold evening in mid-January, Nishio presented himself to Division Leader Hayashi in his quarters and asked for special permission to leave the base.

Hayashi stared at him. "What! Are you crazy? You know there are no exceptions to the curfew! Now, get the hell out of here!"

Nishio had not thought it would be easy, but he was shocked that Hayashi had shouted at him so vehemently. Then Hayashi, very deliberately, grinned at him, and Nishio knew that he had just been putting on a show for the other division leaders in the adjoining quarters and that he had tacit approval to carry out his plan.

Nishio bowed deeply, then hurried back to the barracks to find his two best friends, Nakane and Yasui.

"I know you think I'm crazy," he said. "But I want to be engaged to Taeko. Will you please come with me and act as my witnesses?"

Under cover of darkness, the three young men left the base by the rear gate and rode their bicycles into Sawara. Arriving at the inn, they took a room, ordered saké, and asked for Taeko.

As soon as Taeko had entered the room and sat down on a floor cushion next to Nishio, she knew from the grave and subdued manner of the men that their time was approaching. When Nishio said he wanted to formalize their engagement, she burst into tears.

"Serve us saké," Nishio said.

In strained silence, Nishio's friends took turns filling the small saké cups. He and Taeko exchanged several drinks in a solemn ritual. In the meantime, other maids in the inn had prepared a bridal bed for them.

There were no words the young couple could say to ease their agony. Finally Nishio stood up. Taeko also got up, as if she were in a trance.

"I want both of you to come with us," Nishio said to his friends.

Nakane and Yasui were shocked.

"You have to be kidding," Nakane said. "We'll wait here and have a drink." Both he and Yasui were embarrassed.

"Please, I beg you!" Nishio urged.

The tone of Nishio's voice and the look on his face told his friends that he was serious, but they could not bring themselves to comply with his request. Finally realizing that they were too embarrassed, Nishio led Taeko out of the room and down a hallway to the bridal room.

Two sleeping mattresses were laid out side by side. Nishio crawled into one of them, and Taeko got into the other. They then joined hands and held onto each other tightly for several minutes, with their eyes closed.

Finally, Nishio opened his eyes and said, "All right. I can go now without feeling any anxiety."

Nakane and Yasui were surprised when he came out of the room so quickly. "Are you sure that was long enough?" they asked.

"It was fine, just fine," Nishio replied.

Taeko had stayed in the room. Still beneath the quilt, she sobbed quietly.

As soon as the three men were back on base, they went to Hosokawa and reported that they had gone AWOL. Nishio was silent. Nakane and Yasui explained what had happened in exact detail.

"Anyway," Nakane said, "we violated the rules, so we should be punished."

Hosokawa fully understood why the men were asking to be punished, but he did not feel like punishing them. "Never mind," he said.

"No, you must punish us. Otherwise the rules will collapse," they insisted. Finally, to satisfy the men, Hosokawa stood up and slapped each of them smartly.

In mid-January, family members of the Thunder Gods Corps were allowed to visit them. Inns and private homes in the vicinity of the base were designated as meeting places. The Thunder Gods were strictly forbidden to talk about their special mission.

Most of the ranking officers in the unit did not ask their families to visit them. As Betty squadron leader, Nonaka had a house in the nearby town. Under direct orders from Commander Okamura, he finally went home late one evening to see his wife and children. It was exceptionally cold and there was a thin layer of snow on the ground. The following morning, standing outside the doorway preparing to leave, Nonaka was suddenly struck by the urge to ask his wife to dance with him. He held her to him as he hummed Johann Strauss Jr.'s beautiful *Frühlingsstimmen*. As they danced they left a double circle of footprints in the snow.

On January 17, the Thunder Gods' base was visited by an emissary from the Emperor, who thanked them for their spirit and said the nation would thereafter revere their souls. This meant that their departure for the front was imminent. Each man began to steel himself for what was soon to be.

In the meantime, the advancing forces of the United States had moved southward from Lingayen Gulf to the vicinity of Clark Field. Ashore, Japanese military units had retreated into the mountains and were being pursued by Filipino and Allied forces in running guerrilla battles.

The Japanese high command knew that in the Philippines the end of the battle was near and that it would only be a matter of time before the increasingly powerful Allied forces would begin moving on Japan itself. On January 20, Soemu Toyoda, commander-in-chief of the Combined Fleet, ordered the 11th Aviation Group, made up of the Thunder Gods Corps and the T-Attack Corps, to move to southern Kyushu, southernmost of the main islands of Japan.

On the same day, the Japanese Army and Navy inaugurated their first joint operational plan since the outbreak of the war. There were two stages in the plan. The first stage covered plans to confront the enemy as far away from the main islands as possible, in particular on Taiwan and the Okinawan Islands. The second stage was the defense of the home islands. Initially, the plan had been to move the Thunder Gods Corps from Japan to Taiwan and then to the Philippines, but this plan obviously had to be abandoned. Taiwan then became the focal point for staging counterattacks against the American forces. Efforts to shore up the defenses on Okinawa and southern Kyushu continued at a feverish pitch.

As the situation worsened, the decision was made to deploy the Thunder Gods as widely as possible to get the maximum benefit. Fifty-eight Ohka planes and Thunder Gods pilots had already been shipped to Takao Base in Taiwan. Arrangements were made to ship 30 more to Shinchiku (Xinzhu) in Taiwan, 40 to Singapore, 50 to Okinawa, and 27 each to Kanoya and Miyazaki in Kyushu by the end of January.

Further deployment of the Thunder Gods was scheduled for February and March, with several going to Miyako and Ishigaki islands in the southwest, to Konoike, Atsugi, and Hachijo islands near Tokyo, and to Shanghai and the Sanya (Hainan Island) district in western China.

As soon as the Thunder Gods Corps received orders to transfer to southern Kyushu, they and their special support groups began converging on the designated bases on that southernmost island.

Altogether there were 158 Ohka pilots involved in the transfer. Two had been killed in training, and one had been jailed as a result of the riot. The main force of the corps went to Kanoya Base and set up command headquarters there. Ohka and Betty Squadron members, as well as all the members of the covering fighter squadron, were dispersed among different bases in the area.

Kanoya Base, newly designated as headquarters for the Thunder Gods Corps, was in the center of Osumi Peninsula, and was the southern mainstay of the Naval Air Base Group in Kyushu. When the Thunder Gods flew into Kanoya, they saw the volcanic cone of Sakurajima Island covered with snow. The airfield was still being expanded, but shelters for the Ohka flying bombs had already been constructed in various places around the plateau. The communications center for the base was deep underground, directly beneath the barracks. A number of trenches had been dug into the adjoining hillsides for use as ammunition storage areas and for the base hospital.

When the Thunder Gods had been assigned their quarters they hoisted their *HI-RI-HO-KEN-TEN* and *NAMU-HACHIMAN-DAI-BOSATSU* banners, and then reported to their respective squadrons for additional training.

The training results were not as impressive as hoped, but there was no more time. From February 1 through 3, the navy department of the military headquarters worked on plans to implement in the other islands in the chain, and southern Kyushu, in case the approaching Allied forces attacked Okinawa.

The Thunder Gods and the T-Attack Corps were designated to spearhead Japan's defense against the impending invasion. According to the Navy Department's strategy, roughly 300 body-crash planes would be needed to mount a successful attack against 16 American aircraft carriers. These would include 100 Thunder Gods and 200 suicide planes from the T-Attack Force. Another 150 carrier dive-and-attack bombers were designated as suicide planes to assist in the attack. The Tenth Naval Aviation Fleet, which was the training air fleet, was also assigned with the suicide attack mission in a bid to bring about substantial damage to the enemy forces.

On February 10 the Naval General Staff reorganized the Fifth Naval Aviation Fleet in preparation for anticipated raids by American forces along the entire theater stretching from the East China Sea to Okinawa and Kyushu. The Thunder Gods and the T-Attack Corps were the main force in the reorganized fleet and were to coordinate their attacks with the Third Naval Aviation Fleet, which was in charge of defending the main islands of Japan.

The decision was also made to utilize training squadrons from around the southwestern area to mount special suicide attacks against any enemy ships that survived the first attack by the Thunder Gods and T-Attack planes.

In addition to assigning the Thunder Gods and special attack planes to the Fifth Naval Aviation Fleet in the East China Sea as its main attack force, the Naval General Staff boosted the strength of the fleet by assigning various other naval and army air units to it.

At this time, there was a total of 162 Ohka planes, 72 mother planes, and 108 Zero T-Attack planes to be used in suicide attacks against the American forces. There were also dramatic shifts in high-ranking personnel as the stage was set for both the navy and the army to fully accept the idea of adopting suicide attacks as their main strategy in the final defense of Japan. Although the use of suicide missions had developed as a voluntary movement within the armed forces, it was presented by the top Navy and Army officers as official policy.

With the status of the Thunder Gods and the other suicide attack squadrons confirmed, Vice-Admiral Matome Ugaki, the commander-in-chief of the Fifth Naval Aviation Fleet, left Atsugi Air Base near Tokyo on February 14, arriving at the Thunder Gods base in Kanoya, Kyushu, that afternoon. On the same day, a patrol plane dispatched from Iwo Jima Island spotted a number of American ships, just west of Saipan, moving northward. The next day, a patrol plane from Kisarazu Base reported U.S. warships south of Iwo Jima, but was unable to get an accurate count or description of the group.

On February 16 American ships visible from the island launched an all-out attack against Iwo Jima. Other American bombers carried out massive raids in the Tokyo–Yokohama area in support of the action on Iwo Jima. One of the targets of the U.S. bombers was Konoike Base, the primary training base of the Thunder Gods Corps. By coincidence, 24 Betty mother planes, under the command of Lieutenant-Commander Nonaka, happened to be at the base on a nighttime training flight. The remnants of the Thunder Gods Corps at Konoike had been reorganized into the 722nd Flying Corps, attached to the Third

Naval Aviation Fleet, to train additional Thunder Gods pilots. The group had been nicknamed the *Tatsumaki* or Tornado Corps. But training had been suspended for several days because of a fuel shortage, and there were some 130 planes housed in various structures around the field, without any fuel for their tanks.

There was no warning of the approaching American bombers. They had found holes in the Japanese observation network and came in at very low altitudes. The first attack occurred at 8 A.M. Eight other attacks were carried out in the next eight hours by a total of 130 bombers. Only two of the sheltered planes were destroyed, but all of Nonaka's 24 Betty mother planes were blown to bits. The night before the attack, Nonaka had stayed up late talking with friends. He knew that raids were imminent, but he expected to have enough warning to get his planes off the ground. The roar of the bombers overhead and the thunder of exploding bombs was the first that Nonaka knew of the attack. He rushed to the airfield but had to stand helpless in the front of an air-raid shelter and watch while his entire squadron was wiped out. Eleven of his Bettys were destroyed by bombs; the other thirteen caught fire and burned.

On the following morning, three lone American bombers appeared and destroyed another Betty.

American air raids on Iwo Jima ended at 3 P.M. on February 17. Then, in one of the fiercest battles of the Pacific, American Marines stormed ashore and took the island. On February 25, the Tokyo-Yokohama area again came under heavy attack by American bombers. At Konoike, two more Betty mother planes went up in flames.

This was the beginning of massive air raids on Tokyo and the surrounding industrial areas by B-29 bombers based in the Marianas. Some of the raids involved more than 200 planes and were designed to destroy the ability of the city to function.

Reconnaissance flights by American planes over Kyushu and Honshu, the main island, were becoming a daily occurrence. American submarines were haunting the shores off the Ryukyu Islands. It was obvious that a full-scale attack on the Japanese mainland was being planned. Taiwan was virtually cut off from the home islands, and the plan to use Taiwan as a base to launch Thunder Gods missions against the Allied forces also had to be abandoned.

The Fifth Naval Aviation Fleet again reorganized the deployment of the Thunder Gods Corps and made new plans for launching their attacks from bases on Okinawa and Kyushu. Under the new deployment program, the headquarters of the Thunder Gods Corps, the main force of Nonaka's Betty Squadron, and the Mitsuhashi and Hayashi Ohka divisions were to stay at Kanoya Base. Adachi's Betty Squadron and the Yunokawa Ohka Division of the Thunder Gods Corps were to move from Miyazaki Base to Usa Base in northern Kyushu. The two covering fighter squadrons were to move to Tomitaka Base.

As the end of February neared, it began to warm up. The snow had disappeared from the top of Sakura Island, and there was a feeling of spring in the air.

At the Thunder Gods' headquarters, Corps Commander Okamura was still dissatisfied with the ability of the covering fighter planes to protect the Betty mother planes until they could reach their targets. He had called Yamana, manager of the Design Division in the Aeroplane Section of the Naval Aeronautical Research Laboratory, and asked him to devise a new engine that would give the Ohka planes a greater cruising range so that they could be launched outside the range of enemy aircraft flying protective cover over American ships.

Yamana turned the task over to Chief Designer Miki, who approached it with the same misgivings he had experienced when he first heard about the Ohka. Okamura ordered that the Ohka be equipped with longer-firing engines, even if it meant reducing the amount of explosives the flying bombs could carry. Yamana brought the final plans for the revamped Ohka to Kanoya.

The new Campini-type jet engine had a range that was three-and-a-half times greater than the range of the engines originally planned for the Ohka. It was also much heavier, however, and it would be necessary to cut the weight of the warhead in half.

"That's all right. As long as we get the distance," Okamura said.

In order to make up for the lower maximum speed, the planes were to be equipped with an explosive rocket under the fuselage for emergency acceleration. Frances bombers, which were faster than the Bettys, were to be used as mother planes.

Yamana still wasn't happy. "The maximum speed will also be lower, but the real problem is in testing the thing. With this new engine, the plane is too heavy to test safely. Even with the weight of the explosives reduced to 600 kilograms, the landing speed would still be over 135 kilometers," he said.

He stopped for a few seconds. "The only safe way is to test it without dropping it from the mother plane," he added.

Okamura scowled. "What good would that do? The pilot wouldn't be able to tell anything about how it would feel or function. No, that's not the way." He paused. "We'll have the pilot parachute out after the test is over. I'm sure Nagano can manage that!" he said, his mind obviously made up.

Okamura knew that the idea was risky, but he felt that he had no other choice. If the Thunder Gods were to have even a fair chance of success, they had to have a better shot at reaching their targets. "Anyway, we want the new model as soon as possible, and will get by somehow with the existing model in the meantime. . . ."

The same day this conversation took place, B-29 bombers made several reconnaissance flights over Okinawa. The staff of the Fifth Naval Aviation Fleet had to spend half of the day underground. The entryway to the underground headquarters was low and narrow, barely wide enough for a man to pass through. The tunnel leading to the underground bunkers was dimly lit with naked electric bulbs. The air in the shelter was stale and humid.

On March 1, the American invasion of Okinawa began. A total of 670 American planes made seven bombing sweeps over the island during the morning, knocking out airfields and destroying all of the Japanese ships in the area. That afternoon, 70 U.S. planes raided targets in Kyushu's Kagoshima Prefecture, including Miyazaki Air Base, where one of the squadrons that was supposed to fly cover for the Thunder Gods was based.

Just before daybreak on March 2, a Japanese scout plane reported an American destroyer at a location of some 200 miles south of Cape Sata on the tip of Kyushu. The Fifth Naval Aviation Fleet took this to mean an American task force was on its way.

Preparations for the first concerted attack by the Thunder Gods Corps and the T-Attack Corps began immediately. The T-Attack Squadron took off from Miyazaki Base in heavy, rain-laden clouds. Half of the fighter planes stationed in the area also took off, along with three of the fighter squadrons designated to fly cover for the Thunder Gods. While the cover fighters were preparing to board their planes, Vice-Commander Igarashi made an announcement. "Don't forget! Our primary responsibility is to protect the Thunder Gods. If you encounter a large number of enemy planes, just disperse and get back safely!"

Shortly after the planes took off, it began to rain. The men on the bases waited, expecting an attack at any moment. None came. The rain continued hour after hour. The planes that had scrambled began to return, their fuel tanks nearly empty and their pilots exhausted from the fruitless search. It was finally learned that the scout plane had mistaken a Japanese torpedo boat for an American destroyer.

Welcoming the postponement of something that everyone knew was inevitable, the Fifth Naval Aviation Fleet ordered a comprehensive training exercise involving all of its pilots. The exercise began on March 5 and ended on March 9. The high command was appalled at the weaknesses revealed by the exercise. It was decided that everything possible should be done to delay an enemy invasion until the Naval Aviation Fleet could better prepare itself.

The only way the fleet could force the Americans to postpone their attack was to destroy as many of their aircraft carriers and other warships as possible, while they were still in port.

On March 9, a reconnaissance plane from the Truk Islands confirmed that large numbers of American ships were gathering in the port of Ulithi in the Caroline Islands. Two days later, 24 Frances Kamikaze T-Attack Corps planes, loaded with 800-kilogram bombs, left Kanoya and headed for Ulithi, 1,360 miles away.

Half of the planes lost their way before they reached their destination, and the results achieved by those that reached the Allied anchorage at Ulithi were "disappointing." A reconnaissance plane sent to assess the damage the next day reported that there appeared to have been no damage at all.

Japanese radio stations in the area began reporting a significant increase in the amount of radio traffic among the various contingents of the Allied forces. The same code words they had heard repeatedly just before the invasion of Iwo Jima began to show up regularly. The movement of American submarines became more intense and was extended closer to Japan. The Fifth Naval Aviation Fleet hurried its preparations to stall the expected attack. The Mitsuhashi and Yunokawa divisions of the Thunder Gods were told they would be the first ones to see action.

At Kanoya Base, Lieutenant Hayashi was told to move his Thunder Gods pilots to Usa Base as a backup for later missions. Hayashi knew it did not become a graduate of the Naval College to feel relief at having his life spared a little longer, but he could not help it. He wondered if he would be able to respond with the same enthusiasm as Mitsuhashi had when his time came. On the eve of his move to Usa, Hayashi was told to report to Nonaka's private room. Lieutenant-Commander Hiroshi Saeki, the base's communications chief, was already there.

The notorious but highly respected Nonaka did not waste any time. Looking Hayashi squarely in the eye, he said bluntly, "Hayashi, the Ohka won't work! In the first place, I don't like the idea of suicide missions. I accepted this position only because they said there was nobody else who could assume the leadership role. I'm going to take the best of the Betty pilots with me on our first attack, but I'm sure we will be vulnerable to enemy planes, especially if we make a daytime raid.

"I'll get through somehow, and deal a blow to the enemy, but we will be annihilated! It'll be nothing more than a sacrifice!" Nonaka continued, practically shouting. His eyes burning with passion and anger, he held Hayashi transfixed. "So, Hayashi, after I'm gone, I want you to somehow put an end to these stupid attacks!"

Nonaka knew it was impossible to shelve the plans for suicide attacks by the Emperor's military forces. He knew the Imperial system was absolute. His own brother, who had revolted against the system, had sacrificed his life in the attempt. Nonaka was also caught up in a dilemma—he would have to obey whatever orders were given. He cursed himself. All he could do was criticize. He was not in a position to take any practical action. His words to Hayashi rang with self-contempt.

Hayashi felt cold. He couldn't think of anything to say. He had heard Nonaka express his opinion of the Ohka planes several times, and knew he favored torpedo attacks instead of crash-diving in uncontrollable flying bombs. Still, he was shocked that Nonaka could express himself so directly and bluntly to a mere lieutenant, and that he was relinquishing his role as leader of the special attack force even before he died.

All Hayashi could do was bow to Nonaka and wish him good luck. Finally, Hayashi and the communications chief left the bitter Nonaka's room together. Outside, Saeki muttered, "This is a terrible responsibility." Then he, too, was silent.

The command of the Combined Fleet reasoned that if the American forces left Ulithi on March 14, they would arrive in the Kyushu area around the eighteenth. The fleet stepped up its reconnaissance patrols, but bad weather around Truk on the sixteenth and seventeenth grounded all scouting patrols. This left the Japanese high command completely in the dark. They did not know the makeup of the American invasion fleet, when it might begin its move northward, where its destination would be, or whether it would herald a full-scale invasion or just a probing action.

The navy department of the military headquarters debated its choices, whether to avoid a direct confrontation with the enemy until the full-scale invasion began or attempt to damage the invasion fleet so badly before the attack began that it would have to be delayed or abandoned. Without additional intelligence, however, it was impossible to decide which alternative to choose.

Finally, a tentative decision was made to preserve as much of the air force as possible until it could be determined whether the American forces were launching the final invasion or still leapfrogging from one island to another. In any event, it was assumed that something would happen on March 18.

The command of the Combined Fleet telephoned the Fifth Naval Aviation Fleet at 8:30 A.M. on March 17, announcing the decision. Vice-Admiral Ugaki immediately called a full alert, ordered the air corps in southern Kyushu to evacuate to Shikoku and northern Kyushu areas, and beefed up night patrols. It was also decided to send 25 of Commander Nonaka's Betty mother planes to Korea as a safety measure. Nonaka refused to go to Korea. Leaving a message that stated, "I don't want a repeat of what happened at Konoike!" he took the planes to Omura, the intermediate base, in Nagasaki Prefecture.

The Fifth Naval Aviation Fleet, on alert since the morning of March 17, was angry at Headquarters because it could not make up its mind about what to do. The staff was afraid that if it attempted a holding action with a minimum of force when it was already plagued by serious weaknesses in every area of defense, whatever aircraft they could preserve would be easy prey for enemy attacks. The majority of the Aviation Fleet staff favored an active policy of attacking the American forces with every means at their disposal. On the afternoon of March 17, Vice-Admiral Ugaki issued orders for the implementation of "First Tactics," which called for a radar-scout patrol that night, a torpedo attack at dawn, followed by an attack by the Thunder Gods and the other special attack corps during the daylight hours.

By this time, the air corps had nearly completed its evacuation to Shikoku and northern Kyushu, and was ordered to return immediately to southern Kyushu. Nonaka's squadron was also ordered back to Kanoya, headquarters of the Thunder Gods. The Thunder Gods' fighter squadrons were ordered to protect the Miyazaki area. Okamura, Iwaki, Saeki, and other ranking officers in the corps moved from Kanoya to Tomitaka, where three fighter squadrons were waiting.

Even though they knew it was imperative that they preserve as many of the fighter planes as possible to provide cover for the first Ohka attack, they also knew they could not just stand by in the midst of the coming calamity.

At 10:45 P.M. that night, a radar patrol plane detected a large number of ships approaching Kyushu from a southeasterly direction. The location of the ships was estimated at approximately 160 miles from Cape Toi. The American ships were also picked up by radar on Tanegashima, a small island some 20 miles south of the coast of Kyushu. Still, navy headquarters would not make a firm decision. The telephone message to Ugaki was the same: "Try to preserve your forces. If you can't, make whatever decision you think is appropriate." Fuming, Ugaki gave the order for an all-out attack at 2:02 A.M. March 18.

At almost the same time, two telegrams were received from the commander of the Combined Fleet. One instructed Ugaki to engage only minimal forces if it was not a full-scale invasion. If the American force included landing troops, however, Ugaki was to commit everything he had to the battle. In the latter case, code-named "Operation Heaven No. 1," Ugaki's Fifth Naval Aviation Fleet was to play the pivotal role with support from the First Naval Aviation Fleet from Taiwan and the Third and Tenth Naval Aviation fleets. The Sixth Army Air Force was also to be placed under Ugaki's command.

Unfortunately, by the time the two telegrams were deciphered, it was almost 4 A.M., and Ugaki had already started his own war.

Fifty-four Jill and Frances planes roared off runways in southern Kyushu at 3:30 A.M., heading for dawn torpedo and suicide attacks against the approaching American fleet. Over Cape Toi the planes ran into a flight of American carrier-based fighters but managed to get through with only a few losses. Twenty-seven Judys, selected for one-way suicide missions, followed them to continue the attack after daylight hours.

At 5:40 A.M. the first of the American carrier-based bombers and fighters appeared over southern Kyushu and Shikoku, and began successive strikes against airfields and other targets. Altogether, a total of 1,460 planes took part in the raids. Only 110 Japanese fighter planes were available to send against the U.S. planes. They fought heroically but were unable to deter the planes from their targets.

In the meantime, the 54 Jill and Frances planes carried out their dawn raid on the American fleet. It was reported to Ugaki that they had managed to sink several American warships, including an aircraft carrier, a battleship, and a cruiser. Ugaki decided to send in the Thunder Gods as well as special attack planes. At 12:13 P.M. he gave the order for them to get ready for their first mission.

Okamura and his fighter squadrons at Tomitaka Base had already made two sorties against attacking American planes that morning, and managed to shoot down a few of them. As soon as he got the message from Vice-Admiral Ugaki that the Thunder Gods Corps was to prepare for an attack, Okamura ordered nine Bettys from Nonaka's squadron and nine from the Adachi squadron to get ready. Nonaka's squadron had not yet completed the move back to Kanoya, however, and because of the intensity of the morning raids by the American bombers, the planes that were already there were not prepared for takeoff. Finally, Lieutenant Adachi was ordered to get 18 of his planes ready to go.

As soon as the admiral's order came down, personnel at Usa, which had not been attacked by the U.S. bombers, pulled 18 Bettys out of their shelters and began bringing the Ohka flying bombs from their secret tunnels. The ground crews were about halfway through the task of fueling the Bettys when another wave of American bombers was reported heading in their direction. There were no fighter planes at Usa. Okamura had not expected the planes there to be endangered as long as he could intercept any enemy aircraft before they reached that area. Now he tried to reach the field at Usa to have the planes evacuated to Omura, but communications had been disrupted and he could not get through.

Reacting to the gravity of the situation, Okamura quickly decided to launch all of the fighter planes that were to be used as cover for the Thunder Gods. Part of the wave of American bombers suddenly left the formation, flew back, and dropped their bombs on Tomitaka Base, where Okamura was struggling to get his fighters into the air. The rest of the American bombers, with the threat from Tomitaka eliminated, proceeded on to Usa unchallenged.

At Usa, preparations to launch the first flight of the Thunder Gods were continuing at a frantic pace. Members of the Thunder Gods Corps not scheduled to go on the mission were helping the ground crews ferry the Ohka bombs across the runway to the waiting Betty mother planes. "This is too fast," Adachi thought as he walked to a hangar for a farewell drink with the Ohka pilots who were to accompany him on the one-way mission. "We have not been given enough time to prepare properly. Something is wrong!"

At just this instant, a group of American dive-bombers burst through the clouds hanging over the field and rained bombs upon the base. The ground crews and their Thunder Gods helpers scattered. The Bettys already on the runway, as well as several of those still in shelters, went up in flames one after the other. Miraculously, none of the Ohka planes was hit. One of the air-raid shelters, where some Thunder Gods pilots had taken refuge, suffered a direct hit, killing several of them. Adachi had sprinted into another air-raid shelter. Now someone yelled, "You'll have to pay for this!"

In the meantime, Tomitaka Base was still under heavy attack by American planes. The Japanese fighter planes from the 306th and 307th squadrons that had managed to get into the air were fighting a hopeless battle. The Ohka Special Fighter Squadron, under Reserve Sub-Lieutenant Hosokawa, was supposed to follow the 306th and 307th into the battle, but was prevented from taking off by Wing Commander Iwaki.

"It doesn't make any sense for you to go now," Iwaki said to Hosokawa. "It's hopeless. You people should die in Ohka attacks!"

A thunderous blast of bombs, a whining of plane engines, and the loud chattering of machine guns filled the air. Tracer bullets crisscrossed the sky. Hosokawa watched one of his former instructors, Petty Officer Umeno, chasing an American plane. Three other American enemy planes suddenly appeared on Umeno's tail. Hosokawa grabbed the land-to-plane phone and began shouting: "Look out, Umeno! Break away!"

At that instant, a trail of smoke gushed from the American plane Umeno was firing at, and almost simultaneously his own plane was hit by the planes behind him. It burst into flames, and he went down.

As soon as the American planes had dropped all of their bombs, they moved off, but they were followed by a second wave, and then a third. A report came in that the enemy planes that had been attacking Kumamoto were now headed for Tomitaka, and that more planes were coming in from Cape Sata.

Most of the remaining Thunder Gods fighter planes were unable to land at Tomitaka for refueling, and had to make forced landings at Kochi, Oita, and in the Kumamoto area, some distance away.

Finally, the battle ended at 4 P.M. Only 32 fighter planes were still capable of flight. Approximately half of the planes that were supposed to provide cover for the Thunder Gods had been destroyed. Okamura, Iwaki, and Saeki found an undamaged transport plane and flew from Tomitaka to Kanoya around 9 P.M. that evening. There were still numerous fires blazing, lighting up all the airfield except the runway. Aiming the plane at the area that appeared to be the runway, the pilot made a rough landing.

When the plane's engines were cut, they could hear the crackling of fire coming from the blazes around the base. They climbed down out of the plane and stood for a few seconds looking at the scene of destruction. Only a few yards in front of the plane they had just landed in was a deep bomb crater.

The American attack on areas in northern Kyushu and southwestern Honshu continued on March 19. More than one thousand planes made repeated attacks on Kure Naval Port and several Japanese warships in the area during the morning, and in the afternoon carried out successive raids against military installations in the Osaka–Kobe, Nagoya, and Kyushu areas.

The Fifth Naval Aviation Fleet had suffered devastating losses and was trying to bring some order out of the chaos, but communications between the bases had been destroyed, making it impossible for fleet headquarters to fully assess the damage. The chief of staff suggested to Ugaki that he suspend all activity in order to reserve the few forces he had left. Ugaki ignored the suggestion. "When you are fighting against heavy odds, you must repeatedly make guerrilla attacks," he grumbled.

Some members of the Naval General Staff began to worry about Ugaki's willingness to expend all of the forces he had. They reasoned that if he continued his tactics, the fleet would soon have no force left with which to resist a landing by American troops. The majority of the staff wanted to issue an order to Ugaki, forcing him to suspend his attacks.

Vice-chief of the Naval General Staff, Vice-Admiral Jisaburo Ozawa, agreed with Ugaki, however, and refused to agree to the motion against him. "Once you have started this kind of operation, it is difficult to stop," he said.

The ferocity of the American attack began to diminish. On the twentieth, only small groups of planes raided the air bases at Matsuyama, Kanoya, Nobeoka, and Aburatsu. Vice-Admiral Ugaki continued to press his attack. He ordered a suicide mission made up of 17 Judy dive-bombers, and followed with night raids against the U.S. fleet. Reconnaissance planes reported that the combined attacks had sunk one American carrier, set another on fire, and damaged a cruiser. It was also reported that the U.S. task force was continuing to move southward at 10 to 12 knots. Ugaki decided to go for a knockout blow. He ordered the Thunder Gods Corps to prepare for an attack.

At 8:10 A.M. on Wednesday, March 21, reconnaissance planes reported sighting two groups of American warships only 320 miles from Cape Toi. One of the groups included two aircraft carriers, apparently with no planes flying cover over them. The weather was clear. Ugaki and his staff reasoned that the carriers must have been damaged in their earlier attack and that there would never be a better opportunity to finish them off. There was tremendous excitement in the underground operations room of the Fifth Naval Aviation Fleet. Corps Commander Okamura, Wing Commander Iwaki, and Betty Squadron Leader Nonaka were summoned to the operations room.

Okamura was worried about the number of cover planes available for the Thunder Gods mission. Chief of Staff Yokoi reported that only 23 supporting planes were available from the 203rd Flying Corps.

"Is that all? Can't we get more?" Okamura asked.

"That's the best we can do right now. All the others are damaged," Yokoi replied.

With the additional 32 fighters from the Thunder Gods Corps, the total number of covering fighter planes was only 55. Frustrated and angry at the turn of events, Okamura said grimly, "I will make do with 32 planes flying direct cover, but only 23 for indirect cover is not enough!"

"Our reconnaissance patrols report that there are no enemy planes covering the ships!" Yokoi retorted.

"We can't count on such reports!" Okamura said bluntly.

"And the ships are said to be slowing down," Yokoi said.

"They may be slowing down," Okamura conceded, "but they are still moving away from us, and if they are too far away the mother planes will not be able to return to base after releasing the Ohkas!" Okamura was determined not to sacrifice the lives of his men for nothing.

The normally outspoken Nonaka remained silent, looking grim. Yokoi nodded his understanding of Okamura's fears, then turned to Vice-Admiral Ugaki. "Sir, shall we wait for another chance?" he asked.

Ugaki stood up slowly, a determined look on his face. He faced Okamura directly. "If we can't use the Ohkas now, in this situation, we will never have the chance to use them," he said resolutely.

Okamura knew from the tone of the vice-admiral's voice that there was nothing else he could do. It was the most difficult thing he had done in his life, but he finally managed to say, "All right, sir. We'll do it!"

The final decision made, Iwaki and Nonaka left the operations room together and headed for the airfield. There was a slight breeze blowing, rustling the leaves of the bamboo trees on the hillside. Walking a few steps ahead of Iwaki, Nonaka was deep in thought, thinking of the life and death of the great hero Masashige Kusunoki. Finally he turned and said to Iwaki, "Wing Commander, there comes a time when things are so hopeless that even warriors have to die."

The official order for launching the first Thunder Gods mission was made at 9:45 A.M. Lieutenant Hiroyuki Kai, senior division leader of Lieutenant-Commander Nonaka's squadron, approached Nonaka and said forcefully, "Sir, I will take the lead today!"

Nonaka ignored him.

Corps Commander Okamura arrived, went directly to Nonaka, and said, "I will take your place today!"

"Like hell you will!" Nonaka replied belligerently. "What's the matter? Don't you trust me?" He walked away before Okamura could reply.

Nonaka selected the best pilots in his squadron for the mission, dividing the 18 into six groups of three. Only 15 of the Bettys were to carry Thunder Gods and their stubby-winged Ohka bombs. Lieutenant Mitsuhashi and his 14 men were chosen to man the flying bombs.

The leader of the 32 direct-covering fighters was Lieutenant Kunio Kanazaki. His division leaders were Lieutenants Mutsuo Urushiyama and Yuichi Izawa.

The 15 Thunder Gods and the mother plane crews took clippings from their fingernails and hair and placed them in unpainted wooden boxes for delivery to their parents so they could hold funeral services for them. They took off their old clothes and burned them, putting on new uniforms. They then sat down and carefully wrote out their death statements.

Lieutenant Kentaro Mitsuhashi, Ohka Squadron
71st Term Graduate, The Naval College, Age 22

When men did their best and left the rest to providence, they were rewarded with divine winds. Will there be other divine winds to protect our homeland now? Of course, I believe there will be. But that happens only when men do their best!

Reserve Sub-Lieutenant 1st Class Yuzuru Ogata, Ohka Squadron
Graduate, Kansai University, Age 23
With my mission now at hand, my dear old town, my dear old people, I now abandon everything and leave to protect this country; to pursue our eternal and just cause, I now go forth. My body will collapse like a falling cherry blossom, but my soul will live and protect this land forever. Farewell. I am a glorious wild cherry blossom. I shall return to my mother's place and bloom!

Flight Petty Officer 1st Class Ataru Shimamura, Ohka Squadron
17th Term, Category B, Graduate Naval Training Course, Age 20
I shall fall, smiling and singing songs. Please visit and worship at Yasukuni Shrine this spring. There I shall be a cherry blossom, smiling, with many other colleagues. I died smiling, so please smile. Please do not cry. Make my death meaningful.

Flight Petty Officer 2nd Class Tomio Matsuo, Betty Squadron 12th
Term, Category A, Graduate Naval Training Course, Age 20
I am going, but I am not feeling lonely because I have the *haramaki* (stomach-band) which mother made to protect me.

Flight Petty Officer 2nd Class Naokichi Kameda, Betty Squadron
18th Term, Category B, Graduated Naval Training Course, Age 19
A man will die sooner or later. The value of being a man is given at the time of his death.

Preparations for launching the flight were finally complete. In front of the headquarters building, all the Thunder Gods who had not been chosen for the first mission were preparing farewell cups of saké for their colleagues. Many of them appeared more pale and nervous than those who knew they were to die that day. One of them, carrying a tray of drinks across the flight line, passed in front of a Betty just as the pilot turned on the engines for the routine pre-flight check. The Thunder

God was sucked into the propeller. The impact threw his body high into the air, killing him instantly. The body was quickly removed from the runway, but word of the accident flashed around the field, creating an even more strained and ominous mood.

A drum roll was sounded, the signal for the Thunder Gods and the crews of the mother planes to line up in front of the headquarters building. The official name of the group had been posted a little earlier as: First Kamikaze Ohka Special Attack Unit, Thunder Gods Corps.

Lieutenant Mitsuhashi, leader of an Ohka squadron, had a white silk pouch around his neck. The pouch was inscribed *Navy Lieutenant-Commander Tsutomu Kariya*, and contained the ashes of Kariya, who had been killed during the training of the Thunder Gods. All of the 15 Ohka pilots were wearing headbands inscribed with the word *Thunder Gods* by the commander-in-chief of the combined fleets, Admiral Toyoda. Each one also had a sword in a brocade sheath strapped to his waist.

Lieutenant-Commander Nonaka, the overall leader of the mission, was wearing a white muffler. He unceremoniously sat down in a chair in front of the headquarters building, holding his saber like a cane, with its tip resting on the tarmac. Beside him was a large blue and white streamer and two large banners, all flapping in the wind. The sky overhead was clear and blue. To the north, there were patches of white clouds. It was a beautiful early spring day.

The assembled men waited, growing more uneasy as each minute passed. Vice-Admiral Ugaki was late. Finally he showed up and solemnly took his place in front of the formation. Commander Okamura was the first to speak, but it was hard to understand him because his voice was choked with tears.

"Today's mission will not be an easy one," he said. "But brave and resolute action will scatter even devils. With your passionate spirit of martyrdom, you will be able to overcome any kind of difficulty! You will succeed! Keep this conviction strong in your minds!"

Okamura's voice failed him completely and he could not speak. Tears flowed freely down his face and he looked as though he were going to go to pieces. He struggled to continue.

"Looking back, your serene state of mind and outstanding behavior since last November has impressed me. I could not be more proud of you. Now you will go into the next world. And just as you have been in this world, I pray that you will continue to be pure, beautiful, healthy, and cheerful. Your colleagues and I will soon be following you. Please remember the ties we had in this world!"

Once again, Okamura had to stop to get himself under control.

"Good luck!" he shouted hoarsely.

Then Vice-Admiral Ugaki, Okamura, and the other officers exchanged farewell cups of saké with the Thunder Gods and mother-plane crewmen.

The fighters had been pulled out of their shelters and were now on line. The ground crews began warming up the Bettys. Their whirling propellers glistened in the sun, and the roar of their engines filled the air.

Lieutenant-Commander Nonaka stalked to the front of the formation and turned to face the men. For several seconds he was silent, staring intently into the face of each man. Then he said in his impressively loud voice:

"We will now make an attack on the enemy's warships! Once you are in battle, do not hesitate. Attack aggressively and destroy your target regardless of all else. Let us fight to the death! Let us fill the Pacific with our blood!"

The division leaders saluted smartly. Lieutenant Mitsuhashi, leader of the Ohka squadron, stepped forward. "I have nothing more to say. Let us die together!" he said.

Nonaka turned to face Okamura, saluting him in his usual brusque fashion.

"We go, Commander!" he said.

Okamura returned his salute, his grief-stricken face drained of color.

Nonaka turned and signalled the men to break ranks and man their planes. The men peeled off and sprinted toward their assigned aircraft. The remaining Thunder Gods, Betty pilots, crewmen, and staff lined both sides of the runway, waving their caps and shouting encouragement to the departing mission.

"Kill them!"

"Sweep the Pacific!"

Some of the mission members shouted back.

The blocks were removed from the wheels of the lead planes. The white flag went down. The roar from the planes' engines drowned out everything else. Nonaka's plane streaked down the runway in a cloud of dust, rose into the air, and careened out over Kagoshima Bay. The other planes followed him, one by one. Some of the Thunder Gods could be seen in the windows, waving. The Bettys, with the heavy Ohka bombs suspended beneath their bellies, lumbered down the runway like fat gooney birds. One of them swayed to the side of the runway, injuring several well-wishers with its tail. As soon as the 18 Bettys were in the air, the fighter planes began taking off. One of them stalled immediately after lifting off, hit the ground, and exploded.

The two squadrons turned from west to east, were joined by the third squadron of 23 assisting fighters that had taken off from adjoining Kazanopara Base, then headed southeast over Osumi Peninsula.

Vice-Admiral Ugaki and his staff, along with Okamura, Iwaki, and other officers of the Thunder Gods Corps, gathered in the underground operations room. In the adjoining telecommunications room, Reserve Sub-Lieutenant Horiuchi adjusted four receivers to the frequency assigned to Nonaka's squadron. Another receiver was for a reconnaissance plane that had left 30 minutes before the Thunder Gods took off.

About half an hour after the mission left, half of the fighters returned to base and made emergency landings. Their fuel pumps had malfunctioned. Because of insufficient time to service them properly, they could not draw fuel from their second tanks. The shock to those waiting at the airfield was considerable. But more was to come. Most of the planes that had taken off from Kazanopara had the same problem and had to return to base. This left only 30 fighter planes covering the entire mission.

Then, as if to make things even worse, a message came in from the reconnaissance plane saying there were three groups of American ships in the area, with three aircraft carriers in one group and two each in the other two groups. Not only was the force much stronger than previously believed, each group was sure to have covering planes.

There had been no word at all from Nonaka.

Several members of the Fifth Naval Aviation Fleet staff wanted to scrap the mission and call Nonaka back. But once again Ugaki refused to accept their judgment.

"The Thunder Gods are right now face-to-face with the enemy. I cannot bring those young boys back now after they have made up their minds to die. It would be too much for them to bear!" he said.

It was then approaching 3 P.M., well after the time the mission should have reached the target area. Still there was no word from Nonaka. If they were still in the air, their fuel would be gone soon.

Ugaki ordered a message sent to Nonaka: "If the enemy has not yet been detected, head for South Daito Island."

There was no response to the message.

It had been agreed beforehand that Nonaka and his squadron would maintain complete radio silence, but now the waiting was almost unbearable. The air in the underground room was stale. The men sat around, not trusting themselves to speak.

Just after dark, guards outside the tunnel reported the sound of an approaching plane. A badly damaged Zero came in low from the bay and made a rough landing. It was followed by a second plane. Both planes were pockmarked with bullet holes and were streaked with oil. The two pilots were exhausted, but between them they managed to tell what had happened to Nonaka's squadron.

At about 2:20 P.M., when the squadron had reached a point some 50 to 60 miles away from the American fleet, it was suddenly attacked by about 50 American fighter planes. Thirty of the fighters covering the Thunder Gods and their mother planes fought back, but nine of the Bettys carrying the Ohkas and their Thunder Gods pilots and two of the special attack bombers were shot down in just over ten minutes.

Unable to match the enemy in number or firepower, the remaining 19 fighters dispersed. Left without fighter protection, the mother planes jettisoned their Ohka bombs, dispersed, and began a battle to save themselves. Within ten minutes, the only survivors were Nonaka's plane and three others. One of the Zero pilots said that the last he saw of these four planes, they were diving wing-to-wing toward the sea. Altogether, 160 Thunder Gods had been lost, including 15 Ohka pilots.

Thus, on March 21, seven months after Ota's proposal was made to Wada and Miki, the Thunder Gods had finally made their first sortie.

Inside the underground communications room, the radioman refused to turn the sets off and sat in his chair, listening for some final word from Nonaka. Outside, searchlights swept the still dark sky. Nonaka's *HI-RI-HO-KEN-TEN* banner swayed quietly in the nighttime breeze.

Meanwhile, in the flight operations rooms of the American aircraft carriers to the south, there was jubilation. The victory by the American pilots had been swift and complete. The main topic during the debriefing session was the fact that the Betty bombers had flown much slower than their normal speed, and all of them had been carrying some sort of winged gizmo suspended beneath their hulls.

As soon as the pictures taken during the battle were developed, it was surmised that the devices beneath the Bettys were winged bombs patterned after the German V-1.

Chapter 5

The operational officers of the Fifth Naval Aviation Fleet could not believe that the first coordinated attack by the Thunder Gods Corps had been totally annihilated—that it had not even been able to reach the enemy fleet. It was particularly bewildering that not one of the Betty mother planes had returned.

Two-grade promotions were authorized for all of the men who died on the mission—not only Ohka pilots but also the crewmen of the mother planes and covering fighters.

There was a strong feeling among the lower-ranking officers that the attack had been badly planned. A group was named to reevaluate the use of the Thunder Gods in future attacks. There were 18 people in the study group, including Vice-Admiral Jisaburo Ozawa, who was vice-chief of the Naval General Staff, and Rear Admiral Toahitane Takada, vice-chief of staff of the Combined Fleet. Okamura, the man who was primarily responsible for the Thunder Gods Corps, was so angry at Vice-Admiral Ugaki, who had ordered the attack, that he could hardly contain himself.

"The attack was a total failure because there were not enough covering planes protecting the Bettys, and because there was no element of surprise or any other war advantage!" Okamura said bluntly. "The whole process of using the Thunder Gods has to be reexamined!"

Okamura also blamed himself for having gone along with the idea of a daytime formation raid. It had been foolish from the start, but he had let it happen because it was an order. With so many planes lost and no possibility of their being replaced, the only recourse was to mount surprise attacks by single planes.

Just before the meeting closed on the morning of the second day, Vice Admiral Ugaki defended his position, saying, "In the present situation, there is no such thing as 'regular tactics.' Changes are normal!"

That same morning, at approximately 8 A.M., 282 American bombers raided Okinawa and South Daito Island. A Japanese patrol plane reported that the planes took off from three American aircraft carriers and that two of the carriers were less than 100 miles southeast of Okinawa.

The navy department of the military headquarters had concluded that five American aircraft carriers, two battleships, one heavy cruiser, one light cruiser, and one unidentified ship had been sunk in the earlier aerial battle off the coast of Kyushu. As a result of these successes, the navy department believed that the Allied forces would have to postpone their attack on Okinawa. Because the raid on Okinawa occurred much earlier than expected, the naval staff officer interpreted it as a retaliatory action by the remnants of the American fleet that was "fleeing" southward to Ulithi in the Caroline Islands. No one on the staff believed that the U.S. intended to follow up the raids on Okinawa with a landing force, whose arrival would mean it was time to launch Operation Heaven No. 1 in the final defense of the southern islands. This was a tragic miscalculation.

The air raids on Okinawa continued throughout the day and were intensified on the following day (March 24), when more than 900 bombers took part in the attack.

In reality, no American aircraft carriers had been sunk in the previous aerial attack off Kyushu. Three carriers had been damaged, but there were seven other large aircraft carriers and six smaller carriers in the fleet approaching Okinawa. The garrison on Okinawa reported the presence of 30 battleships and destroyers in the fleet, which were then shelling military targets along Okinawa's southwestern coast.

The navy department of military headquarters finally realized that the attack against Okinawa was an all-out invasion. Having lost more than 60 percent of its 350 operational planes, the Fifth Naval Aviation Fleet was hurriedly reorganized in preparation for the launching of Operation Heaven No. 1. With Nonaka's death, the Thunder Gods Corps was also reorganized. Lieutenant-Commander Jiro Adachi, leader of the 708th Betty Squadron, was ordered to also take over Nonaka's 711th Squadron. Vice-Commander Igarashi fell ill and was transferred to the Tornado Corps at Konoike Air Base. Wing Commander Iwaki was promoted to vice-commander of the corps.

The Thunder Gods Corps' Mitsuhashi Division members pose for a group photo before the first Ohka sortie, March 21, 1945. *Back row, second from right,* Saburo Dohi; *front row, third and fourth from right,* Hachiro Hosokawa and Kentaro Mitsuhashi. (Thunder Gods Association)

The Thunder Gods Corps' Mitsuhashi and Yunokawa divisions pose with Admiral Toyoda (*front row, center*) at Konoike Air Base. (Thunder Gods Association)

Hachiro Hosokawa, the only reserve officer of Mitsuhashi, Hayashi, and Yunokawa divisions to vive the war. He was 24 when this photo was ta▶ (Thunder Gods Association)

Hirokazu Ushikubo (*right*), the unlucky Thu: God who crashed during takeoff. His friend ◀ Teizo Imai died in the third Ohka at▶ (Thunder Gods Association)

Masazo Okubo, the pilot who refused to switch from an Ohka to a fighter-bomber. (Thunder Gods Association)

Keisuke Yamamura, the pilot who survived three Ohka sorties, wearing the extra-long *hachimaki* (headband) that declared his determination to die for his country. (Thunder Gods Association)

'hunder Gods pilots (Motoji Ichikawa t rear, with the pipe) at Kanoya Air ase. The sign declares them to be *orps Commander Okamura's Patri-tic Samurai*. (Thunder Gods Association)

Kinshi Yano (*left*) and Fujio Hayashi at the command post (*shikisho*) where the Thunder Gods pilots received their orders. Yano died in the first Kemmu (fighter-bomber) special attack. (Thunder Gods Association)

Motoharu Okamura, commander of the Thunder Gods Corps, poses with four of the young pilots who were members of the 1st Kemmu (fighter-bomber) Squadron. (Thunder Gods Association)

Mitsutaka Nishio, the young pilot who "married" the maid of a local inn before leaving the training camp at Konoike Air Base. (Thunder Gods Association)

Vice-Admiral Takijiro Onishi. (U.S. Naval Institute, Annapolis)

Betty pilots are briefed before leaving for a special attack against the American force invading Okinawa. (U.S. Naval Institute, Annapolis)

Thunder Gods pilots being served the ritual farewell cup of saké before a sortie. In the foreground is Vice-Commander Kunihiro Iwaki. (Thunder Gods Association)

Division Leader Kentaro Mitsuhashi salutes as he and his men prepare to take off on the first Ohka mission, March 21, 1945. Their target was the American force invading Okinawa. (U.S. Naval Institute, Annapolis)

An Ohka crew waiting for takeoff. The Ohka can seen suspended beneath the Betty bomber in the background. (U.S. Naval Institute, Annapolis)

A typical farewell for the Ohka pilots taking off on their one-way missions against the Americans in Okinawa. (Thunder Gods Association)

The gun camera of an American fighter plane made these remarkable shots of a Betty bomber carrying a piloted Ohka bomb. The photos were processed on July 20, 1945. (U.S. National Archives)

A Zero fighter approaches the battleship USS *Missouri* on an unsuccessful suicide attack off Okinawa. April 28, 1945. (U.S. Navy)

American ships firing medium-range rockets during the invasion of Okinawa, April 1, 1945. (U.S. Navy)

Close-up of rockets firing (U.S. Navy)

Crewmen on the deck of the aircraft carrier USS *Bunker Hill* fight fires caused by the impact of kamikaze planes, May 11, 1945. (U.S. National Archives)

A photographer on the heavy cruiser USS *Wichita* took this shot of the battleship USS *New Mexico*, just after it was hit by a kamikaze plane at dusk on May 12, 1945. She did not sink. (U.S. National Archives)

The destroyer USS *Hazelwood*, seemingly on the verge of sinking after taking a kamikaze hit on April 29, 1945. She was kept afloat and towed to a moorage in the Philippines. (U.S. National Archives)

Fire on board the carrier USS *Saratoga* after it was hit by a Zero fighter. The outline of the Zero can be seen in the fire. The plane in the foreground is an American Grumman F6F. February 21, 1945. (U.S. National Archives)

Type-11 Ohka at Kadena Air Base, Okinawa, April 1945. (U.S. Navy)

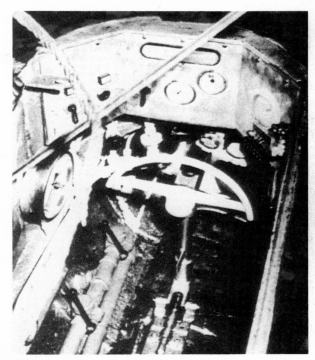

Cockpit of the Type-11 Ohka (U.S. Navy)

The Ohka used to train the pilots at Konoike. Note the runners under the fuselage—the actual Ohka was not equipped with wheels. Photographed at the U.S. Navy Memorial Museum, Washington. (U.S. Navy)

The larger, improved Ohka Type-22 Campini; it was still being worked on when the war ended. Photographed in Japan. (U.S. National Archives)

Type-11 Ohka at Kadena Air Base, Okinawa, April 1945. (U.S. Navy)

The Ohka plane was called Baka (Crazy) Bomb by the Americans. It was the biggest attention-getter in a parade down Pennsylvania Avenue, Washington, D.C., in honor of Fleet Admiral Chester W. Nimitz. October 1945. (U.S. Navy)

Present-day Yasukuni Shrine, Tokyo

A Shinto priest leads surviv members of the Thur Gods Corps in prayers their dead colleagues Yasukuni Shrine, March 1985. This is the most for part of the annual reun (Thunder Gods Association)

Memorial to the dead Ohka pilots at Kenchoji Temple, Kamakura.

Okamura's suggestion that the Thunder Gods be used only in individual surprise attacks had been accepted, and there was now intense study on how to make the best use of them. With large-scale Ohka attacks abandoned, he no longer had to hold several dozen Thunder Gods pilots in reserve. The special Ohka fighter squadron was disbanded. He then divided the Thunder Gods into two groups: one to fly the Ohka bombs, and the other to fly special attack fighter planes loaded with bombs.

The whole idea of the Ohka flying bomb had been to improve on the destructive power of ordinary fighter planes used in crash-dive missions. Now that the Fifth Naval Aviation Fleet no longer had command of the airspace around Japan, the special attack fighters were more practical than the short-range, non-maneuverable Ohkas.

Besides the flying and maneuvering advantages of regular planes, if one of them was lost, it was only one plane and one pilot, but in Ohka attacks the loss often involved not only the Ohka pilots but also eight crew members of the Betty mother plane. The high command of the Fifth Naval Aviation Fleet enthusiastically endorsed Okamura's newly proposed tactics.

On March 24, while the bombardment of Okinawa by American warships continued, all Ohka pilots who had been dispersed in the Kyushu area were ordered to report to Tomitaka Air Base. The airfield itself had been almost totally destroyed, but the raiding planes had left the barracks virtually untouched, attesting to the skill of the enemy bombers. The Thunder Gods gathered in the open area outside the billets just as the sun was setting. There was a cool breeze, and it was quiet. So far 27 of the Ohka pilots had died—15 of them in the first Ohka attack led by Nonaka, and 12 others in accidents and air raids.

Okamura stepped up on the podium in front of the assembled Thunder Gods and told them that the original plan for using the Ohka bombs in mass raids had been scrapped. The men were surprised and began glancing around at each other. In some of them there was a tiny glimmer of hope that they would not have to play out their final role. Then Okamura went on to explain that the decision had been made to divide the corps into two groups, one of them flying bomb-laden planes in special suicide attacks. The faint hope was crushed.

Okamura continued, "But the 250-kilogram bombs that were used in special attacks in the Philippines were not particularly effective, so I have decided that we will use 500-kilogram bombs. I think that it's possible if we use the latest model of the Zero. A final decision will be made about the size of the bomb as soon as we make a test flight."

Okamura then instructed the division leader of the Thunder Gods to divide them into two groups, assigning one group to fly regular fighter planes and the other group to man the Ohka bombs.

"All those who prefer the fighters, raise your hands!" the division leader yelled.

Only four hands were raised.

"All those who want to board the Ohka bombs no matter what, raise your hands!" the lieutenant shouted.

This time only three hands went up.

The men were now confused and bitter. They had all made up their minds to die on the Ohka bombs. They had merged their consciousness with the bomb and saw themselves as one: as cherry blossoms that would explode themselves against the enemy in one glorious burst for the Emperor and their homeland.

Now they were suddenly struck by acute psychological instability. The introduction of the fighter-bomber idea broke the relationship they had developed with the Ohkas. The knowledge that they were now regarded as nothing more than a means to mount suicide attacks against the enemy, regardless of the method, made many of them angry and resentful.

The lieutenant repeated Okamura's point that it was far more practical to fly a bomb-rigged plane than a winged bomb, and that their chances for success were far greater. The men began to argue among themselves. Finally, in desperation, one of the reserve sub-lieutenants groaned, "If our lives are needed, does it really make any difference whether we die in an Ohka or in a plane? Let's just get it over with and agree!"

The argument continued for several more minutes, but finally the majority of the men were won over by the sub-lieutenant's point and they agreed to accept Okamura's plan. Among those who insisted that if they were going to die they would die only on an Ohka was Higher Flight Petty Officer Keisuke Yamamura, who earlier had refused an offer to change from the suicide corps of pilots to the fighter squadron flying cover for the mother planes. To dramatize his resolution to die on an Ohka, Yamamura had made himself a headband with a long tail that hung down to his waist. One side of the band he inscribed, "Heaven's retribution, the Thunder Gods' Ohka Squadron, Higher Flight Petty Officer Keisuke Yamamura." On the other side was his death statement: "Turning myself into a fireball, I shall now take revenge for 100 million people!"

The test flight of a new Zero loaded with a 500-kilogram bomb was scheduled for March 25. The pilot revved the engine all the way up and began taxiing down the runway. He first pushed the control stick forward to see if the nose of the plane would go down. No matter how hard he pushed, the nose stayed up. Just as the plane was approaching the end of the runway, the pilot managed to get it off the ground. It was all he could do to maintain level flight, but since the plane was not expected to do anything except fly directly into its target, the test was regarded as a success.

A new squadron was formed for the special 500-kilogram-bomb-carrying attack planes. Commander Tadashi Nakajima, who had been involved in the use of planes in suicide missions in the Philippines, was brought in to provide operational guidance, and the group was named the Kemmu Squadron. In the meantime the American forces kept up their attacks on Okinawa, both from the air and from the sea. The commander-in-chief of the Combined Fleet ordered that preparations be made to launch Operation Heaven No. 1, and on March 26, when American troops began landing on the Kerama Islands off the southern coast of Okinawa, the final order for the implementation of Heaven No. 1 was given. The Third Naval Aviation Fleet was placed under the command of the Fifth Naval Aviation Fleet, and all planes belonging to the two fleets began to assemble in southern Kyushu.

On March 27, a contingent of 30 Ohka pilots gathered at Kanoya Air Base to get ready for attacks against the American forces invading Okinawa. Most of the buildings on the base had been destroyed by successive bombing raids, so the pilots were housed in the requisitioned Nozato Primary School, just west of the airfield. Concussion from exploding bombs dropped on the air base had blown out most of the school's windows, and there were bullet holes in the walls and ceiling. Wind whistled through the rooms. The men slept on the floor on blankets. The cherry trees in the school yard were in full bloom, reminding the men that, like the fragile pink blossoms, they, too, would soon be gone.

Some petty officers in the group, billeted in farmhouses near the school, hung their banners up outside their makeshift quarters. In addition to Nonaka's two favorite slogans, there was a third one that read: "OKAMURA'S PATRIOTIC SAMURAI!"

The remaining Ohka pilots moved to Tomitaka Base, led by Vice-Commander Iwaki and Division Leader Yunokawa. Adachi's Betty Squadron was sent to Komatsu Base in Fukui Prefecture along the coast of the Japan Sea. Both groups were to dispatch planes to the staging area of Kanoya Air Base in Kyushu as needed.

American carrier-based planes, joined by B-29 bombers that had been carrying out daily raids on the industrial centers of Tokyo and other major cities to the north and east, began hitting air bases in southern Kyushu on March 28 and continued the diversionary attacks throughout the twenty-ninth.

Japanese garrisons detected several troop transports just southwest of Okinawa on the twenty-ninth. In the week before this, more than 3,000 American bombers had rained bombs on Okinawa's two main air bases. Naval bombardment of the areas by U.S. warships began on March 25 and continued through March 31. Okinawa's ground defense was in the hands of the 32nd Army Corps, which was short-handed and had run out of most supplies. The commanding general decided to send most of his remaining troops into the hills around Shuri Castle, and to deploy only small forces around the two airfields, to destroy them and prevent American planes from landing there. The troops were also ordered to destroy ten Ohka planes that had been brought to the airfields earlier.

With the Operation Heaven No. 1 now in effect, the combined naval aviation fleets on March 31 issued a directive outlining the goal of the plan. "First, the enemy warships will be exterminated, followed by annihilation of the enemy troopships to frustrate the enemy's invasion plans."

Operation Heaven No. 1 called for attacks against the American task force by planes from the Third and Fifth Naval Aviation fleets, and attacks by planes from the Tenth Naval Aviation Fleet on Allied troopships. The Kemmu Squadron of the Thunder Gods was assigned to attack aircraft carriers, while other Ohka pilots were to sink warships in the vicinity of Okinawa. But more time was needed for the naval aviation fleets to assemble their remaining planes and coordinate their attacks. Somehow the American invasion of Okinawa by ground troops would have to be delayed. Ugaki decided that the only way to cause the American forces to postpone their landing on Okinawa was to immediately attack the warships then shelling the island. He ordered the Thunder Gods to prepare for a sortie.

Okamura instructed Lieutenant Hayashi to make up the roster of the Thunder Gods to go on the mission. The burden of whom to choose to die weighed heavily on Hayashi. He could not help but feel some resentment against Okamura, who had only to tell him the number of men who were to die. Hayashi was only 23 and he felt that the task was too cruel. Hayashi remembered the last thing that Nonaka had said to him. The outspoken commander had virtually ordered Hayashi to find some way to end the Ohka program—thoughts and words that were treasonous and unthinkable to a graduate of the Naval College. He also remembered a comment by his friend who had become engaged to the girl he loved in order to accept his own death more calmly. Nishio had said, "If suicide attacks are all that is left to us, I would rather see the war end with our defeat!"

At that time, Hayashi had replied, "I envy you being able to say that so frankly. We graduates of the Naval College cannot say that, even if it is what we feel."

Finally, Hayashi admitted that the only way he could resolve the dilemma was to die as Nonaka had done. He wrote his name on top of the sortie list and handed it in to Okamura. The corps commander looked at the list, grabbed a pen, and crossed Hayashi's name out.

"You go last! When I go!" he said brusquely.

Hayashi was silent. Okamura's words were the equivalent of an order, condemning him to play the role of executioner until his own death. It took all his mental strength and spirit to keep his feelings under control. He went into the officers' dining room and wrote the names of the Ohka pilots chosen for the mission on a large blackboard.

It was April, several hours before daybreak. A heavy mist hung over the air base, almost obscuring the distant moon. Six Thunder Gods pilots and 42 mother plane crew members boarded a truck in front of their school-building quarters. As the truck stopped in front of the headquarters building, the men climbed out and lined up in formation.

Yamamura, the higher flight petty officer who had made himself a long-tailed headband to declare his intentions to the world, stood in the forefront of the Thunder Gods. Some of the members had broken off twigs from the cherry trees near the billets and stuck them into the backs of their uniforms. Commander Okamura made a short speech, asking the men to do their duty and reminding them that if they were unable to reach the enemy ships with a good chance of mounting a successful attack, they should return to base. Farewell cups of saké were exchanged. Then the order was given for the doomed men to board their planes.

The lead mother plane lifted off at exactly 2:21 A.M., disappearing quickly into the mist as if it had been swallowed up by the world. The five other planes followed at two-minute intervals, all heading directly toward different warship targets that were still pounding Okinawa with their great guns. Yamamura, wearing his long headband, was aboard the leader's plane, sitting behind the pilot. The vibration from the plane's engines permeated his body. As the mother plane left the runway, he looked out the window and saw cherry trees in full bloom flashing by. For the first time, tears came into his eyes. "I'm going to die! I'm going to die!" echoed in his mind. Tears began to flow down his cheeks, and he made no attempt to stop them, caught up in the poignancy of the moment.

As the plane passed out over the ocean the mist changed to heavy fog. The pilot began descending, finally finding a rift in the fog at about 3,000 meters. Yamamura took off his life jacket so he would be ready to climb through the hatch into the Ohka bomb when they reached the target area.

A sudden burst of machine-gun fire, coming from behind the plane, jerked Yamamura out of his reverie. The pilot quickly went into a steep dive, trying to reach the cover of the fog at about 1,000 meters. Just before they reached the fog, Yamamura saw the red exhaust of an American fighter plane just a few hundred meters from his window. The pilot had also seen the enemy fighter and wheeled the plane over in a sliding dive, making its metal joints squeal in protest. At the same time the pilot jettisoned the heavy Ohka bomb that was meant to carry Yamamura to his death.

The plane was still descending. Yamamura looked over the pilot's shoulder. The altimeter was rapidly approaching zero.

"Pull up! Pull up!" Yamamura shouted frantically.

Suddenly the plane was out of the fog, but it was too late. The glistening black surface of the sea was rushing up to meet them. Yamamura saw that the speedometer was registering 220 knots.

The next thing Yamamura knew, his eardrums felt as though they were going to explode, and he was underwater. Not knowing how deep he was, Yamamura began battling with all of his might to reach the surface. In just a few seconds his head was above water, but he found himself in a sea of flames. The heat seared his eyebrows and hair. He quickly ducked back under the water, swallowing a huge mouthful in the process, and swam frantically for several yards. When he surfaced, he was still in the midst of the burning fuel. Again he ducked back under the water, again gulping a mouthful as he gasped for breath. He had to come up within the burning area two more times before he was finally clear. The water was biting cold, and he did not feel the pain of his burned flesh. Without his life jacket he knew he would be able to last only a few minutes. Then, miraculously, he bumped into some debris from the plane. It was a seat mat. He grabbed on to it.

Yamamura heard someone shouting, calling out a name. Other voices called out. Within a few minutes, four other crew members of the plane had managed to come together. They had all sustained various injuries. All were covered with oil and were wide-eyed with shock and fear. Some of them were in such bad shape that they were being kept afloat only by their life jackets. The body of another crew member drifted nearby. There was a big hole where the face should have been, so it was impossible to tell who it was. Yamamura cursed, swam to the body, awkwardly removed its life jacket, and put it on. The body sank immediately.

There was nothing the men could do except try to stay together. They held on to each other. A few minutes later a partially inflated rubber lifeboat, dropped by one of the American planes, drifted up to them. Taking turns blowing into the air valve, they managed to get the small boat fairly well inflated, but only one of them was able to climb into it. Yamamura's legs and chest were badly bruised. His right hand had almost been torn apart—it was split between the thumb and first finger—and his little finger had been ripped nearly off. Working with his good hand, he managed to tie his right wrist to the boat with his watch strap, and then let himself toss on the waves. His watch had stopped at a little past 2:30 A.M.

All the men were in intense pain from their wounds, made worse by the stinging seawater. After what seemed like forever, dawn came, but it was so foggy that their vision was limited to a few yards. A few minutes later, one of the crew members died. The other men tied his body to the lifeboat. The minutes dragged on. The weaker of the men, barely able to hold on to the raft, said their goodbyes. "Hold on!" Yamamura urged. "Hold on for just a little longer!"

Suddenly they could hear voices coming to them faintly through the fog. The voices were asking, "Japanese? American?"

Yamamura and the other men yelled back at the top of their voices, "Japanese! Japanese!"

A fishing boat slowly emerged from the fog and sidled up to the floating men. It was from Kurosu Village on Cape Sata. The fishermen pulled the injured men and the body of the dead man aboard their boat. Yamamura lost consciousness while he was being pulled onto the vessel.

The next thing Yamamura remembered was his own voice yelling "Goodbye! Goodbye!" He woke up in excruciating pain. He was naked, lying on top of a bed. A splint had been attached to his little finger to hold it in place. It took several moments for his head to clear, and then, with the realization that he had survived, that he was alive, his heart began to beat rapidly and his body flushed with relief and joy.

Later, Yamamura learned that of the five planes in his group, one had become lost and returned to base. Another had made a forced landing at sea. A third one had crashed into a mountain on Osumi Peninsula and gone up in flames, and the two others had simply disappeared and were never heard from again. The mission had been a total failure. The "Effects" sections of the Thunder Gods Corps' "Fighting Results Report" remained blank.

At approximately the same time that Yamamura had been tied to a life raft off the coast of Kagoshima, American warships began an intense bombardment of airfields in the northern and central areas of Okinawa. Hundreds of American carrier-based planes filled the sky over Okinawa, adding their bombs to the assault. The noise from exploding bombs and shells was almost continuous. A thick layer of smoke and dust blanketed the coastline and swelled up into the air. From the air, one could see huge fires burning in every direction. The Heianzan Naval Battery, on the south side of the central airfield, was reduced to smoking debris in a few minutes. The small groups of army troops deployed around the airfield to deny its use to airborne American troops were shattered and abandoned their positions.

The first contingent of American troops landed on Okinawa at 8:30 A.M. on April 1. They were followed by wave after wave of landing barges and other ship-to-shore vessels, and in less than an hour there were some 16,000 American soldiers ashore. They were followed immediately by a large number of tanks.

The ground troops and tanks began to move inland, and by 2:30 in the afternoon had succeeded in capturing and securing all of the central and northern airfields on the island. There was practically no organized resistance. The bombardment by the American warships and planes during the early hours of the morning had demolished most of the Japanese military installations on the island. The two main airfields looked like dumping grounds for destroyed military aircraft and equipment. Among the wreckage was a number of decoy planes made of canvas over bamboo frames, which brought much laughter from the American troops.

At the central airport, hidden in earthen bunkers, the Americans found four intact Ohka planes, and soon identified them as the manned rocket bombs that the Allied forces had originally believed to be remodeled German V-1's. They had nicknamed the Ohka "Baka," which means crazy or foolish. The Ohka planes were later packed up by the American Occupation forces in Okinawa and shipped to the United States, where they were inspected by the Technical Air Intelligence Center. On June 17 the center issued a report on the design of the Ohka. Thirty years later, when Miki, the chief designer of the Ohka, saw the report, he was astonished. "It was even more detailed than the specifications we had made," he said.

Following the detailed analysis of the Ohka plane's structural design and performance, the American report went on to suggest alterations to the plane that would improve its performance capabilities. Among the suggestions was a new engine that would make it possible to launch the Ohka directly from ships or land, and an improved guidance system. Practically all of the suggestions were points the Japanese designers of the plane had been considering or were working on before the war ended.

Rapid progress was indeed being made on developing a Campini-type jet engine that would greatly improve the flying bomb. The design work was completed in late March, and the Aichi Aircraft Company in Nagoya was ordered to begin production. This new version was called Ohka Type-22 to differentiate it from the conventional Type-11. Several other versions of the Ohka were also under way, but it was finally decided to concentrate on Ohka Type-43B fitted with turbojets modelled after the German-made Schwarlbe. It was to be catapult-launched from sites along the coasts of the main islands. This new, land-based version of the Ohka was to have a speed of 300 miles per hour, with a cruise range of nearly 400 miles. The designer at the Naval Aeronautical Research Laboratory and representatives of Aichi Aircraft Company were told that the Ohka Type-43B was to be the key weapon in the coming decisive defense of the home islands, and was being depended upon to bring final victory to the Empire of Japan.

The announcement explained: "When the enemy, believing that it has destroyed all Japanese planes, warships, and other defensive weapons, gathers its large fleets around Japan proper for its final invasion, the Ohka Type-43B, kept in various seashore shelters, will be launched from catapults all at once so as to bury the enemy invasion troops in a watery grave."

Work on the Ohka Type-43B, along with the launching catapults, proceeded at fever pitch, almost exactly as the American aerial technicians had predicted in their report. Chief Designer Miki drove himself an average of 20 hours a day, in part because it was only by losing himself in the work that he could forget the moral and intellectual dilemma that threatened his sanity. He knew it was insane to think that suicide bombs would save Japan from the final ignominy of defeat by the United States. He knew it was a morally objectionable waste of innocent young life to pursue the course of suicide down to the last man.

And yet, he had no choice but to work on this cruel project, ordained by those in command as the last chance to save Japan from invasion. Miki, the designer of their coffins, saw himself as much a victim as the young Thunder Gods who were required to hurl themselves against the enemy as living bombs. The contradiction was almost more than he could bear.

The Thunder Gods Corps was now virtually the last resort in the battle against the American forces landing on Okinawa. On April 2, the day after the invasion began, the first Kemmu Squadron, made up of four fighter-bombers laden with 500-kilogram bombs, carried out a raid against the U.S. ships that were part of the invasion fleet. On the following day, eight planes making up the second Kemmu Squadron were launched in a twilight attack against American ships south of Amami Oshima Island. Two of these planes returned to base because of engine trouble.

In both of these raids, half of the suicide bombers were destroyed by American fighter planes before they reached the area of their targets. Another 50 percent of the survivors were shot down in the airspace over their targets. This meant that out of the total of 12 bombers launched in the attacks, only 3 managed to crash-dive into American ships. Each one of the bombers was limited to 200 bullets to use in self-defense against American fighter planes.

The enthusiasm of even the most dedicated Thunder Gods pilot was now considerably diminished. However, even while knowing that most of them would die in vain, that their deaths would be meaningless, they were still caught up in the mystique of giving their lives for their country, and in the system that created the myth of their divinity.

The burden of waiting and the anticipation of certain death became even heavier. During the two-and-a-half-hour flight from the bases in Kyushu to the target area, each of the Thunder Gods pilots selected to fly regular planes in kamikaze attacks was silent, staring alternately at the sky in front of him and the hard, glistening surface of the water below.

The pilots were supposed to report their first contact with the enemy in pre-arranged abbreviated codes, but several of them were never heard from after they left the air base. The messages that did come through were ghost-like:

"Enemy aircraft sighted."

"Enemy ships sighted."

"I am beginning my dive."

"I am now crash-diving into an enemy warship."

"I am now crash-diving into an enemy aircraft carrier."

Japanese reconnaissance planes continued to report an unbelievable buildup of American ships in the vicinity of Okinawa. There was no indication whatsoever that the raids by the Thunder Gods had succeeded in reducing the number of U.S. ships in the area. The American invasion fleet, using techniques developed in the recapture of the Philippines, was protected by three rings that were almost impossible for the Japanese to penetrate. The outer ring consisted of squadrons of carrier-based interceptor fighter planes. Second was a picket line of radar patrol ships made up of destroyers and other vessels, and third was a wall of anti-aircraft guns on warships guarding the carriers and troopships.

American landing forces continued to battle their way inland on Okinawa, securing one area after another. On the day following the first landing, they were already using some of the airfields for smaller aircraft. The Japanese navy high command knew that U.S. construction battalions would have the airfields cleared of debris and patched

147

up so that they could be used by large bombers in just a matter of hours. As each hour passed, the possibility of the Japanese forces being able to make an effective counterattack against the American ground troops became less and less likely. It was also obvious that as soon as the American ground forces had secured Okinawa and were able to use the airfields, the carriers and their supporting warships would be able to withdraw out of the range of both the Thunder Gods and the remnants of the Japanese air force.

Fully aware of the gravity of the situation, the Tenth Naval Aviation Fleet was put under the command of the Fifth Naval Aviation Fleet in Kyushu. Efforts to strengthen the Army's Sixth Air Force and throw it into the fray continued at a frenzied pace. Admiral Toyoda knew that the next ten days would decide Japan's fate.

On April 3, the navy department of the military headquarters and Combined Fleet headquarters dispatched some of their top personnel to the Thunder Gods air base at Kanoya, with instructions to implement Operation Kikusui No. 1, which called for a last-ditch series of aerial attacks against the Allied forces. In concert with these aerial attacks, the order was given to send the great battleship Yamato to Okinawa, where its huge guns could wreak havoc among the American ships surrounding the island.

On the morning of April 4, Admiral Toyoda announced that the long-awaited counterattack would begin the next day. He sent the following telegram to all commanders:

> The Combined Fleet will continue its attacks against the enemy invasion ships and landing forces, taking advantage of every opportunity. At the same time, we will mount aerial attacks against all enemy warships stationed around Okinawa. Our objective is to totally destroy the offshore support ships, aircraft carriers as well as battleships, and to capture and annihilate the enemy landing forces.

That afternoon, when it became obvious that preparations could not be completed before April 6, the date of the counterattack was postponed until then.

Vice-Admiral Ugaki, the man directly responsible for implementing the counterattack, gave order after order to speed up the preparations. The Thunder Gods pilots stationed at Kanoya, as well as Army and Navy pilots in Taiwan, were to spearhead the attack in a series of joint suicide missions.

Ugaki knew it was his last big gamble. If the operation did not succeed, there could be no Operation Kikusui No. 2 or No. 3. Every aircraft that could fly, including old Zero planes from the Tenth Naval Aviation Fleet being used as training craft, were commandeered for the suicide attack operation. At Kanoya, several additional squadrons of Thunder Gods fighter-bombers laden with 250-kilogram bombs were formed of the additional planes that came in. The newly arrived Thunder Gods pilots from the Tenth Naval Aviation Fleet were put up in makeshift barracks at Nozato.

The primary targets of the fighter-bomber squadron now attached to the Thunder Gods Corps were to be American warships at anchor in Okinawan ports and offshore. The pilots of the Ohka Exploding Cherry Blossoms were to go after aircraft carriers and other warships cruising in the vicinity.

On April 5, the day before Operation Kikusui was to be launched, Japan's government fell apart. The Koiso Cabinet resigned en bloc, and 79-year-old retired Navy Admiral Kantaro Suzuki was appointed prime minister. Suzuki had been the grand chamberlain and privy councillor at the time of the infamous February 26 Incident in 1936, when a group of rebellious officers including Nonaka's brother, staged an unsuccessful coup against the government, killing several high-ranking officials and wounding Suzuki and others.

Well aware of the Emperor's desire to end the war, Suzuki appointed ministers he could trust to do his bidding. It was his plan to seize the right moment at the end of the war, knowing that he would probably be assassinated by military extremists immediately thereafter. At the same time he strongly supported the plan for a last-ditch stand against the Allied forces in Okinawa. He knew the outcome of that battle would determine his chances for ending the war any time soon.

Southern Kyushu was partially covered by clouds on the morning of April 6, but the weather over Okinawa was fair. At Kanoya and other bases in the area, activity was at a high pitch. The noise from the ringing of phones and the roar of aircraft engines was incessant.

At 8 A.M., the first batch of fighter planes left Kanoya Air Base and headed southward along the islands stretching toward Okinawa. Their mission was to attract enemy fighters away from Okinawa. Three more groups of fighter planes took off in succession. Their goal was to secure command of the air over and around Okinawa. Army fighter squadrons were also dispatched to patrol the airspace over Amami Oshima and

Kikaigashima islands to intercept any enemy aircraft that might be headed for Kyushu. Other planes were sent to drop metallic foil off the west coast of Okinawa to prevent American radar from picking up the approach of Japanese aircraft.

Shortly after the departure of these planes, reconnaissance reports came in with the news that four groups of American warships had been spotted in waters north of Okinawa. Sixty navy planes, along with 18 aircraft from the third Kemmu Squadron of the Thunder Gods Corps, were hastily launched to make suicide attacks against the American ships. Only four of the attacking Thunder Gods managed to break through the fighter planes and ring of fire sent up by the American vessels and to radio the fateful message, "Now crash-diving onto the target." But the attack by the Thunder Gods and other planes succeeded in tying up large numbers of American carrier-based aircraft.

Approximately 60 army planes, and 150 navy planes, including Thunder Gods fighter-bombers (with 250-kilogram bombs), were dispatched in a massive raid against American naval forces around Okinawa.

At approximately 12:30 P.M. the Japanese planes encountered the first ring of the American fighter planes. Several of the Japanese aircraft were shot down before the main force was able to break through and proceed on its way toward Okinawa. Then came the picket line of American radar patrol vessels, which succeeded in blowing several other Japanese planes out of the air. Nevertheless, more than half of the Japanese aircraft survived the defensive rings set up by the Americans, and began their final approach to Okinawa. The American ships in the vicinity immediately began zigzagging, laying smoke screens, and peppering the sky with anti-aircraft barrages. Those that were at anchor in harbors and offshore joined in with their batteries of anti-aircraft guns.

The ensuing battle was a nightmare of exploding planes and ships, with smoke, fireballs, and metallic debris filling the air. Despite the defensive maneuvers of the American ships and the almost solid wall of anti-aircraft fire, several dozen of the Thunder Gods and other suicide pilots managed to hit their targets, setting some of them ablaze and sending others to the bottom in a matter of minutes.

The Japanese interception center at Kanoya Base picked up desperate messages from American ships on the picket line and around the island:

"Mayday! Mayday! We are under heavy attack!"
"Five planes are diving toward us! Five planes. . . !"
"We need air cover! Two kamikazes have hit us!"
"We are in need of a tow . . . we need medical assistance. . . !"

When the carnage was over and the last of the Thunder Gods was gone, two American destroyers, a minesweeper, and two ammunition carriers had been sunk. Ten destroyers, one destroyer escort, one light carrier, seven minesweepers and a number of other American vessels had been heavily damaged.

At 4:30 P.M. Admiral Toyoda, commander-in-chief of the Combined Fleet, arrived at Kanoya Air Base from Tokyo to take direct command of the operation. At 6 P.M. he ordered the battleship *Yamato* and eight destroyers to leave the protection of Bungo Channel and head for Okinawa.

The following morning, just after 8 A.M., the fighter planes from the Fifth Naval Aviation Fleet flying cover over the *Yamato* had to return to base for refueling. Almost immediately the *Yamato* and accompanying destroyers came under attack by two American flying boats, which were driven off.

Shortly after noon, in a steady drizzle, a wave of carrier-based American planes broke out of the clouds and made torpedo and bombing runs against the *Yamato* and its escort vessels. Moments later a second wave appeared, followed soon thereafter by a third wave, each one unleashing a ferocious attack against the giant battleship.

Approximately two hours later, having been hit by six bombs and ten torpedos, the world's largest battleship exploded and sank, without ever having been engaged in a naval battle. It was another devastating blow to Japan.

In the meantime, aerial suicide attacks against the American forces around Okinawa continued. Sixty army planes and 10 navy craft again managed to penetrate the American defenses and attack American ships at berths in Okinawa. Another 40 navy planes, along with 12 fighter-bombers from the Thunder Gods Corps' fourth Kemmu Squadron carried out an attack against U.S. ships in the vicinity of Kikaigashima Island between Okinawa and the main island of Kyushu.

One of the Thunder Gods pilots who died in this raid was Reserve Sub-Lieutenant Mitsutaka Nishio, the young man who had become engaged to Taeko, the inn maid, while still at the Thunder Gods Corps' training center near Tokyo.

Monitoring the enemy's communications showed that the concentrated kamikaze attacks were having both a demoralizing and destructive effect upon the American forces. They had no real defense against such suicide tactics and had suffered heavy losses. The 32nd Army Corps in Okinawa reported that approximately 70 American warships had been seriously damaged or sunk. The number of carrier-based American bombers raiding the southwestern islands declined dramatically.

On April 8, Military Headquarters in Tokyo announced that in the past three days, Japanese aerial forces had sunk two special aircraft carriers, one battleship, one destroyer, five troop transport ships, and six unidentified vessels, and had put three additional battleships, three cruisers, seven transport ships, and six other unidentified vessels out of commission. They were to learn later that the actual number of American vessels sunk or damaged during this three-day period was three destroyers and three other vessels sunk, and two aircraft carriers, one battleship, 21 cruisers, and seven other ships heavily damaged.

Vice-Admiral Ugaki was pleased with the success of Operation Kikusui No. 1. He had concluded earlier that if the first special Kikusui mission against the invading American forces did not succeed, it would be totally senseless to launch further attacks. Now he reasoned that there was still a chance of destroying so many of the enemy's warships by continuing the concentrated suicide attacks that the Americans would stop the invasion.

He sent a coded telegram to Admiral Toyoda, saying: "It now seems advisable to overcome all of our difficulties and mount an all-out offensive against the enemy. Utmost efforts are now being made to round up the necessary materials and planes to continue special suicide attacks."

Toyoda agreed with Ugaki, and replied, "There is every indication that the enemy's forces have been thrown into disarray, providing a delicate war opportunity." On April 9, he ordered the immediate launching of Operation Kikusui No. 2.

Ugaki was aware that once it was agreed to pursue suicide tactics in defending the homeland, it would be virtually impossible to stop until every last plane and Thunder Gods pilot was gone—which was exactly what had occurred in the Philippines.

Now, with the full support of the Combined Fleet and the Naval General Staff, he plunged headlong into launching an endless aerial suicide operation against the American forces.

The rain that had started to fall on the day the battleship *Yamato* was sunk continued for three days. The first phase of the Kikusui No. 2 suicide operation began on April 11, the day the rain stopped. Sixty navy planes, including 16 Thunder Gods fighter-bombers from the fifth Kemmu Squadron, attacked American ships in the vicinity of Kikaigashima Island. Three of the Thunder Gods were unable to reach the area of their targets and returned to base.

On the following day, just after noon, the main Kikusui No. 2 attack was launched. Altogether 50 navy planes, 70 army planes, and 9 Bettys carrying Ohkas began leaving Kanoya Air Base at one- to two-minute intervals, headed for American ships berthed around Okinawa. Another 19 Thunder Gods fighter-bombers were to go after enemy ships in the waters around the island. Ohka pilot Reserve Sub-Lieutenant Saburo Dohi was on the second Betty making up the third Ohka Squadron. Until just moments before the takeoff, he had been helping set up bamboo-frame cots for officers in the Nozato school building adjoining the air base. He had been expecting the delivery of six more bunk frames and fifteen tatami reed mats, and only had time to yell at his superior, "Please receive them for me!" Airborne from Kanoya, Dohi's plane first headed out toward the East China Sea, intending to swing around and approach the coast of Okinawa on a north–south course. Two hours after their takeoff, the Thunder Gods squadron was spotted by American aircraft, which immediately attacked them. Several of the Bettys with their Ohka planes were riddled by enemy fire and went down in smoke and flames.

Reserve Sub-Lieutenant Kitataro Miura, chief pilot of the Bettys carrying Dohi and his Exploding Cherry Blossom, ordered the pilot to veer away and dive for cover in a bank of clouds below them. Hidden from the sight of the attacking American warplanes, the Bettys continued on toward Okinawa. Dohi sat with his arms folded across his chest and his eyes closed. He looked as if he were asleep.

At 2:45 P.M. Flight Petty Officer Zenjiro Sugano, the assistant lookout on the plane, spotted the wake of ships on the horizon. Adjusting his binoculars, he counted seven American ships steaming in the direction of Okinawa.

Dohi opened his eyes, rose, and peered out the small window. Without binoculars he was unable to see anything, but he knew his time had come. He took off the aviator's cap he was wearing, removed his life jacket, then tied his Thunder Gods band around his head. He removed the pistol strapped to his waist and handed it to Sugano.

"I don't need this anymore. Please give it to Reserve Sub-Lieutenant Terashita with my regards," he said quietly.

Sugano laid the pistol aside, then opened the floorboard hatch leading to the Ohka plane suspended beneath the Betty. Pale and silent, as if in a trance, Dohi nodded to Sugano, then lowered himself into the tiny cockpit of the Ohka.

Peering down from above, Sugano's eyes caught Dohi's in a last glance. He saluted and quickly closed the hatch.

A few seconds later, Dohi signaled that he was ready.

Anti-aircraft shells began exploding around the plane, creating clouds of purple smoke that obscured the pilot's vision. One of the blasts was so close that it severely jolted the Betty. The plane was then flying at an altitude of 6,000 meters, and was an estimated 18,000 meters from the target ships.

Sugano tapped out a signal to Kanoya Air Base that they were ready to launch Dohi and his bomb-laden Ohka. Chief Pilot Miura sent a "drop" signal to Dohi, then pushed the button to detach the Ohka. There was no explosion. The charge failed.

"Sugano!" the captain yelled. "Pull the detach wire!"

Sugano scrambled up the stairway that led to the front navigator's seat and quickly yanked the trip wire attached to the clamp holding the Ohka. The Betty immediately lifted, indicating that the heavy little plane had been dropped.

The Ohka shot ahead of the Betty in a straight dive toward the American ships on the horizon. Sugano got a quick glimpse of the red rising sun on the Thunder Gods band as the little plane spurted forward, leaving a trail of smoke as it sped toward the line of ships below.

The Betty veered sharply to the right to get away from the anti-aircraft fire from the American ships. Sugano kept his eyes glued to the trail of smoke left by Dohi's Ohka. The trail suddenly ended, and a split second later a column of dense black smoke began rising from the surface of the sea. As the seconds passed, Sugano could discern a growing oil slick around the base of the pall of smoke. It glittered brightly in the afternoon sun. He saw tiny dots in the water.

"We did it! We did it!" he yelled to the rest of the Betty crew.

Aware that the plane was not equipped with an aerial camera to record the scene (it had been removed to reduce the weight), Sugano added:

"Hurry! Sketch the scene so we can show we made a hit!"

Miura grabbed a pencil and writing pad and quickly drew a representation of the burning ship. Sugano then prepared a coded message that said, "One battleship sunk," and transmitted it to Kanoya at 3:15 P.M.

A few minutes later the Betty's port engine caught fire and began smoking. The pilot immediately pulled back hard on the stick and held it there until the plane had reached its maximum altitude. He then shoved the stick forward and went into a nose dive. The maneuver put the fire out.

The pilot set a course for Kagoshima Bay and, flying at 1,500 meters, managed to land the plane at Kanoya Air Base at 5:45 P.M. After the Betty landed, the crew found that the plane had been riddled by shrapnel and had more than 50 holes in it, some of them a foot in diameter.

When the weary but excited crew of the Betty entered the headquarters building to report, they were welcomed by squadron leader Yagita, who almost shouted, "Is it true that you sank *two* battleships?"

Miura was surprised. "No, sir. One battleship," he replied.

"But your radio message said two!" Yagita insisted, holding up the message that had been received from Sugano.

It was immediately obvious that Sugano had made a mistake and in his excitement had misread the cipher book when coding the message.

The officers of the Betty were given time to clean up and rest, then ordered to report to the underground operations room of the Fifth Naval Aviation Fleet. The room was filled with staff officers, including Vice-Admiral Ugaki, who had been asleep on a cot when the crew arrived. An aide woke him. It was the first time that any of the Ohka mother planes had returned with a specific eyewitness account of the success of one of the Ohka pilots. It was therefore an auspicious occasion, and the staff members of the Aviation Fleet were eager to hear firsthand the details of the attack.

The questioning began immediately. In rapid succession the staff officers asked one question after the other, hardly giving the crew time to respond. Chief Pilot Miura finally became exasperated at the officers and their questions. He and his crew had not been able to see the actual impact of the Ohka against the American warship and therefore could not be precise as to where Dohi had hit the ship and the nature of the explosion that followed. They were not even positive that it had been a battleship.

"What the hell do you people expect of us?" Miura finally shouted.

One of the staff officers shouted back: "You idiots can't even count, much less identify the type of ship!"

Miura became white with anger, seeking to control his temper. Vice-Admiral Ugaki was sitting there staring at him intently, but Miura was unable to completely suppress his anger and wanted desperately to yell something like "Why don't you go on one of these missions for yourself?" He restrained himself, but the meeting ended with a considerable amount of ill will between the crew of the Betty and the fleet staff officers. In the meantime, another Betty had radioed back that its Ohka pilot had succeeded in hitting a second battleship. Two other Bettys that had made forced water landings had reported similar successes. Altogether, the attack made up somewhat for the failure of the first two Thunder Gods missions. It owed its success to the earlier successes of the fighter planes and suicide missions in reducing both the number of American aircraft carriers and the ability of the American forces to send up such overpowering numbers of planes against them.

The Naval Aviation Fleet staff officers finally agreed that a total of 11 American ships had been sunk by Operation Kikusui No. 2, including one aircraft carrier, one battleship, two cruisers, and seven other ships that could not be identified. In actuality, the American ships sunk that day were one cruiser and one unidentified vessel, while two battleships, ten cruisers, and one other ship were heavily damaged and rendered virtually useless for the time being.

The fact that so many destroyers were on the list of damaged vessels meant that the kamikaze planes were attacking the first line of enemy ships to come into view after they penetrated the wall of fighter planes protecting the enemy fleets—in other words the destroyers making up the picket line. The Thunder Gods mother planes in particular had so far not been able to get beyond the picket line of American ships because of their slow speed and vulnerability to both enemy fighter planes and anti-aircraft fire from the cruisers.

The ship that Dohi hit was actually the destroyer *Mannert L. Abele,* which was dead in the water as a result of an earlier hit by a kamikaze plane that had impacted on the starboard side and exploded in the engine room. Dohi also struck the ship on the starboard side, near the front stack. The resulting explosion cracked the ship in two, and it sank within three minutes. One hundred and fourteen American seamen and officers on the cruiser were killed. It was Dohi's success that demonstrated the superiority of the Ohka planes over regular kamikaze planes in terms of their explosive impact.

American naval records acknowledge a total of four Thunder Gods attacks on this day. One of the Ohkas targeted the destroyer-mine sweeper *Jeffers*, which was on its way to rescue the crew of the destroyer *Abele*. This Ohka missed the ship and hit the water some 50 meters off the starboard side. The explosion was so powerful that the impulse wave traveling through the water warped the upper deck of the *Jeffers*.

The two other Ohkas attacked the destroyer *Stanley*, which was stationed on the first picket line of the American forces. An anti-aircraft shell from the destroyer's guns ripped the wing off one of the Ohkas as it dived toward the *Stanley*. It careened over the ship, side swiped the second stack (knocking off the *Stanley*'s insignia), bounced off the water, and exploded some 1,800 meters off the ship's starboard side. The other Ohka hit the starboard bow of the *Stanley*, but went right on through the hull of the ship and exploded over the water on the port side. The Ohka had been designed to pierce the heavy armor of large warships, and simply bored through the *Stanley*, leaving a gaping hole that was serious but not fatal.

Chapter 6

In the 20 days following the disappearance of Lieutenant-Commander Nonaka and his squadron on March 18, 11 Thunder Gods pilots died in "Exploding Cherry Blossom" attacks, and 49 crew members of Betty mother planes gave their lives. Altogether, 172 men, including fighter-bomber pilots assigned to the Thunder Gods Corps, were killed during this period.

Iwaki led the remaining Ohka pilots in their move from Tomitaka to Kanoya Base on April 12, the day of Dohi's raid. There were now only 70 men left in the corps—2 division leaders, 5 reserve officers, and 63 petty-officer pilots.

An urgent order for more men to be assigned to the Thunder Gods Corps went out to various air corps squadrons, including the Tornado Corps at Konoike Base.

It was announced that Operation Kikusui No. 2 was to be followed by a new effort called "All-out Running Attacks Against the Enemy Task Force." Names of the Thunder Gods pilots selected to go in the first attack were posted.

Higher Flight Officer Bansaku Tamura was one of the Thunder Gods picked to go on the mission. He started out to visit a neighboring farmhouse to thank the family for the kindness they had extended to him. A blue mist was hanging over Kanoya. Dandelions and violets bloomed in profusion along the runway. Tamura could hear the chirping of larks in the intervals between the roaring of airplane engines.

Tamura walked to the farmhouse as if he were in a dream. There, the farmer's wife, Fuki Kakimoto, served him tea and tidbits of food—all she could manage as a result of the strict rationing. Her daughter Sachiko, a student, made a cherry blossom out of a piece of pink flannel and sewed it onto Tamura's flight jacket.

Mrs. Kakimoto could see that Tamura was close to tears, but she could not bring herself to say, "For the sake of our country . . ."

When he got up to leave, Tamura handed Mrs. Kakimoto an envelope containing several ten-yen notes and his death statement. "I have no more use for this. Please take it," he said.

Mrs. Kakimoto tried to return the envelope to Tamura, but he refused, and left, fighting back tears. Tamura had a lover in his hometown and had once told his pilot friends that he did not want to die under any circumstances. But there was no hint of this in his death poem.

In the officers' dining room at Nozato Primary School, five reserve officers sat around a table. They were the only ones left from the original group of 21 who had been the first to come to Kanoya from Konoike, the training area. It was midnight. They were eating stew. In the group was Katsuhei Terashita, the man who had caused the riot at Konoike, and Hachiro Hosokawa, the man who had failed to heed the warnings that friction between the reserve officers and regular officers was coming to a head.

"So now there are only five of us left," someone muttered.

"Until tomorrow. Then there will only be four," another man said, staring at Hisaki Nakane, the man chosen to lead the Sixth Kemmu Squadron mission the following day.

In a corner of the room was a cluttered pile of plain wooden boxes containing the private articles of the Thunder Gods who had already died. Each time a group of the pilots took off on one-way missions they asked those left behind to see that their possessions were kept safely so they could be returned to their families. But those who made the promises soon followed their comrades, each time passing on responsibility for the boxes.

"I heard that Roosevelt died yesterday. I wonder if that will change the course of the war."

"It won't change anything. Besides, the outcome of the war has nothing to do with us."

Another of the men spoke up. "Whatever happens, all of us graduates of the 13th reserve officers training class will die in body-crash attacks."

"The 13th class, indeed! And wouldn't you know it! Today is Friday the 13th," commented another.

"Every day is Friday the 13th for us!" someone else said.

The men were quiet for a few minutes, then began to make disjointed comments, trying to sound natural, trying to stay in control of their feelings.

"I don't know who wrote the haiku, 'Falling cherry blossoms; the remaining cherry blossoms will soon be falling cherry blossoms,' but it's appropriate, don't you think?"

"I'm afraid it will hurt when I crash."

"No, you won't feel anything. You'll be scattered into a million pieces before you can feel any pain."

Terashita picked a piece of pork out of his stew with his chopsticks, held it up, and said, "The pigs beat us to it."

The other four men burst out laughing.

Terashita addressed Hirokazu Ushikubo, a former Zero fighter pilot. "You're not good enough to follow the fate of this pig. Chances are you'll self-explode before reaching your target!"

"That's a stupid thing to say. You always did overdo things!" Ushikubo said, bristling.

"Never mind," Terashita soothed. "It won't make any difference whether you hit your target or crash into the sea. We'll all meet at Yasukuni Shrine. So, Nakane, you go first and wait for us at the shrine."

Nakane stood up. "I think I'll go take a bath. I don't want to show up at Yasukuni so grimy my friends will laugh at me."

April 14 dawned bright and clear. The order was given for a daylight attack. Seven Ohka planes, the sixth Kemmu Squadron, and two squadrons of Thunder Gods fighter-bombers (laden with 250-kilogram bombs) took off and headed for a fleet of American aircraft carriers that had been sighted some 85 miles east of Tokunoshima Island. A total of 125 fighter planes had been gathered from various air bases to provide cover for the suicide attack against the American ships. One of the unit of fighters was commanded by Captain Minoru Genda, who had been transferred from the Naval General Staff and had been a key planner in the attack on Pearl Harbor four years earlier.

As Genda's squadron approached Kikaigashima Island, air tremors indicated the presence of other planes, and the signal was given to attack. The attack was well under way before it was discovered that the "enemy" planes they were attacking was the Japanese fighter squadron they were supposed to rendezvous with. By the time the error was discovered, Genda's planes had used up so much fuel that they had to return to base. The planes they attacked had jettisoned their outside fuel tanks in preparation for battle. The plane of the squadron leader had been seriously damaged in the attack, and when he turned and headed for home, the other planes followed him. This left the Thunder Gods and their mother planes without any fighter protection whatsoever, but they continued. A short time later, two of the fighter bombers developed engine trouble and returned to Kanoya Base. None of the other planes was ever heard from again.

In the meantime, another 15 Thunder Gods fighter-bombers were dispatched to attack two remodelled aircraft carriers at anchor in Kerama. Six of these planes developed engine trouble and returned to base. A short time later, one of the other nine planes radioed, "Enemy aircraft sighted. . . ." That was the last word from them.

In these two missions, 83 Thunder Gods perished.

While mission control at Kanoya Base was still waiting for word from the ill-fated daylight sorties by the Thunder Gods, two transport planes arrived at the base, bringing in Sub-Lieutenant Hiroshi Shinjo, 16 reserve officers, and 25 petty officers. They were all immediately incorporated into the Thunder Gods Corps and ordered to stand by for a mission the next day. The assignment was an order to prepare for death, shocking the newcomers by its abruptness.

"Wait just a minute!" Sub-Lieutenant Shinjo blurted out. "Let us at least have a short break!"

But time had run out. The newcomers were trucked to the Nozato Primary School, where they were to bunk that night. Among the still surviving members of the original Ohka squadrons were several of their friends who had gone through a number of "immediate standbys," and others who had gone out on sorties and returned because of engine problems or failure to find their targets. The men had grown surly and disrespectful.

Higher Flight Petty Officer Ichikawa, the man who had been reluctant to volunteer for the Thunder Gods and had been left behind when his friend Tamura was called first, was among the newcomers. As soon as he entered the barracks he asked about Tamura, and was told that he had missed him by just a few hours—that he had taken off that morning as a member of the fourth Ohka Squadron. Ichikawa went to the control tower alongside the runway, hoping that Tamura's mother plane would return so he could find out something about Tamura's last moments. The plane did not return. Back at the school, Ichikawa wandered around, looking into the abandoned classrooms. On the blackboard in one of the rooms he found Tamura's death statement.

On the following day, the Thunder Gods Corps held an athletic meet, partly to help the men get their minds off their impending deaths, and also to welcome the new members. All of the men, especially the ones whose names had been picked for the next day's mission, played with all their strength, determined, it seemed, to vent all of their fears and frustrations and get as much as possible out of the exercise. Commander Okamura put on a sword play exhibition, his specialty.

Just before 2 P.M., when the meeting was scheduled to end, the loudspeaker suddenly began squawking, "All hands, take cover! All hands, take cover!"

It was an enemy air raid. Approximately 80 American planes appeared suddenly and began bombing and strafing the base. The Thunder Gods and support personnel dived for the nearest ditches, frightened by the bomb blasts and showers of bullets that plucked at the earth around them. Even those who were doomed to die the following day were frozen with fright.

No sooner had one wave of American planes made a run on the base than another wave would come in. The attack lasted for nearly two hours. Additional fuel tanks could be seen on all of the attacking enemy planes, so it was surmised that they had come all the way from airfields on Okinawa. While the attack was going on, orders were given for as many fighter planes as possible to follow the attacking planes back to their base and attack them before they could refuel and replace their ammunition. The attacks were only minimally successful. Most of the fighter planes were shot down. That evening a squadron of Betty bombers was dispatched to attack the same bases, with similar results.

The next morning 70 navy planes and 50 army planes made suicide attacks against the same ships in Operation Kikusui No 3. Six Ohkas and 20 Thunder Gods fighter-bombers participated in the raids. Of them, 4 Ohkas and 10 planes were lost. In addition, 40 other navy planes, including Kemmu Squadron and fighter bombers, attacked an American task force east of Kikaigashima Island. Of these 40 planes, 21 were lost.

Shortly after the first group took off from Kanoya and headed south to meet the enemy, the base came under attack by approximately 100 American carrier-based planes. The raid continued until midday. Immediately after it ended, a second group of kamikaze planes took off to follow the American planes and attempt to close with their base carriers. In this second group there were 34 Thunder Gods planes (12 from the eighth Kemmu Squadron and 22 Thunder Gods fighter-bombers), 15 of which were shot down or crash-dived into the enemy.

Commander Hosokawa stood in front of the headquarters building, watching Ushikubo, the ex-Zero pilot and leader of the eighth Kemmu Squadron take off his final mission. The plane was nearing the end of the runway and still had not lifted off.

"What the hell is he doing?" Hosokawa shouted.

"Ushikubo, get the nose up!" he yelled again.

The plane continued straight ahead, plunged off the end of the runway into a grove of mulberries, and exploded into a ball of red flames. The sound of the explosion could be heard for miles. A huge cloud of black smoke and dust rose up from the point of impact. The other planes taking off had to fly through the smoke.

As Hosokawa ran toward the crash site he thought, "Why in hell did he have to prove Terashita right?" Sprinting down the side of the runway, Hosokawa saw a path of oil leading directly to the downed plane. The explosion of the 500-kilogram bomb had blown a hole in the ground that was deeper than the height of a man. The air reeked with the odor of gunpowder. Bits and pieces of the plane and its crew were strewn all around the hole. The only thing that survived the crash and explosion was a lifeboat, which appeared to be undamaged.

Hosokawa picked up the bones and chunks of flesh that could be found and placed them in the lifeboat. The largest pieces he found were an ankle and a part of a spine with some burnt flesh still on it.

Two of the mother planes that had left early in the morning limped back to the base while Hosokawa and the other men were still looking over the crash site of Ushikubo's plane. The two planes had been attacked by enemy fighters as well as hit by anti-aircraft fire, and were badly damaged. One of the aircraft had served as mother plane for Ohka pilot Terashita, who had jokingly predicted just hours earlier that Ushikubo would blow himself up before he could reach an enemy target. The commander of the mother plane later reported that after dropping Terashita in his Ohka flying bomb, they had spotted a column of black smoke, but had been unable to determine whether he had hit an enemy ship.

The other mother plane had not succeeded in dropping its dangerous Ohka cargo: both the explosive bolts and the manual trip wire had failed. Now, as it approached the runway, the Ohka still suspended beneath its belly, the base personnel scrambled into ditches and behind other barricades, fearing that it might explode when the plane landed. Miraculously, the mother plane made a soft landing, then managed to avoid the bomb craters on the pockmarked runway.

Suicide attacks against the American ships in the vicinity of Kikaigashima Island continued the following day, April 17. One of the fighter planes shot down that day was piloted by Lieutenant-Commander Yanagisawa, who had refused to accept the position of flight leader in the Thunder Gods Corps.

From April 6 through April 17, the Thunder Gods and other special-attack forces succeeded in sinking 5 American cruisers and 4 other unidentified vessels, and seriously damaging 4 aircraft carriers, 6 battleships, 54 destroyers, and 14 other ships. When added to the ships damaged in ordinary attacks, the toll of American ships damaged numbered nearly 100. The headquarters of the Fifth Naval Aviation Fleet knew that its kamikaze tactics were having a serious effect on the American forces because radio messages flying between American ships and planes indicated that the crews of the ships were exhausted from having to stand watch 24 hours a day and contend with repeated suicide attacks against which they had no effective defense. The sight of a single Japanese plane raised terror in the hearts of men on the enemy vessels. Meanwhile, the number of damaged American ships tied up at berths in the Kerama Islands continued to grow at a staggering pace. Some of the ships were barely afloat, and the waters around them were covered with oil. Those that could still navigate under their own power began the long voyage back to Hawaii and the U.S. mainland for badly needed repairs and new crews.

The Thunder Gods and other special-attack forces had succeeded in disrupting the Americans' schedule for capturing and securing Okinawa. The Japanese Fifth Naval Aviation Fleet Headquarters picked up messages from the American forces on April 17, asking for all-out support for the invasion of the strategic island. One of the intercepted messages said that the Japanese suicide attacks were worthy of close attention in terms of method and outcome. The American forces were exhausted, and it was feared that this might lead to a crisis. In order to fight off the suicide attacks, the message requested all-out air support.

As soon as he received this message, Admiral Nimitz ordered the B-29 squadron based in the Mariana Islands to support the invasion of

Okinawa. The huge bombers were then diverted from their daily raids on Japan's major industrial cities to attacks against Kanoya and other southern Kyushu bases supporting the suicide missions against American vessels around Okinawa.

In the meantime, the losses of planes and pilots by the Thunder Gods Corps, as well as Japan's other aerial forces since the beginning of Operation Kikusui, had been so severe that the whole effort was on the verge of collapse. To make matters worse, the heavily reinforced American troops on Okinawa opened a new front designed to divide the Japanese forces and render them incapable of an effective defense.

Despite the successes of Operation Kikusui, the Japanese high command was acutely aware that the fight to stop the American advance in Okinawa had failed, and began talks about staging Operation Ketsugo, the final defense of the Japanese homeland.

When the B-29s began their raids on Kanoya and other air bases in the southern Kyushu area on April 17, Admiral Toyoda ordered part of the planes of the Tenth Naval Aviation Fleet, which were under the Fifth Naval Aviation Fleet command, reassigned to Operation Ketsugo (*ketsugo* means "last resort") in preparation for the anticipated American invasion of the home islands. Vice-Admiral Ugaki was furious, but there was nothing he could do. He said that taking the planes away was like removing the ladder while his other forces were still on the second floor.

This move by Admiral Toyoda was interpreted by most of the staff of the Fifth Naval Aviation Fleet as an indication that the Navy had been pushed aside by the Army, which was determined to stage the last decisive battle on Japan proper.

On April 18, the headquarters of the Tenth Naval Aviation Fleet withdrew from Kanoya to Kasumigaura, transferring its standby squadrons to the Fifth Naval Aviation Fleet. Special suicide attacks against American forces in Okinawa continued. The Fifth Naval Aviation Fleet was down to fewer than 600 planes, of which only 350 were operational.

Twenty new pilots were conscripted for the Thunder Gods Corps, including Reserve Sub-Lieutenant Minoru Tagi from the Tornado Corps stationed at Konoike Base. Over half of this group were pilots of fighter-bombers and had had no Ohka training at all. Other squadrons from the Tenth Naval Aviation Fleet were formally incorporated into the Thunder Gods Corps. Some were "attached" to the 306th Fighter

Squadron, which had survived in name only, since all of its members had died with Lieutenant-Commander Nonaka. All Ohka members not already assigned to missions were ordered to move back from Kanoya to Tomitaka Base to train new Ohka members. Vice-Commander Iwaki was again put in charge of the move. Of the first group of 158 Ohka pilots that had arrived at Kanoya, only 37 were still alive. The only surviving reserve officers were Hachiro Hosokawa and Susumu Ohashi.

Being left at Kanoya meant death. Being assigned to Tomitaka meant that life was extended for a little while. The daily anticipation of death was almost more than Hosokawa and Ohashi could stand. If they were still doomed to die, they wanted to die as soon as possible. Yet they also wanted to live as long as possible. Hosokawa knew that if he was left at Kanoya, that would seal his fate. It all depended on the whim of Lieutenant Yunokawa, his commanding officer. Finally, much to Hosokawa's surprise, Yunokawa ordered him to move to Tomitaka and Ohashi to stay at Kanoya. Hosokawa had felt sure that he would be the first to fly because Ohashi had a closer relationship with Yunokawa. He wondered if Yunokawa was trying to tell him that the Thunder Gods were beyond such petty discrimination.

Walking with Ohashi from the divisional leader's office back to their billets, Hosokawa rationalized that Yunokawa's decision was based on the practical need to preserve the lives of former fighter-plane pilots for as long as possible, and that he was chosen over Ohashi only because he had been a leader of the Ohka Special Fighter Squadron and had experience as a mediator between reserve officers and petty officers. "We are both destined to die. It's just a matter of who goes first," he said to himself.

Ohashi suddenly turned and punched Hosokawa in the face.

Hosokawa was more shocked by the action than hurt. He stared at Ohashi in disbelief.

Ohashi had tears in his eyes and was near the breaking point. Finally he said, "I'm sorry!" then turned and walked away.

Hosokawa rubbed his cheek and watched Ohashi walk away, trying to fathom the depth of his feelings. The sound of Ohashi's footsteps echoed in his mind. It occurred to him that Ohashi's reaction was more rational than a polite, composed farewell, and he was strangely pleased.

On April 20, Division Leader Yunokawa led the main force of the special-attack pilots from Kanoya to Tomitaka. The once-crowded billets at Nozato School were now ghost-like. Bombings by the American B-29s had become a daily occurrence, and the base now bristled with red flags indicating the location of unexploded time bombs.

All of the operational aircraft were safely hidden in tunnels well away from the airfield. Those that were not operational were left on the field as decoys. The weather worsened and rain was predicted. At varying intervals, one of the time bombs would go off, keeping everyone on edge. It was no longer safe to sleep in any of the billets, so the pilots and other personnel moved their blankets into ditches dug into the hillsides and slept on the damp ground, their rest disturbed by both bombs and infestations of lice.

On April 25, the navy department of the military headquarters set up a Navy General Headquarters to supervise the activities of all navy units. Admiral Toyoda, who was already head of the Combined Fleet, was given the additional duty of commander-in-chief of the new organization. The new Navy General Headquarters was patterned after the Army General Headquarters, which was in charge of the final defense of Japan. Toyoda immediately ordered a joint meeting with the Army to study the current situation and make recommendations.

Conflicting opinions abounded. Some of the staff members insisted that the Thunder Gods had caused so much damage to the American navy that Japanese forces were now advancing. Several plans were suggested but none of them was specific. Finally, it was generally agreed that the new Type-22 Ohka plane under development would be a decisive factor. One group suggested that its development be rushed even more, because with it they would be able to destroy the enemy forces with one single stroke.

In reality, there was a serious problem with the new Ohka rocket engine. It took too long to start. At last they decided to start the engine while the plane was still on the ground, using fuel from the mother plane and switching to its own inboard rocket system just before it was dropped.

Then another problem developed. When the Ohka reached an altitude of 4,000 meters, fuel would not feed smoothly into the engine, causing it to jerk and vibrate.

In the meantime, development of the catapult-launched Ohka Type-43B, which was to be used in the final defense of Japan proper, was progressing rapidly. Its design was completed on April 26, and plans were made to set up a small catapult at Takeyama near Yokosuka Naval Port, to test the new flying bomb and familiarize pilots with its characteristics. Another site was needed for glide training. Tourist areas with cable-cars that could repeatedly haul test models to the tops of mountains were ideal for this purpose.

Mt. Ikomasan in Osaka Prefecture offered the best prospects, but there was a tunnel on the way to the top of the mountain that was too narrow for the plane to go through even with its wings folded. Finally, Mt. Hieizan, a famous religious center, was chosen despite the limited amount of space around the terminal of the cable-car system. The planes could glide to a landing at the Shiga Air Corps base at the foot of the mountain, and plans were made to use a mechanical catapult to launch the test planes from the mountaintop. The humidity in the area was a serious problem, however, causing machinery to rust and making it impossible to keep the gunpowder dry.

In the meantime, the training of new Thunder Gods pilots at Tomitaka proceeded at a frantic pace, using a Japanese carrier in Beppu Bay as a simulated target. Many of their mornings were spent in tunnels on Cape Hososhima to escape continuing raids by B-29s. More recruits for the Thunder Gods Corps were sent in from Konoike. Most of the newcomers were fighter-bomber pilots and had received no Ohka training.

The air-raid tunnels were equipped with phones connected to Kanoya Base, and they were either ringing or out of order because of the humidity. The nerves of everyone, already on edge, were being further tried by the incessant shouting of the communications personnel as they attempted to make themselves heard over the faulty phone lines.

Vice-Commander Iwaki finally lost his temper and yelled for the officer on duty. "That telephone operator is worthless! All he does is shout 'Hello!' Go kill the son-of-a-bitch!"

Twelve of the Thunder Gods pilots being held on standby at Tomitaka were ordered to report back to Kanoya to board fighter-bombers laden with 500-kilogram bombs. The order angered Sub-Lieutenant Shinjo, who felt that his group should have been picked because it had been at Tomitaka longer than the others.

"I insist that the selection be made in the order of our arrival here," he said to Vice-Commander Iwaki.

"Don't be so concerned about order," Iwaki replied. "Your turn will come soon enough. In the meantime, why don't you get in some more training?"

The response did not please Shinjo. " 'Soon enough' won't do!" he yelled. "I insist that you change the order and replace Tagi's group with us right now! That is only reasonable!"

Iwaki's face turned red. "I will decide what is reasonable!" he shouted. "Now get out of here!"

Shinjo walked away, smoldering. He was well aware that the best trained of the Thunder Gods were being held back, as were former fighter pilots and members of the Ohka Special Fighter Squadron. He wondered if they were being saved for the new versions of the Ohka plane they kept hearing about.

On April 28, the order for Kikusui No. 4 came down, calling for a new wave of special attacks against American warships tied up at berths around Okinawa. The special-attack force was made up of 40 navy planes and 40 army planes, along with 4 Ohkas from the Thunder Gods Corps. It was to be a night raid.

The Thunder Gods pilots chosen for the mission readied themselves by writing their death statements, turning their personal belongings over to friends, and then saying farewell. Many of those seeing them off cried openly. For some, it was harder to stay than to go.

There was considerable grumbling among the Betty pilots about the decision to make the raid at night. The planning staff was obviously thinking that the mother planes and their precious cargo would have a better chance of avoiding enemy fighter planes and anti-aircraft fire in the darkness of the night, but that same darkness would make it virtually impossible for the pilots to sight their targets.

The planes took off. Besides the darkness, there was a vast cloud cover blotting out the ocean below. Even when a rift appeared in the clouds, it was still too dark for the Thunder Gods and crew members of the mother planes to see anything on the surface of the water.

Suddenly a yellow light exploded near the plane carrying Flight Petty Officer Naohiko Yamagiwa.

"Anti-aircraft fire! The enemy is right below us!" the plane's observer shouted.

A crew member immediately opened the floorboard hatch leading to the Ohka suspended beneath the plane. Without reflecting on what he was doing, Yamagiwa crawled into the tiny cockpit of the flying bomb and closed the hatch. Keiichi Sakai, the chief pilot, began circling to the left, trying to get a glimpse of the American ships below. He reached for the speaker tube connected to the Ohka.

"Yamagiwa, can you hear me?" he yelled into the tube.

"I hear you!" Yamagiwa replied.

"Can you see the enemy warship?"

"No, I can't see a thing."

Shells began bursting all around the plane, sending flashes of yellow light into the cockpits of both the mother craft and the Ohka.

"Sir! Sir!" Yamagiwa yelled. "Detach the Ohka! I'll dive at the flashes of light from the anti-aircraft guns!"

Almost without thinking, Sakai hit the switch, releasing Yamagiwa, then banked to the right in an attempt to watch his descent. But he could see nothing. He was suddenly filled with intense regret at having dropped Yamagiwa without a second's thought into the blackness of the night. His reaction had been mechanical, without consideration of the lives involved.

A crew member's shrill voice suddenly pierced through the roar of the engines.

"We've done it! We've done it!"

Swiveling his head around to look backward, Sakai saw a pillar of red fire shooting up from the surface of the sea. He immediately ordered the radio operator to inform headquarters that Yamagiwa had hit and sunk what appeared to be a large warship. Sakai then headed the plane for home.

The celebration in the mother plane was short-lived, however. As it was approaching Amakusa Island it came under attack by several American fighter planes, was heavily damaged, and was forced to make an emergency landing at sea.

Of the three other Ohka attack planes in Sakai's squadron, one had to jettison its Ohka and make an emergency water landing west of Kyushu. A second one came under attack by enemy fighter planes before reaching its assigned target, abandoned its Ohka, and returned to base. The third plane reported engine trouble, then dropped its Ohka and headed for home but was never heard from again. This plane and its crew members were excluded from the announcement of meritorious deeds accomplished by the corps, and the missing men were not given posthumous promotions.

The good weather continued. On April 29, the Thunder Gods Corps was ordered to launch still another attack, this one a twilight sortie against enemy ships cruising off the east coast of Okinawa. The raid was conducted by four squadrons, the ninth Kemmu Squadron with 12 planes and three Thunder Gods fighter-bomber squadrons with a total of 21 planes carrying 250-kilogram bombs. Only two of the planes from the Kemmu Squadron returned to base. Only four of the other planes returned. By this time, the Thunder Gods planes had little or no fighter protection. The few fighters left had been split up as a result of continuing B-29 bomber raids on the home islands.

The good weather broke on April 30, and by May 1 a torrential rain was falling. Japanese newspapers carried stories reporting the unconditional surrender of Germany to the Allied powers in Europe. They also informed their readers that the American forces had for the first time publicly acknowledged that the Japanese were using manned bombs against them in the Pacific.

The men of the Thunder Gods Corps could not fathom the reason for the government's decision to allow this foreign news dispatch to be carried by the Japanese press, because the ability of the corps to carry out its special suicide attacks was diminishing daily at a rapid rate. It seemed that Fifth Naval Aviation Fleet Headquarters was pinning its final hopes on the success of the more powerful 1,200-kilogram bombs to be used in the advanced version of the Ohka.

The weather began to clear up on May 4, and the order was given to implement Operation Kikusui No. 5. The 32nd Army Corps, which had been driven into the mountains of southern Okinawa, began an all-out counterattack against the American forces. Seventy navy planes, and 50 army planes carried out coordinated suicide attacks.

The American forces later reported that one of the Ohka pilots had succeeded in hitting his target, and another one had come close. The Ohka piloted by Reserve Sub-Lieutenant Ohashi hit the bridge of a minelayer-destroyer, penetrated the superstructure of the ship, and exploded, killing 118 crew members. The Ohka manned by Higher Flight Petty Officer Masayoshi Ishiwata dived at the minesweeper *Gayety*, but hit the water nearby. The resulting explosion injured artillerymen on the ship. The mother plane, seeing the tower of smoking rising form the explosion, assumed that the ship had been sunk and was able to return to base by using clouds as cover.

Only one of the other Ohka attack planes returned to base. Two were never heard from after their takeoff. Two others disappeared after radioing that they had launched their Ohkas and were being pursued by enemy planes. By this time the death toll in the Thunder Gods Corps had reached 587.

Admiral Toyoda returned to Kanoya Base on May 8, determined to take some action that would break the deadlock with the enemy forces on and around Okinawa. But the only air force available was the Thunder Gods Corps. Orders were given for the remaining Ohka pilots to prepare themselves. Three days later, on May 11, the order for Operation Kikusui No. 6 was given. It was heavily overcast at dawn and soon began to rain.

Ohka pilots Mitsuo Yamazaki and Koji Katsumura were ordered to take off first and crash their Ohka bombs onto the runway of the northern airfield in Okinawa. Commander Okamura explained that this would temporarily prevent the Americans from using the airfield, and give the other Ohka planes a better chance of reaching their targets. Yamazaki and Katsumura began complaining about being asked to commit suicide by diving onto a runway.

"I understand your feelings," Okamura said, a painful expression on his face, "and I'm sorry to have to give this kind of order, but we are short of special-attack planes and now have to depend on the power of the Ohka. Please understand."

Reluctantly, the two pilots agreed. The first mother plane took off at 1:56 A.M., and was followed eight minutes later by the second plane. But as fate would have it, Yamazaki's plane developed engine trouble and had to return to base before reaching its target. A short while later, Katsumura's mother plane also returned, reporting that the cloud cover over Okinawa was so heavy, it could not locate the airfield.

This was the third time that Katsumura's mother plane had failed to launch its Ohka, and its chief pilot, Higher Flight Petty Officer Naomi Kamata, was reprimanded by Operations Officer Nakajima.

"Why didn't you go below the cloud cover and find a way to launch the Ohka?" he asked sarcastically, implying that Kamata was a coward.

The main attack force, made up of 30 navy planes (including Ohka and mother planes), 40 army planes, and 26 Kemmu Squadron and Thunder Gods fighter-bombers, whose targets were American ships off the east coast of Okinawa, began taking off at 5 A.M.

In the truck taking him and other Thunder Gods pilots to the airfield, Sub-Lieutenant Shibata, leader of the tenth Kemmu Squadron, alternately boasted that he would skim the surface of the sea and crash into the exact center of his target, and then cried out, "Mother! The Navy is trying to kill me!" Shibata's strange behavior was typical of the mixed emotions of the young Thunder Gods pilots.

Well before the two attack forces reached their target areas, they were intercepted by an especially large number of American fighter planes. Most of the special-attack planes were shot down in the next few minutes. Only one mother plane heading for American ships at berth managed to launch its Ohka, which scored a near miss on a destroyer, causing heavy damage. One other mother plane developed engine trouble and returned to base.

The force heading toward the American ships at sea had better luck. One bomber-fighter managed to get through the ring of American planes and anti-aircraft fire and dived into the flagship carrier *Bunker Hill*, hitting it on the starboard side near the third elevator. The bomb-laden plane pierced the deck and exploded inside the ship, destroying most of the planes on deck and disabling the carrier. The flag was moved to the carrier *Enterprise*.

On May 12, the day after the launching of Operation Kikusui No. 6, the Navy General Headquarters merged the remainder of its planes, mostly training and reconnaissance aircraft, except for the Thunder Gods Corps, into a single fleet and named it the Heaven Air Unit. The new unit was to be used to continue the attacks against American forces in Okinawa. The day after the inauguration of this new unit, the Americans launched a series of six air raids, employing a total of some 900 planes, against the southern Kyushu air bases being used by the new Heaven Air Unit. The raids continued into the second day, but the Thunder Gods managed to launch a new attack made up of 28 planes from the eleventh Kemmu Squadron and Thunder Gods fighter-bombers. Once again, one of the planes managed to break through the American defenses and succeeded in crashing into the USS *Enterprise*.

The suicide plane hit the *Enterprise* near the front of the first elevator and pierced the deck. The explosion that followed blew the elevator some 120 meters into the air, warped the deck, and set the hangar on fire. The flag was once again moved, this time to the carrier *Randolph*.

Despite the dramatic decline in the number of Japanese suicide planes being sent against them, the American naval forces moved southward beyond the range of Japanese scout planes in order to avoid the possibility of suffering more damage. In the meantime, the American Army Air Force began launching daily raids on southern Kyushu from airstrips in southern Okinawa. The B-29 bombers, which were stationed in the Marianas and had been participating in raids on

Okinawa, now resumed their fire-bombing attacks on major cities in the home islands. The American forces also stepped up their minelaying operation.

Vice-Admiral Onishi, commander-in-chief of the First Naval Aviation Fleet, who had been stationed in Taiwan after the fall of the Philippines, was ordered to report to the Naval General Staff at Atsugi Air Base outside of Tokyo. His plane was scheduled to make a stopover at Omura Air Base in Kyushu, then diverted to Yonago city when it was learned that Omura was under attack by American fighter-bombers. The pilot of Onishi's plane informed him that he intended to stay well west of the main cities to avoid any chance encounter with American fighters, but the vice-admiral ordered him to fly directly over Nagoya, which had been raided by B-29 bombers on the previous day.

Vast stretches of the once populous city had been reduced to rubble. Among the major buildings, only the Mitsubishi Nagoya Aircraft Factory near the port still had its roof.

Onishi had used every resource at his command to continue the special suicide attacks against the American forces, and continued to adhere to his belief that this was the only way Japan could hope to win the war.

"The gods will provide us with victory only when all Japanese are devoted to the spirit of special attacks. Death is not the objective, but each person must be resigned to death, and try to destroy as many of the enemy as possible. This is the best way to defend the Empire and will lead the nation to victory," he said.

On May 19, Onishi was appointed vice-chief of the Naval General Staff, a post he had demanded at the time the Koiso–Yonai cabinet was formed. The other hard-liners in the army and navy who agreed with Onishi about the use of special suicide tactics were overjoyed at his appointment.

The 32nd Army Corps in the mountains of southern Okinawa was on the verge of collapse. As a last resort, the central army authorities planned to land airborne troops on the northern and southern airfields on May 24, in concert with Operation Kikusui No. 7, to be carried out by the new Heaven Air Unit of special-attack planes. The combined attack force consisted of 100 navy planes and 20 army planes, including 12 Ohka mother planes from the Thunder Gods Corps. Among the pilots lined up on the runway on May 25 was Higher Flight Petty Officer Yamamura, who had made a forced water landing after an aborted

Ohka attack on April 1. He was now pale with fear and shivering as if he had a serious chill. He could not even hear what Commander Okamura was saying.

Yamamura was still in a sort of daze when he climbed aboard the mother plane, which took off just before dawn. The weather changed rapidly and soon they were caught in torrential rain. Water was hitting the windshield so hard that Yamamura could not hear the roar of the engines. Someone handed him a lunch box. He forced himself to take a few bites, then gave it to one of the crew members. The plane finally reached what appeared to be the target area. The floorboard exposing the cockpit of the Ohka was opened. A blast of cold, wet air hit Yamamura in the face, nearly knocking him down. Holding tightly to the entryway, he climbed into the Ohka and closed the hatch. He then pulled a photograph from his pocket and put it on the dashboard in front of him. It was a photograph of an actress whose name he did not know. She was smiling sweetly up at him. Yamamura sent a "ready" signal to the mother plane and sat staring at the red light, waiting for it to go on. The rain was now heavier. He could see nothing outside of the tiny cockpit. He took a deep breath, waiting for the flash of red light that would mean he had only a few seconds left to live.

The light did not go on. Unable to bear the suspense, Yamamura yelled into the speaker tube. "What's happening?"

"Visibility is so poor, we can't see anything!" a voice replied.

Yamamura dug into his pocket, pulled out a cigarette, and lit it, puffing tensely. The waiting was almost more than he could bear.

"Petty Officer! Petty Officer!" came the voice through the speaker tube. "Return to the mother plane. We can't make a drop in this weather!" Yamamura felt as though he were dreaming. He unlatched the cockpit hatch, and crew members pulled him back into the plane.

Nine other mother planes, also unable to locate any targets because of the weather, returned to base. Three others disappeared without a trace. The weather also forced several of the special-attack planes to return to base.

That evening at 7 P.M., 12 army planes loaded with airborne troops took off from Kumamoto Air Base and headed for Okinawa. They were to land on the American-occupied airfields in northern and southern Okinawa and inflict whatever damage they could. The planes were equipped to signal accompanying scout aircraft with a red light if they succeeded in making a landing on the designated airfields.

The scout planes returned to base and reported that four of the planes had succeeded in landing in northern Okinawa, and two of them had landed at a central Okinawa airfield at about 10 P.M. In reality, only one plane made a successful landing on the northern airfield. The plane immediately came under attack by small-arms fire, but the troops aboard managed to get off and destroy several American planes and fuel dumps before they were shot to death one after the other.

The eighth Operation Kikusui attack, against enemy ships at berth in Okinawa, was ordered on May 27. It was to begin at dusk, continue until the following morning, and be carried out by 50 special attack planes, most of which were reconnaissance aircraft. For the first time, the Thunder Gods Corps was not involved in the operation.

On the twenty-eighth, it was announced that the army would no longer participate with the Naval Aviation Fleet in Operation Kikusui. The ostensible reason was that the commander-in-chief of the army's Sixth Flying Corps was senior to the incoming commander-in-chief of the Combined Fleet, but in actuality the army was abandoning any attempt to recapture Okinawa. Admiral Toyoda, who had been commander-in-chief of the Combined Fleet, was appointed chief of the Naval General Staff.

Also on May 28, the Navy Ministry for the first time made public the activities of the Thunder Gods Corps. The announcement read:

> Since the end of March 1945, the members of the Thunder Gods Corps have made sorties to waters south of Japan proper, and around Okinawa, and have threatened the enemy forces with their admirable fighting spirit and the formidable power of one-hit sinking. With much appreciation, the commander-in-chief of the Combined Fleet announces their meritorious deeds to the entire force.

This announcement was followed by a list of the names of the Thunder Gods pilots who had died in the first through the fourth Ohka squadrons and the first through the sixth Kemmu squadrons. There were 332 names on the list. The announcement was carried in all of the major newspapers on May 29, with big headlines and praise for the Thunder Gods Corps.

From May 30, the papers carried continuing stories about the first Ohka Attack Squadron, along with a detailed profile of the escapades of Lieutenant-Commander Nonaka. No mention was made of the fact that he and his entire squadron had been annihilated. Special Service

Sub-Lieutenant Ota, the man who had initiated the Ohka flying bomb program, was described as a veteran pilot who had devoted all of his energy to help develop the weapon. Ota was not a pilot but had allowed the authorities to think he was in order to gain credibility for his plan.

The annual spring rainy season now began in earnest. The launching of the ninth Kikusui operation was repeatedly announced on successive mornings and cancelled in the afternoon. The morale of the remaining Thunder Gods pilots became lower each day, and they went about their assigned duties with less and less enthusiasm.

American bombers stationed on Okinawa continued to raid the main islands regardless of the weather, operating what was dubbed "a regular flight service." The main forces of the American naval fleet, now under the command of Admiral Halsey, who had replaced Admiral Spruance, gathered in the vicinity of Okinawa. Aircraft from the various carriers made "show-off" flights over Kyushu.

On June 2, an amphibious plane, escorted by some 20 fighters, landed in Kagoshima Bay to rescue the crew of an American bomber that had been ditched following a raid. Following the broad-daylight rescue, the plane "took off in a leisurely manner."

There were few Japanese planes left to defend the islands from the daily American raids. Being forced repeatedly to run for air-raid shelters and spend hours in hiding lowered the morale of the Thunder Gods Corps even further. At Tomitaka Base, many of the pilots began ignoring the air-raid warnings. This infuriated Commander Iwaki. On one occasion, when enemy aircraft were detected coming toward the base over Hyuga Bay, several of the pilots continued lounging in front of the barracks. Iwaki rushed into the mouth of a tunnel and dashed back out with a machine gun in his hands.

"So you people want to die, huh? Okay! I'll help you fulfill your dreams!" he shouted. With that, he opened fire, spraying the ground in front of the pilots with a burst of bullets. The startled pilots jumped up and ran for the shelter.

This was just one of the incidents that indicated the growing problem of keeping the corps together. At Kanoya, more and more of the petty-officer pilots began leaving the base without permission, drinking and carousing in nearby inns. One evening Higher Flight Petty Officer Kyusaku Koshiro, who did not drink, was the only one left in the Nozato billet. He was playing a card game when an orderly rushed in and told him that Commander Okamura wanted to see him.

Koshiro hurriedly reported to Okamura's office, where he was ordered to assemble all of the pilots of the Ohka Squadron. Frantic, Koshiro borrowed a bicycle and pedaled furiously into Kanoya Town, four kilometers away. There he was able to find only about half of the pilots, all of whom were so drunk they could hardly stand, much less walk back to the base. With the help of a military policeman who happened by, Koshiro got a lumber dealer to drive the Ohka members back to their billets in his truck. All the way back, the drunken pilots sang loudly.

Still reeling and complaining loudly, the pilots did their best to line up in the schoolyard. Because half of them were still missing, Koshiro persuaded several members of the maintenance division to stand in for them, hoping that Okamura would not notice the difference in the darkness. He then knocked at Okamura's door.

"Ohka Squadron has lined up!" he yelled. By this time it was 10 o'clock.

"All right," Okamura replied. "There are some sweetened bean cakes at the paymaster's office. Go get them and give them to the men," he added.

Koshiro was confused. "Thank you very much, sir. But what was it you wanted with us?"

"Nothing. That's all," Okamura said, shaking his head. "The men haven't had anything sweet for a long time, and since the corps got some sugar, I ordered bean cakes prepared. When you're done eating, dismiss the men and let them go to bed."

The following morning Koshiro was further confused when Operations Chief Nakajima harangued the Thunder Gods pilots for their conduct. There were just too many contradictions for him to understand. He later was told by Sohachi Yamaoka, a popular novelist who had been assigned to the Thunder Gods Corps as a reporter, that Nakajima had confronted Okamura many times about the behavior of the Thunder Gods Corps and repeatedly asked him to discipline them and be more strict. Okamura was more understanding of the extraordinary position of the pilots and tended to be lenient with them, saying that when the time came they would all give their lives without complaining. Koshiro presumed that Okamura had ordered the late-night "bean paste" assembly just to get Nakajima off his back.

On June 7 there was a break in the weather, and the ninth Kikusui operation was finally launched. Again the Thunder Gods Corps was

178

kept out of the action, which involved 46 planes, only 10 of which managed to reach their designated target areas. It was becoming increasingly obvious that the Thunder Gods Corps was being held back to take part in the battle for Japan proper. At least, that is what the majority of the pilots believed.

Just before noon on June 8, some 270 American planes raided dozens of targets in Kyushu, including Kanoya Base, where several planes were set afire and 40 others were damaged. Vice-Admiral Ugaki believed the attacking American planes had come from somewhere southeast of Okinawa. He decided to launch an attack against the area using the Thunder Gods. Because of the distance, the fighter-bombers would have to take off from Kikaigashima Island, south of Kyushu. Four fighter-bombers laden with 500-kilogram bombs arrived at Kikaigashima Island on the same day the main American naval force left the waters of Okinawa for Leyte Gulf, signalling the end of their direct support of the Okinawan invasion.

Meanwhile, American forces on Okinawa had driven the last of the 32nd Army Corps away from the ruins of Shuri Castle to Kiyan Peninsula at the tip of the island. The naval troops stationed in the Koroku area, now completely on their own, staged a final raid on June 11 and were never heard from again.

On June 12, the Naval General Staff presented its draft of a plan for the final defense of Japan. Called Operation Ketsugo (Last Resort), the keynote of the plan was to stage all-out suicide attacks against the enemy. At this time, too, the Thunder Gods Corps was notified that the new Ohka Type-22 would be tested on June 14 and 15. Iwaki, Yunokawa, and Hayashi were ordered to report to Konoike Base to witness the tests. En route to Konoike, their plane had to dodge a flight of American bombers.

The initial ground tests were a failure. The remodeled rocket vibrated so much it had to be shut down, and the flight tests were postponed. Iwaki and his party returned to the Thunder Gods base at Kanoya, sorely disappointed. It was soon discovered that a basic mistake had been made in the design, and the project was quickly put back on line.

The navy department of the military headquarters was at last forced to admit that the battle for Okinawa was a lost cause. The Kikusui suicide operations were to be suspended after the completion of Operation No. 10. Orders were to be given for small guerrilla forces to stage nighttime attacks against the American forces on Okinawa, to keep them busy while more preparations were made for the defense of the home islands.

The last Thunder Gods attack against the enemy in Okinawa was made up of six Ohka planes and eight Thunder Gods fighter-bombers carrying 250-kilogram bombs. The pilots lined up in front of a tunnel at 3 A.M. on June 22. A dim light was turned on. Yamamura, who had returned from two unsuccessful Ohka attacks, was in the front of the lineup. The memory of his last flight, when he had sat in the cramped cockpit of the Ohka, waiting for the red light that meant his doom, loomed large in his mind. He was both angry and sad.

"Damn!" he said. "Hurry up! Kill me! Get it over with!"

One of the pilots who had been chosen for the Ohka mission, Kiyomi Katagiri, was not there. The final instructions of the commander and the exchange of farewell cups of saké were to start. Division Leader Hayashi rushed into the school building. The only one there, as usual, was Koshiro, asleep in his bunk. Hayashi shook him.

"Get up, Koshiro!" he said loudly. "Katagiri is missing and I want you to go for him!"

Still half asleep, Koshiro began struggling to get his uniform on, grumbling about being picked to die for someone else who was out having a good time. Yamaoka, the reporter, who had followed Hayashi into the billet, remembered that Katagiri often hid in an air raid shelter to sleep off his drunken binges. Yamaoka ran to the shelter and tripped over Katagiri, asleep on the floor, still in his uniform.

A torch attached to the side of the tunnel flickered crazily. Katagiri jumped up, blinking. Yamaoka told him quickly what was going on.

"Shit!" Katagiri yelled. "I overslept! Thanks, reporter, and goodbye!" he yelled, dashing off toward the formation of other pilots. A doll hanging from his belt swayed back and forth as he ran. On the back of his uniform was written in white paint: "I'll gather with friends at the river Styx and have a party!"

Back at the billet, the departure ceremony was over. The pilots were climbing into a truck to be driven to the airfield. As Koshiro took his place in the truck, Okamura's final words were echoing in his mind. Someone grabbed him by the belt and began pulling him off the truck. It was Katagiri.

"It's my turn! Not yours!" Katagiri said emotionally. As the truck pulled away he yelled *Abayo!* (Goodbye) to Koshiro several times.

This time, when the 14 planes left the base, they were accompanied by 66 fighters from Kazanopara, the first time since the annihilation of Nonaka's squadron that the Thunder Gods were flying in formation with fighter protection.

The sight of the fighters was a welcome change to the crew members of the six Betty mother planes and the eight fighter-bombers, but within less than an hour 25 of the fighters had engine trouble and had to return to base. A short while later the two squadrons came under attack by American planes, scattering most of the other fighters. The squadrons continued on toward Okinawa with virtually no protection.

The Ohka squadron was to approach Okinawa from the west, and the fighter-bomber squadron from the east. Just as it was approaching Iejima Island, north of Okinawa, the mother plane carrying Yamamura and his Ohka spotted the wake of an enemy warship. Suppressing his desire to scream out his refusal, Yamamura once again climbed into the cockpit of the winged bomb suspended beneath the Betty.

Once again he yelled "Ready!" into the speaker tube and kept his eyes glued to the red light on the instrument panel. This time the light began flashing. He grabbed the control bar. There were three short flashes, followed by a long one and then a final short flash. His mouth and throat were dry. There was a sharp pain in the pit of his stomach as he waited for the falling sensation.

But nothing happened. The Ohka was still attached to the Betty. He began rocking from side to side, trying to shake the plane loose and roaring like a wild animal. It was no use. The Ohka remained locked to the Betty, which, along with two other mother planes, returned to base.

The mother plane carrying Katagiri was approaching three enemy cruisers when it was attacked by two American fighters. It caught fire and exploded. Nothing was heard from the three other Bettys. One of the eight fighter-bombers was ditched at sea. The others were apparently shot down before they could reach the target area.

The final sortie of the Thunder Gods Corps against the enemy on Okinawa thus ended in complete failure. On the same day, the remnants of the 32nd Army Corps pinned down on the southern tip of the island began killing themselves. At dawn on June 23, Commander Mitsuru Ushijima and Chief of Staff Isamu Cho committed harakiri. The battle for Okinawa was over.

Chapter 7

Approximately 9,440 navy planes had taken part in the aerial battles off Kyushu from the beginning of the battle for Okinawa in March to the tenth Kikusui operation in June. Of this number, 1,320 planes were lost. A total of 1,840 special-attack planes (those assigned suicide missions) also took part in the battles, out of which 960 were either destroyed by enemy gunfire or crashed into their targets. The sacrifice by the Thunder Gods Corps was particularly enormous. Of the total of 185 planes used in Ohka attacks, 118 were destroyed, taking the lives of 438 persons, including 56 Thunder Gods pilots and 372 mother-plane crew members. Out of 368 fighter-bombers used during this period, 284 planes and their crews were shot down or crash-dived into the enemy.

It was later reported by the U.S. Navy that out of 240 American warships damaged or sunk by Japanese forces during the battle for Okinawa, 192 of the ships were hit by kamikaze planes. A booklet published on May 28, 1945, by U.S. Navy Operations stated that the suicide attacks by fighter planes and manned bombs resulted in damage far in excess of that caused by conventional aerial attacks.

Still, the damage inflicted by the kamikaze planes was superficial. Most of them hit the superstructures of their targets, and only a total of 15 ships were sunk, none of them larger than a destroyer. As for the Ohkas, they succeeded in sinking only one destroyer and damaging five others—not nearly extensive enough to compensate for the enormous expense and loss of life. The Ohkas were indeed "spears hard to handle."

The advanced Type-22 Ohka had not come on line in time for the battle of Okinawa. On the date of Operation Kikusui No. 10, only 10 of the Type-22 Ohkas were at the testing stage, and they proved to be defective. In the first test, the booster rocket fired before the detach signal was given, sending the Ohka into a tumbling dive toward the earth. Nagano, the test pilot, barely managed to kick himself free from the falling aircraft, but his parachute did not fully open and he was seriously injured when he hit the ground. When the Frances mother plane landed, it was found that the bottom of the fuselage had been ripped off. Inspection of the wrecked Ohka showed that the rocket had been set off before the Ohka was released from the mother plane.

Nagano was still conscious when the members of the test crew and other witnesses reached him. As he was being carried to the base infirmary he said clearly, "I did not touch the ignition button!" He died that evening just before 6 P.M. Because the Ohka was so badly damaged in the crash, it was impossible to determine the cause of the premature ignition of the booster rocket engine. Why Nagano's parachute failed was also a mystery. It had been folded by two veteran employees of the parachute manufacturing company while Nagano watched to make sure that it was done right. Rumors began to float around that it had been sabotaged. A two-day inquiry into the accident was unable to clear up either mystery.

Review of the problems of the Type-22 Ohka led to a decision to dispense with the booster rocket and to suspend all test flights until the problem of the propulsion system could be resolved. In the meantime, progress was being made on the catapult-launched Type-43B Ohka, which was fitted with a turbojet engine adapted from a German-made jet-propelled plane. The turbojet engine was also to be used in the newly designed Kikka plane. The first model of the Kikka was completed by Nakajima Aircraft's Koizumi Factory in Gumma Prefecture on June 29, three days after Nagano's accident. As soon as the turbojet engine was tested in the Kikka, it would be ready for use in the Ohka Type-43B.

Construction of land-based launching catapults for Ohka planes on Mt. Hieizan and the beach at Takeyama were already well under way. The first test of the catapult at Takeyama, using a two-seater Type-11 training plane, was held on June 27. Chief Designer Miki himself went along as an observer on a test flight, seated in the rear of the plane with a commanding view of Miura Peninsula below. He and the pilot, Commander Hiromitsu Ito, who served as liaison for the Ohka and Kikka planes in the Naval Aeronautical Department, were tremendously impressed with the plane. After they landed, Ito said jocularly, "How about starting an aerial sight-seeing company with this plane after the war is over!"

The construction and testing of the flying bombs and special-attack planes continued at a feverish pace, hampered by shortages of materials and beset by continual air raids. In addition to problems of production, there were problems of handling and maneuverability of the fighter-bombers. One of the problems of special concern was the difficulty the pilots had in keeping the nose of their planes down so they could strike an enemy ship in a vulnerable location. Diving into a ship at a 60-degree angle gave the pilots the impression they were in an almost completely vertical fall. Since most of the remaining pilots were barely capable of sustaining horizontal flight, it was too much to expect them to be able to execute a perfect dive against an enemy ship.

In an attempt to discover the most vulnerable area of a ship, bombs were placed in several locations on a partially completed aircraft carrier at the Kure Naval Dockyard. After several types of bombs were exploded at different angles without seriously damaging the ship, a Type-22 Ohka warhead was exploded beneath the lower deck near the rear elevator. This caused heavy damage to the flight deck, but did not sink the ship.

The military headquarters presumed that the American forces would begin their invasion of Japan proper in southern Kyushu. Orders were given for all available men in the area to be mobilized. The shortage of artillery weapons was so acute, however, that little real progress was made in fortifying the coastline. The army and navy air corps were expected to play a leading role in the defense of the home islands, but their numbers had been seriously depleted by the battle for Okinawa. Most of the remaining planes were in need of repairs, and the surviving pilots were exhausted. The Naval Flying Corps in particular had trouble restructuring itself, and it was late June before it finally began deploying its remaining forces in Kyushu.

The remaining 145 members of the fighter-bomber squadron were spread around among bases in Kyushu and Shikoku. Seventy-five Ohka pilots and 400 Betty crew members in the Thunder Gods Corps were ordered to move to Komatsu Base on the coast of the Japan Sea in Ishikawa Prefecture. Some of the Ohka officers were billeted in the home of a well-known banker, Chogoro Matsumura, while the Betty officers were put up in a temple. When Hosokawa made a courtesy call on the banker to thank him for the use of his home, the banker commented on the buildup of army and navy forces in the area, and asked if this meant the forces were retreating.

It was the first time that anyone had asked Hosokawa outright if they were losing the war. Always before, everyone had given him exceptionally deferential treatment because of his role in the Thunder Gods Corps. As the only surviving member of the 21 reserve officers who had left Konoike Base in the first group to come to Kyushu, Hosokawa was acutely embarrassed. He replied:

"That's not the case at all. Since the decisive battle on Okinawa has ended, we're moving here to protect Japan proper."

"So it has come to that," the banker said sadly.

During this deployment, the Tornado Corps at Konoike Base was also being reorganized. On July 1, half of the members of the corps who had completed conventional Ohka training were sent to the Shiga Flying Corps to undergo training for the Type-43B turbojet-propelled Ohka. Others were assigned to Type-22 Ohka planes or to a new special steel attack plane (KI-115) developed by the Army if the Type-22 Ohkas were not ready in time. Division Leader Hayashi was transferred to the Tornado Corps, as an Ohka Type-11 instructor.

On July 10, the American invasion fleet, which had been undergoing preparation in Leyte Gulf, began launching a new series of airborne attacks against the Tokyo area. On July 14 and 15, American carrier-based planes sank most of the ferryboats that connected the northernmost island of Hokkaido with the main island of Honshu. Meanwhile, American warships bombarded the steel factories in Muroran and Kamaishi. On July 17 and 18, the Tokyo district was hit once again.

American planes based on Iwo Jima Island and Okinawa coordinated their efforts with the carrier-based planes, and now had almost complete control of the skies over Japan. A raid on Misawa Air Base in northern Honshu resulted in the destruction of most of the 25 Bettys being adapted for Operation Ken (Sword), which was to be a surprise attack on the American-controlled Mariana Base by airborne troops. Consequently, the launching of the surprise attack was postponed for nearly a month.

While this was going on, the army and navy departments of the military headquarters agreed to combine their remaining forces into a fleet consisting of approximately 5,000 planes, to be used primarily in suicide missions against the expected American invasion fleet. A total of 230 Ohka planes (170 Type-11 and 60 Type-22) were to be included in the attack force—90 of them deployed in Kyushu and Shikoku, 40 in the Kinki area, 20 in the Chubu area, and 80 in the Kanto area. The number of land-based catapults for launching Type-43B turbojet-propelled Ohka planes, due to come on line in September, was increased to between 50 and 60 and were to be located from the Boso to the Kii peninsulas, along the Pacific coast.

On the morning of July 27, Radio San Francisco announced the Potsdam Declaration, which called for the unconditional surrender of Japan, to be followed by military occupation, demilitarization, and the loss of all overseas territories. The call for Japan's unconditional surrender brought a burst of derisive laughter from the Fifth Naval Aviation Fleet's Vice-Admiral Ugaki. "We should be the ones calling for the unconditional surrender of the United States, Great Britain, and China!" he shouted.

But Ugaki's boast was hollow. The size and frequency of American air raids against the home islands increased dramatically. On July 28, a total of 3,200 planes carried out successive raids on targets in Honshu. American warships standing offshore began bombarding coastal cities for the first time. In the meantime, the Fifth Naval Aviation Fleet continued its hasty withdrawal from southern Kyushu, bringing harsh criticism from local residents, who felt they were being abandoned to the enemy and would have to suffer the brunt of the coming American invasion.

Bad weather struck the area on August 2, further delaying the move by staff members of the Fifth Naval Aviation Fleet. Vice-Admiral Ugaki's headquarters were moved to Oita Base. Because of the threatening typhoon, Ugaki had to travel by car and train and was delayed several hours by air raids. His new headquarters outside the rubbled city of Oita was a mosquito- and flea-infested tunnel.

The Thunder Gods Corps had completed its redeployment, but was unable to continue its training programs because of continuous enemy air raids and lack of fuel. The men spent their time swimming, fishing, and visiting local tourist attractions.

Following a decision by the Army Flying Corps to use suicide troops in Operation Ken, several planes from the Thunder Gods' Betty Squadron were sent to Chitose in Hokkaido, where their crews joined navy land combat troops and army airborne troops in nighttime exercises aimed at destroying B-29 bombers and setting fire to oil tanks and powder magazines. The execution of Operation Ken was scheduled for sometime between August 19 and 23, when the moon would be at its brightest.

Tests on the Ohka Type-22 were still being delayed by mechanical problems. The first aerial test ended before the mother plane got off the ground. The Ohka came loose from the remodeled Frances bomber while it was taxiing down the runway, and was seriously damaged. The Campini-type jet engine of the second test model vibrated so badly it could not be controlled, and quit completely when the speed was reduced. By August 1, six unsuccessful tests had been carried out.

The air raids and coastal shellings by the enemy continued virtually unopposed. Operation authorities insisted that the Ohka Type-22 be ready for its first drop test by August 12 despite the fact that the vibration problem had not been solved. They increasingly saw the Thunder Gods Corps and the other special-attack forces as Japan's last hope. A special unit was moved from Konoike Base to Mt. Hieizan, in order to man the Ohka Type-43B planes that were to be launched by catapult. The catapult was approaching completion. The unit of Thunder Gods pilots was billeted in the priests' quarters at the center. The device was to be tested from Mt. Hieizan before final adjustments were made.

A wooden model of the Ohka Type-43B was placed on the catapult cart on the mountain, and three tubes of gunpowder were ignited. There was an ear-shattering explosion that shocked the assembled Thunder Gods pilots, reminding them in a very graphic way of the fate that awaited them. The cart bearing the Ohka plane was propelled to near the end of the catapult by the blast. The necessary adjustments were determined and made.

The pilots then awaited the arrival of the training planes. As soon as the pilots had undergone one test flight, they were to be dispatched to different catapult sites around the country to wait for the beginning of Operation Ketsugo—the last defense of Japan. In preparation for their deaths, the pilots cut their hair and fingernails, and buried them beneath the main building of the temple where they were staying.

All of the catapult launch sites were on the Pacific Coast side of the islands. Fears began to rise that the American forces might also approach from the Japan Sea side. On August 5 the Naval General Staff hastily revised its plan, calling for the construction of catapults along Tsushima and Tsugaru straits on the west side of the island before continuing with new sites on the Pacific side. The plan called for 24 catapult sites to be constructed along the Tsushima Straits, with 360

Type-43B Ohkas and pilots to man them, and eight launch sites spread along the Tsugaru Straits, with 120 Ohkas and pilots assigned to them.

The turbojet Kikka plane, which was the key to the successful deployment of the Type-43B Ohka, was to undergo its first test flight at Kisarazu Base in Chiba Prefecture on August 7. The weather was good that morning, but at 10:20 A.M. some 40 American bombers came in over Sagami Bay and raided targets in the Kanagawa area for more than an hour. The air-raid alert was not lifted until well after noon, but it was decided to proceed with the test of the Kikka.

The radically new jet plane was wheeled out of its shelter at 1 P.M. and, with both sides of the runway lined by members of the Tornado Corps and various high-ranking officers, was given the "go" signal. The plane made a smooth takeoff, soared to 600 meters, circled to the north of the base and then landed. It was in the air for only 12 minutes, but the test had been successful and the Kikka was the first Japanese-made jet plane to fly. The assembled officers, crewmen, and other personnel jumped and danced with joy in celebration. A full test flight was scheduled for August 10.

At approximately 3:30 P.M., while the celebration was still going on, a message was received from military headquarters about an air raid that had taken place on Hiroshima. The fact that the announcement came directly from military headquarters meant that it was of special significance, since such announcements generally came from the local military district. The announcement said that a small number of B-29 bombers had raided Hiroshima and that a new type of bomb had been used, causing substantial damage. The message added that the incident was being investigated. Another message reported that the new bomb might have been an atom bomb. There had been some speculation about an A-bomb, but no one believed such a weapon would materialize during the war.

At midnight on August 9, Russian troops crossed the border into Manchuria in a surprise attack against Japan.

At 11 A.M. on the following day, a second A-bomb was dropped on Nagasaki.

American warships, which had not been seen in the area for more than a week, suddenly reappeared and began shelling targets in the Tokyo-Yokohama areas.

Vice-Admiral Ugaki, who had been appointed commander-in-chief of the Combined Naval Aviation Fleet, recognized the shelling as the beginning of the enemy's planned invasion of the home islands. On the morning of August 11, he received instructions from Navy General Headquarters to launch attacks immediately against the American ships off the main island of Honshu as well as against those still at berth in Okinawa. This meant the policy of preserving the remaining planes and pilots for use during the actual land invasion had been abandoned. Ugaki ordered six planes from the Thunder Gods' fighter-bomber squadron, laden with 500-kilogram bombs, to stand by on Kikaigashima Island to carry out a preliminary strike against U.S. ships in Okinawa ports.

That afternoon Ugaki received a copy of a message broadcast by San Francisco Radio that Japan had agreed to surrender on condition that the Emperor be retained.

Furious at this unexpected turn of events, Vice-Admiral Ugaki shouted at his aides, "Why didn't they consult with me, the com-mander-in-chief, before making such an important decision? This must have been plotted by a small group of people in the government—why surrender while we still have forces in reserve? I will never follow such shortsighted cowardice! I will not surrender! We will carry on guerrilla action throughout the nation and will not lose this war! The enemy will get tired and give up!"

More broadcasts followed, some of them covering on-the-scene celebrations in London and Honolulu at the prospect of the war ending in a matter of days. This made Ugaki even more furious.

Meanwhile, the Thunder Gods pilots on the tiny island of Kikaigashima who had been ordered to carry out an attack against American warships in Okinawa had not been kept informed about what was going on. They had been on the front line for two months, and only occasionally received word about the movement of enemy ships. When they did, the messages were often meaningless, because no one had thought to inform them of code changes. On one occasion a message they received placed the enemy fleet in the center of China. They did not know that Operation Kikusui had ended, that all forces at home were being deployed in the expectation of an invasion, or that Japan had apparently accepted the Potsdam Declaration.

Under the circumstances, then, they presumed that the order from the Fifth Naval Aviation Fleet to attack ships in Okinawa was part of Operation Kikusui. One of their planes had been destroyed during an air raid. This meant there were only five planes available for the mission, which they scheduled for August 13. Other lower-ranking navy personnel were also unaware of the movements to end the war and continued feverishly to prepare for battle.

The first full test of the Kikka jet plane, one day behind schedule, began on the morning of August 11. As the fully loaded plane taxied down the runway, test pilot Takaoka noticed that there was a directional defect in the booster rocket, but it was too late to stop. The plane overshot the runway, hit the side of a ditch, snapping off the landing gear, and crashed into the ocean.

At Konoike Base, the detaching test of the Type-22 Ohka continued. When the mother plane reached 4,000 meters, test pilot Hirano entered the Ohka, settled himself, gave the "ready" signal and turned on the rocket ignition. The Ohka began shaking savagely. "Hold it! Hold it! Don't drop the plane!" Hirano screamed, pressing the emergency button. It was later discovered that three of the four bolts holding the engine were cracked, but no other defects could be found. It was decided to make some general improvements in the plane and test it one more time on August 15. If it failed that test, it was to be junked.

On the same morning (August 12) Radio San Francisco predicted that the Allies would not accept Japan's demand that the imperial system be preserved as a condition of its surrender. Vice-Admiral Ugaki at Oita Base hoped that the news would quash the plot to surrender Japan to the enemy. He also suspected that the movement might have just been a trial balloon to see how the Americans would react. Under orders from the Navy General Headquarters, he continued preparations for the last-ditch defense of the country.

There was a flurry of broadcasts on August 13, urging Japan to surrender and avoid more bloodshed and destruction, but Ugaki ignored them. When he learned that the arrival of his successor, Vice-Admiral Ryunosuke Kusaka, had been delayed by air raids, Ugaki sent a telegram to the Navy Personnel Bureau virtually refusing to vacate his post. He was obsessed with the idea of defending Japan to the death.

On the same day, the five Thunder Gods fighter-bombers took off from Kikaigashima Island, headed for Okinawa. Shortly after the first group of three fighters-bombers were airborne, oil was seen leaking from the first plane, and the landing gear of the third plane had not properly closed. The two planes, escorted by the third plane in the squadron, dropped their bombs into the ocean and returned to base. The plane with the bad landing gear crash-landed and was damaged beyond repair.

At approximately 6:50 P.M. radio messages came in from the two other planes that had continued on toward Okinawa. They radioed that they were making their dives.

The three pilots who had returned stood on the coral beach and stared out at the surface of the sea glimmering in the moonlight. "We'll try again!" one of them said. But there were to be no more missions by the Thunder Gods Corps.

At Vice-Admiral Ugaki's headquarters in Oita, members of the Foreign News Section of the Communications Corps were manning their shortwave radios throughout the night, hoping for more news about the ending of the war. On the morning of August 14, the news about Japan's defeat and imminent surrender became more specific. It was reported that General Douglas MacArthur, supreme commander for the Allied Powers, would soon be arriving in Tokyo. Ugaki finally accepted the idea that Japan's surrender had been arranged without anyone having consulted him even once.

At approximately 10:30 A.M. some 200 B-29 bombers could be seen from Ugaki's headquarters, flying northward. A short while later it was reported that Iwakuni Air Base and other targets in the vicinity had been bombed. That evening the mayor of Oita called on Vice-Admiral Ugaki to talk about what they would do when the war ended, but Ugaki refused to make any commitments.

Later that night Navy General Headquarters sent a message to all installations in the islands, saying that an enemy landing was at hand and putting the entire country on alert. Ugaki did not believe that the enemy was actually preparing an invasion. He reasoned that the continuing attacks were meant to intimidate Japan into surrendering, and that there would be no invasion. Just before midnight on August 14, he received orders to cease all hostile actions against American forces on Okinawa and against Soviet forces in Manchuria.

Chapter 8

Just before daybreak on August 15, Vice-Admiral Ugaki, who had been awake all night, summoned the staff officer on duty and ordered him to have five Judy bombers prepared for an attack. Shortwave broadcasts that Ugaki had heard during the night had announced that the Emperor would make a radio address that day, declaring that Japan had accepted the Allies' terms of surrender.

The staff officer immediately informed Senior Staff Officer Takashi Miyazaki of the vice-admiral's order. Miyazaki quickly went to Ugaki and tried to get him to rescind the order. Other ranking officers were informed of Ugaki's order, including Chief of Staff Yokoi, who had been in bed with dengue fever, and the commander of the 12th Aviation Group, who had been Ugaki's classmate at the Naval College. They rushed to his office to try to dissuade him from taking such rash action. Ugaki listened to the pleading of his officers and friends with a quiet smile on his face. All he wanted, he said, was a place to kill himself.

As noon approached, a radio was placed on Ugaki's desk. He and all of his staff officers lined up in front of the desk and stood at attention. The commencement of the Emperor's broadcast was announced. The national anthem was played. Then the Emperor's high-pitched, lifeless voice was heard, frequently inaudible because of static, calling on the people of Japan to lay down their arms and "bear the unbearable."

Ugaki and his men experienced the most profound emotion of their lives. Tears flowed from their eyes. When the address ended, Ugaki went to his room. Chief of Staff Yokoi had given up on the possibility of changing Ugaki's mind. He ordered the planes readied, then drafted a written statement that said:

The Oita Unit of the 701st Flying Corps will attack enemy warships in Okinawa with five carrier dive-bombers. I shall lead the attack myself.

Signed: Commander-in-Chief of the Fifth Naval Aviation Fleet Naval Vice-Admiral Matome Ugaki

He took the statement to Vice-Admiral Ugaki for his signature. The vice-admiral then began to make the last entry in his diary. A short while later, saké was brought into the headquarters tunnel from the barracks outside, and farewell cups were passed around. The men drank and wished those who were about to die a better life in the other world. Ugaki had his staff cut his badge of rank from his uniform.

Three cars were used to drive Ugaki and his staff to the airfield. Senior Staff Officer Miyazaki asked the vice-admiral for permission to accompany him on the mission, but his request was refused and the vice-admiral rebuked him strongly. At the airfield 11 Judy dive-bombers were lined up on the runway instead of the five that Ugaki had ordered.

Ugaki faced the crewmen, who were lined up in front of their planes.

"Commander-in-Chief, we will accompany you!" shouted Lieutenant Tatsuo Nakatsuru, his face flushed with emotion.

Ugaki gazed at the men proudly. He nodded his head several times, then addressed the men, thanking them for their devotion to duty and country, and then added, "With the strong belief in the immortality of this divine land, I therefore order that you accompany me, although I feel it is a pity. Come with me!"

The crew shouted and rushed for their planes. Ugaki boarded Lieutenant Nakatsuru's plane and ordered the observer, Warrant Officer Endo, to get off and let him have his seat. Endo refused to leave the plane, but after a short argument he let Ugaki have his seat then squeezed himself onto the floor between the vice-admiral's legs. As the plane taxied down the runway Ugaki raised a dagger he had received from the late Admiral Isoroku Yamamoto, and waved it at the men lining the field. It was 5 P.M. when the plane lifted off.

At 8:24 P.M. a radio message came in from Ugaki's plane, saying "We have succeeded in making a surprise attack." That was the last word heard from the vice-admiral. Of the remaining ten planes, three were forced to make emergency landings because of mechanical problems and seven were never heard from again.

In the meantime, the statement signed by Vice-Admiral Ugaki had been sent to all air corps within the command. The commander-in-chief of the Navy General Headquarters, Ozawa, was furious when he heard of Ugaki's action. "It was wrong of him to take his men with him as companions to the other world, knowing the Imperial mandate through the Emperor's broadcast. If he wanted to commit suicide, he should have done it alone!"

Ugaki and the 16 men who accompanied him were refused the double posthumous promotions that were normally given to kamikaze pilots. Ugaki was not promoted at all. The 16 men who died with him received one-grade promotions.

In the Aeroplane Section of the Naval Aeronautical Research Laboratory, where the Ohka plane had been designed, Division Manager Yamana and his men had also gathered to hear the Emperor's broadcast. After the Emperor finished speaking, Yamana read a poem from the *Manyoshu*, an anthology compiled more than a thousand years before:

The Sun is setting on the beautiful clouds of the Sea God.
Tonight's moon will be very bright.

"The spiritual basis for the reconstruction of Japan lies in the purity of that poem," Yamana said, with tears in his eyes.

Miki, chief designer of the Ohka, was in the forefront of the group of men, his shaven head bowed low. He knew that just shaving his head was not penance enough for having designed the Ohka, even though he had acted under orders. He had already resolved to write down in detail the story of the design of the Ohka—for himself, not for anyone else—and then store it away and forget about it.

At the Yokosuka Flying Corps field, adjoining the NARL, Hirano had been preparing for the final test of the Type-22 Ohka. Now his mind was in such a state of confusion that he did not know what to do. He was angry that Japan had been defeated and was disturbed by the fact that he had survived when so many others had not. There was also a deep sense of relief that he no longer had to risk his life in the dangerous detaching test of the new Ohka.

At dawn that day several small Japanese aircraft had flown over the base and dropped leaflets calling on all the personnel on the base to fight to the death.

On the morning of August 15 at Kanoya, headquarters of the Thunder Gods Corps, 36 fighter-bombers laden with 250-kilogram bombs were being prepared for an attack. The pilots were readying themselves for their last flight, knowing that the order might be cancelled as it had been so often in the past. It was sheer coincidence that Reserve Lieutenant Kazuo Kayaki, commander of the group, was near a radio when the Emperor began to speak, otherwise he would not have known that the war had ended.

There had been rumors that Japan was going to accept the Potsdam Declaration, and he had been advised by the commander of the Kyushu Flying Corps that the war might end soon and to behave carefully. Now, despite the address by the Emperor, he did not believe that Japan had surrendered. Driven by anger and fierce fighting spirit, he was determined to fulfill his mission of crash-diving into the enemy. He tried several times to call the commander and vice-commander of the Thunder Gods Corps to get their approval, but he was unable to get through because of deterioration of the communications system. Finally he reached the headquarters of the 701st Flying Corps, and was told that Vice-Admiral Ugaki and 16 men from Oita were on their way to attack enemy ships in Okinawa.

Kayaki was shocked at this news, and presumed that Vice-Admiral Ugaki must have gone mad to make a suicide attack against the enemy just when the final battle for the home islands was about to take place. He summoned the other pilots who were on standby. "Today's attack has been suspended and is now scheduled for tomorrow. You are dismissed," he said.

The pilots began grumbling and arguing about taking off on their own, without waiting for orders. Kayaki became worried about what they might do and gave orders that none of them were to be allowed to leave the barracks.

At Komatsu Air Base the Emperor's broadcast was so garbled that it was impossible to understand what he said. Yunokawa, divisional officer of the Ohka Squadron, ran to a nearby private home to find out if the occupants had heard the Emperor's message more clearly. He imagined that it was a call for the entire nation to take up arms in the final struggle against the Allied invasion forces. When he heard that the Emperor had ordered everyone to lay down their arms and cease fighting, he was sorely disappointed. He returned to the base and summoned the other Ohka pilots.

"The Emperor's broadcast apparently means that the war has ended, but I don't know if it is some kind of a plot or actually was the

Emperor's decision. If it is true, what have we been fighting for at such an enormous cost? What about the blood shed by all of our friends and fellows?" His voice choked and he was unable to continue.

Adachi thought that the broadcast might be a declaration of war against Russia. He and Yunokawa made several attempts to reach Corps Commander Okamura at Matsuyama or Vice-Commander Iwaki at Tomitaka to find out exactly what was going on, but they could not get through. Yunokawa suggested that they send a telegram to Okamura, saying they would continue their training, in the conviction that the only way to protect the empire was to pursue the war.

Shortly after dawn on August 16, the squadron learned about Vice-Admiral Ugaki's death in a suicide mission against American forces in Okinawa. Yunokawa remembered that his former instructor, Lieutenant-Commander Hisashi Watanabe, was the son-in-law of Vice-Admiral Zenshiro Hoshina, chief of the Bureau of Military Affairs. He was in a nearby hospital, convalescing, and might have heard some news. He drove rapidly to the hospital at Yamashiro Spa to see Watanabe.

"Is it really true? Is the war over?" Yunokawa asked.

"It is true," Watanabe said. "I've received word from my father-in-law that the Emperor himself decided to end the war and that there was no plot by senior statesmen. He added that I should obey the Imperial mandate wholeheartedly, and not commit myself to anything rash. You should do the same."

At his official residence in Tokyo, Vice-Chief of Naval General Staff Onishi was writing a suicide note. Despite a strong reprimand from Minister of the Navy Yonai, Onishi had done everything he could to continue the suicide attacks against the enemy. He had even begged Prince Takamatsu to dissuade the Emperor from making the surrender broadcast.

"Even the Emperor sometimes makes foolish mistakes," Onishi said to Rear Admiral Sadatoshi Tomioka of the Naval General Staff.

On the night of August 14, Onishi went to see his close friend Kazuo Yatsugi, and said bluntly "It was not I who lost the war, but the Emperor."

Unable to prevent the Emperor from ending the war, Onishi knew that he was finished. Unwilling to do the same as Vice-Admiral Ugaki, who had ended his farewell message with "Long live the Emperor!" Onishi prayed: "To the spirits of the departed special-attack pilots, my heartfelt appreciation for our brave accomplishments. You have departed in the firm belief that we would win the final victory. However, your conviction failed to be realized. I apologize to your spirits and to your bereaved families with my own death."

At 3 A.M. on the morning of August 16, Vice-Admiral Onishi cut his stomach open in the time-honored harakiri ceremony. He was 54.

All during the day of August 16 and 17 the rumor spread throughout Kyushu, the southernmost of Japan's main islands, that the vanguard of the American invasion forces would land in the Hakata Bay area on August 18. The population was in total confusion.

Vice-Admiral Kusaka, who had been assigned to replace Ugaki before the Emperor made his broadcast, arrived at Oita not knowing that Ugaki had led 16 men on an unauthorized suicide attack against American ships in Okinawa. Kusaka immediately ordered all remaining military personnel in the district to abide by the Imperial edict and cease all hostile activity. But hundreds of the men, including Commander Saburo Nishimura, vice-commander of the Seikai Flying Corps, which was in charge of base missions, refused to accept the Emperor's mandate.

Nishimura had an oracle made at the famous Taihei Shrine, outside of Beppu, and took it to Kusaka, urging him to continue fighting. "The Imperial edict was a mistake," Nishimura insisted. "His Majesty is now repenting and will move the capital to Taihei Shrine in a few days. When that happens, a great navy leader will appear and take command of all ground, sea, and air forces around Kyushu to meet the enemy. The general I am talking about is none other than you, Vice-Admiral Kusaka!"

Commander Okamura, head of the Thunder Gods Corps and one of the men who had been a prime figure in promoting and implementing the concept of suicide missions against the enemy, along with Commander Genda, flew to the district headquarters at Omura and pressed Chief of Staff Yokoi to ignore the Imperial command. "If you accept this ignoble order to end the war, you have no right to call yourself chief of staff!" Okamura shouted.

The Imperial edict was especially galling to Okamura. He had personally ordered more than 40 percent of all the special suicide attacks, and he knew the souls of the young pilots who had sacrificed their lives, shouting *Banzai!* as they died, would not be able to rest in peace. He had repeatedly pledged to his men that he would follow them in death—a pledge that was not only personal but also represented the navy and the entire nation. Now this pledge was being ignored by the Emperor himself. The only way to reward the young souls of the dead was to fulfill the pledge and fight to the death.

On the tiny island of Kikaigashima the three surviving members of the Thunder Gods Fighter-Bomber Squadron finally picked up a radio message that the war had ended. The shock was so intense the three nearly went out of their minds with anger, desperation, and sadness at the loss of so many comrades. On the following morning, Reserve Sub-Lieutenant Kanae Okamoto, the ranking member of the group, ordered the other two petty officers, Matsubayashi and Hosozawa, to return to the headquarters of the Thunder Gods Corps at Kanoya, saying he would stay on Kikaigashima with the guard troops and maintenance crew until they were all relieved. "And Matsubayashi, since your plane is no longer in working order, you take mine," Okamoto added. The two young men refused to go without Okamoto.

"Don't be stupid!" Okamoto barked. "There is nothing more you can do here! Return to Kanoya immediately! That's an order!"

When the two Zero fighter planes were ready for takeoff, Okamoto said, "Be careful. If you encounter any enemy planes, just try to get away. And Matsubayashi, this plane has an oil leak, so you be especially careful!"

The two planes took off and circled the tiny island once before heading northward toward Kyushu. As they approached the island of Yakushima, Hosozawa noticed smoke beginning to stream out of Matsubayashi's plane. Before he had time to warn his friend, the plane burst into flames and began falling virtually straight down. It crashed into the water off the southeastern tip of the island and disintegrated into flying metal, fire, and spray.

At Komatsu Air Base, the members of the Thunder Gods Corps had received no news or orders since the Emperor's announcement. Rumors were flying and confusion was rife. Several of the pilots besieged Wing Commander Adachi in his room and insisted that the Imperial edict be ignored and the war continued.

"Don't do a damn thing until we receive official orders!" Adachi shouted at the men. "Now get the hell out of here! This will all be settled very soon!" But after the angry men left his room, Adachi admitted to himself that he had no idea of what was going to happen to them.

Senior Reserve Officer Hosokawa's uncle had arrived at the base and was pleading with him to leave the base and return home because his father was worried about him. His uncle continued pleading with Hosokawa for several hours, embarrassing him in front of his men. Finally, Hosokawa got his uncle to agree to go to an inn in Katayamazu Spa and wait for him. But while escorting his uncle to the train station, he met his father walking up the road toward the base with a knapsack on his back. After a brief reunion with his father, Hosokawa managed to get both his father and uncle to agree to go to the spa and wait until he could find out what was going to happen. Back on base, Hosokawa was approached by a young orderly who was pale with fright. "Sub-Lieutenant Hosokawa," he said in great agitation, "I've just been told by a newspaperman that under the enemy occupation all officers will be shot and all petty officers will be castrated and sent to the southern islands as slaves! What shall we do?"

Hosokawa did his best to reassure the young soldier.

Lieutenant Yunokawa called in a reserve officer who had majored in law and asked him for a legal definition of the end of the war. The officer replied that the ending of the war was merely a truce and that Japan had not yet officially surrendered. With this in mind, Yunokawa made up his mind to rally the men and attack any American forces that landed in the area, capturing them if possible but killing them if they resisted. He assembled the Ohka pilots in the main building of the Korin Temple, and asked them to express their views individually. The squadron was divided into three factions: those who wanted to continue the war immediately without waiting for orders; those who preferred to wait for further developments; and those who said they would abide by the Emperor's order to stop fighting. The men argued loudly. Yunokawa knew there was no way he could get them to agree to his plan and gave up.

In Tokyo, the Suzuki cabinet resigned on August 15, and the new interim Prince Higashikuni cabinet was formed to work out concrete measures for ending the war. Admiral Toyoda, chief of the Naval General Staff, ordered all naval units to cease all hostile activity, and sent Vice-Admiral Asazo Kikuchi, vice-chief of staff of the Combined Fleet, to Oita Base to explain the circumstances of the Emperor's decision to end the war. But Kikuchi did not fare so well at Oita. He was bombarded by questions and accusations. Many of the officers expressed vehement disapproval of the Potsdam Declaration, which they said would force Japan to change its national polity. Others insisted that the Emperor had not made the broadcast of his own free will.

Finally, Vice-Admiral Kusaka, commander-in-chief of the Fifth Naval Aviation Fleet, stepped in to calm the shouting officers. "It doesn't do any good to yell at Vice-Admiral Kikuchi. If you are still not convinced that the Emperor's actions were legitimate, Chief of Staff Yokoi himself can go to Tokyo to learn the facts!"

The men then agreed that the Fifth Naval Aviation Fleet would defer its decision on whether or not to accept the Potsdam Declaration until Yokoi had ascertained the facts. Yokoi and Kikuchi left for Tokyo on August 18.

On that same day, Vice-Admiral Kusaka ordered all commanding officers and executives to report to Fifth Naval Aviation Fleet Headquarters at Oita by noon the following day. The order caused considerable dissension among the men at Komatsu because it meant that only Adachi as the commanding officer was to go to Oita. Rumors had spread that Koreans in the area were going to start riots. Yunokawa insisted that he should be allowed to go to Oita with Adachi. He desperately wanted to hear with his own ears what was really going on so that he could make up his mind about what to do.

At Konoike Air Base, Special Service Sub-Lieutenant Ota, the man who had initiated the Ohka program, was also tormented with concern about what was happening and what he should do. Since stories about him had appeared in the newspapers and he had become a famous figure, he had been living high and fast. All that ended with the Emperor's announcement that the war was over. The only thing he had left was the terrible guilt of having sent hundreds of young men to die in exploding balls of fire for nothing. He now began to fear that he might be charged with murder.

Ota had read an article about the Potsdam Declaration which declared that war criminals would be severely punished. He did not know exactly what was meant by "war criminals," and the thought that he might be included obsessed him. On August 18, the torment in his soul was so overpowering that he could no longer eat. He wrote a suicide letter and, just after noon, made his way to the airfield. There he gave the letter to a member of the base corps division. Waiting until he was alone, he climbed into a Zero-type training plane, started it, and began taxiing awkwardly down the runway. He was not a pilot, but as a veteran air navigator he knew enough to get the plane off the ground. In the meantime the letter had been delivered to one of the corps' reserve officers in the headquarters building. The officer opened it immediately. "What the hell! That idiot Ota says he is going to dive into the Pacific Ocean!" he exclaimed.

Okamoto, the corps wing commander, grabbed a pair of binoculars and rushed outside. He caught a glimpse of Ota's plane disappearing over the northeastern horizon. A search of the waters in the area was launched immediately, but no trace of Ota or his plane was found. He was listed as killed in a training accident, and his name was erased from his family register.

When Hayashi, the former division officer of an Ohka squadron who had been asked by the notorious Commander Nonaka to find some way to end the kamikaze program, heard about Ota's death, he pitied him, but the feeling was shallow and passed quickly. Hayashi was no longer able to feel anything deeply. Everything had become meaningless to him. Unlike most of the surviving members of the Thunder Gods Corps, he had not been able to shed a tear even when listening to the Emperor announce Japan's surrender.

When the ranking officers of the Naval Flying Corps gathered at Oita in response to Vice-Admiral Kusaka's order, there were several junior officers, in addition to Yunokawa, in the group. The Thunder Gods Corps was represented by Okamura, Iwaki, Adachi, Nakajima, Yunokawa, and Kayaki. Everyone noticed how exhausted Okamura looked.

Kusaka prepared for the meeting with the officers by changing to fresh clothing, having already resigned himself to being killed or taking his own life once the meeting was over. Just as he was about to leave for the meeting hall, Chief of Staff Yokoi returned from Tokyo. Walking to the conference room together, Kusaka told Yokoi to tell the assembled officers everything he had learned in Tokyo.

The conference room was filled with tension and excitement. The officers were dressed in their dress uniforms with swords and pistols dangling at their sides. Many of them stared at Kusaka and Yokoi with hostile eyes as the two walked into the room. Their hands were on their weapons.

Yokoi went directly to the podium, greeted the officers, and began his report. "The Navy insists on continuing the war, but the Emperor is remaining firm in his resolution that the war end. Even Prince Takamatsu's efforts to dissuade the Emperor failed. At a meeting on August 14 to discuss the question of ending the war, no consensus could be reached. It was at this time that the Emperor stepped in and made the Imperial decision that the war should be concluded immediately. And that has resulted in the present situation."

Yokoi's tone of voice suggested that he, too, was unhappy with the Emperor's decision to end the war, and when he stopped talking many of the officers began shouting, "Continue the war! The decisive battle should be on Japan proper!"

Yokoi held up his hands. "Wait! I'm not finished !" he shouted. He then began to read aloud the Emperor's decision, which was announced at the Imperial conference on August 14. ". . . so please agree with me," the Emperor said. "Issue an Imperial edict to the population. I am fully aware that it will not be easy to control the Army and the Navy. So issue the Imperial edict to them as well so they may understand my feelings. I will broadcast the announcement if that is necessary. I will do whatever is necessary. . . ."

By the time Yokoi finished reading the transcript, many of the officers in the room were crying.

Vice-Admiral Kusaka immediately went to the podium. "As your commander-in-chief, I came to Kyushu with the firm intention of dying with all of you. However, whether we fight or not is absolutely subject to the Imperial mandate. If the Emperor says stop fighting, I must do my utmost to bring the war to an end. I hope you will understand and cooperate. At the same time, I know some of you feel differently. But I will have my own way as long as I live. If you disagree with that, kill me before you take any action! I'm ready. Do it immediately!"

Kusaka then sat down on a couch and closed his eyes.

The men who wanted to continue the war were torn between their desire and their duty to obey the Imperial mandate. The contradiction in their feelings was more than they could bear. Sobbing turned into wailing.

Yunokawa did not bother to wipe away his tears. He let them flow. They were not tears of sorrow or repentance. They were tears for all of his pent-up feelings; they were tears for the divine Empire of Japan, for all Japanese then and before.

The higher-ranking officers began filing out of the room. Kusaka remained on the couch with his arms crossed, watching the men leave the room. Yunokawa finally rose to his feet and headed for the door, saluting Kusaka as he approached him.

Kusaka spoke. "Whatever happens, do not act blindly or in haste. Be as patient as you can. Hard times are waiting for all of us, but everything is up to you young people. Do your best!"

Suddenly, Yunokawa understood. "Commander, I have been over-wrought with excitement!" he cried. "I swear I will see to it that the members of my squadron obey your wishes!"

From the conference room, Yunokawa sought out Okamura and Iwaki, the two top officers in the Thunder Gods Corps, for whom he had considerable respect. The parting with Iwaki was particularly hard, as he had served as his assistant at Tomitaka.

"Vice-Commander, what do you plan to do?" he asked.

"I don't know," Iwaki said in a resigned voice. "Probably farming."

On August 20, the commander-in-chief of the Navy General Head-quarters issued a long series of instructions to all military personnel, em-phasizing that the ending of the war had been decided by the Emperor and detailing how they were to behave in the days and months ahead.

On August 21, a party of Japanese military envoys who had been sum-moned to the Manila Headquarters of General Douglas MacArthur returned to Tokyo and reported that the first American forces would ar-rive at Atsugi Air Base southwest of Tokyo on August 26. The navy minister ordered all commanders to demobilize all military units under their command.

Meanwhile, at Atsugi Air Base, Captain Yasuna Ozono and a group of junior officers insisted on continuing the war on their own. But Ozono suddenly suffered a severe malarial relapse and was hospi-talized. Their leader gone, the group of dissidents fell apart. Rumors began flying that the elite Thunder Gods Corps was going to take over Atsugi Air Base and thwart the attempts of the American forces to land there. It was also rumored that the Allied powers intended to take special punitive action against the Thunder Gods Corps because of the extraordinary destruction and death the corps had rained upon the Allied forces. On August 22, the commander-in-chief of the Fifth Naval Aviation Fleet quickly ordered that the Thunder Gods Corps be disbanded immediately and that all equipment and documents relating to the corps be destroyed.

At Komatsu Air Base, Wing Commander Adachi called the Ohka and mother plane pilots together and announced that both squadrons were demobilized and that the men were to return to their homes as quickly as possible. Officers were issued 3,300 yen; petty officers received 2,800 yen. Betty planes were designated to take the men to the airfield nearest their homes the following morning. All their pistols were col-lected, then dumped into a nearby lake. All propellers were removed from the remaining planes.

That night a farewell ceremony was held. Hosokawa had each one of the members sign his name in a notebook. All of the members pledged that they would meet at Yasukuni Shrine in Tokyo at 10 A.M. on March 21, 1948, the anniversary of the annihilation of the Nonaka squadron.

Back in his room after the ceremony, Higher Flight Petty Officer Ichikawa, the man who had been one of the most reluctant of the Thunder Gods, lay down on his bunk, his mind awhirl with memories of the past year. He thought of the riot at Kanoya and of his friend Tamura who had died in the fourth Ohka attack. He had survived, but he was still not able to feel that he was actually alive. His pledge to die "as a falling cherry blossom" weighed heavily on him. He took out a notebook in which he had recorded his thoughts during the war years, and wrote "Farewell." He then added: "Farewell to Victory! Farewell to the Efforts for Victory! Farewell to the Achievement of Defeat!" He then closed the notebook.

Early on the morning of August 23, the roar of engines echoed throughout Komatsu Base. One after the other, the Bettys carrying the Thunder Gods away from the war, away from their lives as "cherry blossoms" subject to the winds of war, soared into the bright, fair sky. Lieutenant-Commander Adachi and several remaining officers stood in front of the headquarters building, the gas fumes strong in their nostrils, watching until the last plane was out of sight.

At Matsuyama Air Base, Okamura, commander of the Thunder Gods Corps, was burning documents. On returning from the meeting with Kusaka and Yokoi at Oita, he had assembled the members of the corps stationed at the base and announced, "We shall abide by the Imperial mandate. Hereafter, be prudent in all you say and do!" Afterward, when anyone questioned him, he gave them all the same answer: "It is the Imperial mandate."

When the order came down to disband the corps, Okamura made the announcement as brief as possible. He then added, "Everything that we were, everything that we have done, is now history!" This, more than anything else he could have said, impressed the members of the corps and helped them accept what was then happening to them.

Okamura continued his burning. The orders that had sent so many men to their deaths went into the flames. The battle reports that he had compiled from radio messages went into the flames. At the end, he threw a large batch of letters into the leaping flames. One of them was addressed to Vice-Admiral Takijiro Onishi.

Two years and seven months later, on March 21, 1948, 30 former Ohka members kept the rendezvous at Yasukuni Shrine. Having lost its official status and government support, the shrine had been neglected since the end of the war. The grounds were overgrown with weeds. Only a few other people were there.

The cherry trees lining the approaches to the shrine were still alive, however. Their buds were bulging and would soon blossom. The ex-Thunder Gods greeted each other quietly, then sat around and talked. One of the men mentioned that he had seen Ota, the man who was responsible for the creation of the Thunder Gods Corps and who was supposed to have died when he crashed his plane into the sea. Several of the other men immediately spoke up and said they, too, had been visited by Ota. One of the men said he had loaned Ota money, which he had not repaid. The men felt strangely uncomfortable talking about Ota, and the subject was soon changed. The talking continued until the men had to leave, promising to meet again the following year.

On July 13, 1948, Commander Okamura committed suicide by throwing himself in front of a train near Mobara in Chiba Prefecture. There was no report of his death in either local or national newspapers. He left no suicide note.

In 1952, a year after the working out of the San Francisco Peace Treaty, the Association of Former Thunder Gods Corps Members donated four cherry trees to Yasukuni Shrine. The trees were designated "Thunder Gods Cherry Trees."

Every year around March 21 the Thunder Gods Cherry Trees bloom, as if in anticipation of the annual gathering of the cherry blossoms who survived.

Epilogue

by Hatsuho Naito

Why and how did Japan's Imperial Navy plan and implement the notorious "special (suicide) attacks" against American and other Allied forces during the closing period of World War II? When asked this question, many of the former Imperial Navy officials who ordered such attacks respond: "I myself was opposed to suicide missions, but given our desperate situation near the end of the war, there was nothing else we Japanese could do."

Those who make such excuses are unanimous in blaming one individual for originating the merciless scheme. None would admit that there was any organized involvement by high-level naval personnel. It is most unlikely, however, that such a massive operation could have been the result of the actions of one individual. One person may have originated the idea, but there was, of course, massive involvement by the navy in implementing the suicide attacks. The navy accepted the suggestion and organized the program with inordinate zeal. The plan was organized so rapidly, in fact, that one wonders if there might have been a hidden scenario among the highest naval authorities.

This casts doubt on whether the Ohka was really invented by Ota. When he ignored the deeply ingrained navy chain of command and went directly to Tokyo Imperial University's Aerial Research Department, the department spared neither time nor money in developing the design for the flying bomb. It is strange that a respected public institution would react so promptly and positively to a request made by a low-ranking Navy officer who did not come to them through regular channels.

By the time Ota appeared with the Ohka plan, the Imperial Navy was already working on submarines and surface vessels that were to be used in "body-crash" missions, but with evacuation procedures designed to save the lives of the crews. There was some hesitancy when it came to developing the Ohka plane because it was designed for the pilot to die in the crash. Navy leaders were afraid that deliberate suicide missions carried out by navy personnel would undermine the foundation of the Supreme Command.

There is the possibility that Ota presented the Navy leaders with a way out of this dilemma. If the aerial suicide attack scheme were proposed by zealous petty officers, the naval authorities may have rationalized that their responsibility would be minimized.

If this is true, Ota was little more than a puppet. The wire-pullers secretly introduced him to the university's Aerial Research Department in order to make sure the scheme would be accepted and move smoothly through the navy's decision-making process.

Whatever the truth, it is certain that high-ranking navy authorities made the financial arrangements for testing the Ohka plane at the Aerial Research Department—a belief shared by many other war historians. If the secret wire-pullers could be identified, it would be possible to uncover details about the first fighter-bomber suicide attacks in the Philippines before the appearance of the manned bombs, and how the Navy got so involved in suicide missions so quickly.

Although there are several "candidates" who are strongly suspected of having been responsible for committing the Imperial Navy to this fateful course of action, most of them are dead, and those who remain alive are not talking. Unfortunately, Professor Taichiro Ogawa of Tokyo Imperial University's Aerial Research Department, who would have known the truth, is among those who died a long time ago.

There is one other person who may know the truth and who may still be alive, and that is Ota himself. Ota stole a plane and took off from Konoike Air Base on August 18, 1945, three days after the war ended, saying he was going to carry out a suicide attack against the enemy. His plane disappeared over the horizon and was never found, but in November of that year Ota showed up at a village near Konoike.

Residents of the village knew Ota well from his glory days at the base. According to the villagers, Ota landed his plane at sea and was picked up by a passing fishing boat. When one of the village elders advised Ota to report his survival to the proper authorities he refused, saying he was afraid he would be arrested as a war criminal.

Ota had been very friendly toward the villagers during the time the Thunder Gods were training at Konoike, often bringing them special foods. Now they respected his wish to remain in hiding. One of the farmers allowed Ota to set up housekeeping in his barn. Another farmer registered Ota under the name of Kaoru Yokoyama in order to get him a residence certificate needed to obtain a rice allotment.

Thus Ota started a new life under a false name, living in a barn owned by a relative of the village head, working in the fields and with the cattle along with the rest of the villagers. Sometimes he went on trips from the village but always returned in a few days. In 1947 his absences became longer, and on one occasion he was gone for several months.

When he returned to the village that time, his face was roughed up. He had obviously been fighting. "I plan to help Chiang Kai-shek in Taiwan," he explained. "Many former navy officers have already gathered there."

Ota then said he had developed a new invention to help the villagers ease the clothing shortage that existed in Japan at that time. "It is an unweaving device," he said. "You unweave your fish nets and use them to make clothing. It will be an ideal side job for your wives." The villagers were wise enough not to follow this suggestion. A report from another source said that Ota was involved in black marketeering in Hokkaido when he was away from the village, which could account for the condition of his face.

Soon after his unweaving invention was turned down by the villagers, Ota left and did not return. It was sometime after this that he began to visit his former colleagues in the Thunder Gods Corps to borrow money from them. None of the money was returned.

After Ota had obtained money from nearly half of the surviving members of the Thunder Gods Corps, one of them remarked to him, "I suppose your family is receiving a pension from the government since you were listed as killed in the war, but since you are alive it is actually an act of fraud, isn't it?" He was not seen again by any of his former colleagues. This was around 1949.

Another report says that a woman believed to have been Ota's wife, along with a little girl, visited the village where he had previously lived and asked numerous detailed questions about his disappearance.

There is some possibility that Ota is still alive. War historians have tried several times to find him through the mass media. The only result was that a woman believed to be his daughter came forward and said she also would like to find him. She said his wife had died years earlier.

There are still occasional efforts to find Ota. If found, he is sure to be welcomed by the mass media as a "surviving hero" and by war historians as the link to the unknown history of Japan's Thunder Gods Corps.

While Ota's presence might help uncover some of the secrets of the hidden scenario, it would not contribute to pinpointing responsibility for this merciless phase of the war. In the Imperial Navy at that time, as in the whole Japanese Empire, ultimate responsibility went around and around and resided nowhere.

Even Emperor Hirohito, at the top of the whole system, was not charged with any responsibility. Once a program was started, the system had no way of stopping it. Instead, it converted individual insanity to organized insanity.

It must be pointed out, however, that the young men who were actually called on to make the mass suicide attacks had nothing to do with the organized insanity. They experienced terrors and trauma that are beyond the imagination of anyone else. I do not believe that any of them shouted "Long Live the Emperor!" as they dived their bomb-filled planes into the enemy.

They agreed to die for the sake of their families and their relatives in the firm belief that their death would contribute to their well-being. Who developed the Ohka plane mattered very little to the Thunder Gods. What is more, none of the pilots are known to have said anything critical to or about Ota when he was living with them at Konoike Air Base. Their minds were filled with thoughts of love and affection for their families.

The pilots knew, of course, that the spirits of those who died in the war were worshipped at Yasukuni Shrine but they did not choose to die to become "gods."

These same sentiments are shared by the surviving members of the Thunder Gods Corps who gather at Yasukuni Shrine every year on March 21, the day the first Ohka attack was made. They gather there not because they believe in Shinto, the "Way of the Gods." Some of them are Buddhists; some are Christians; others are atheists. They gather there because the last thing their dead comrades said to them was, "I will be waiting for you at Yasukuni Shrine."

They gather there to recall their youth, when they innocently believed that the sacrifice of their lives would make a difference. Their comrades, without a shred of flesh or bone remaining, can never return. If there is such a thing as spirit, their spirits might be wandering Yasukuni Shrine with nowhere else to go.

The survivors visit the shrine to talk to the spirits of their dead friends, feeling indebted to them for having survived. The parents of dead Thunder Gods also visit the shrine on this day.

Neither the surviving Thunder Gods, nor the families of those who died, ever directly criticize the Imperial Navy's suicide-attack program. The way they separate their pain and sorrow from their anger at the authorities who were responsible for the program is sometimes irritating to other people. It is as though they believe that the only way to comfort the spirits of the dead is to recall the days when they all willingly accepted the suicide missions. They believe that anything said today about the kamikaze attacks is irrelevant because things have changed so much. But from any perspective, the special suicide attacks during World War II were a sad milestone in Japanese history.

We war historians and writers must try to reveal more than the accepted version of Japan's history shows. The enigma of Japan is partly a result of an unwillingness to scrutinize unpleasant facts. It is our duty as historians to revive half-forgotten memories, no matter how unpalatable, in order to apply to the present that which was learned in the past.

Although I take full responsibility for the selection and interpretation of data and testimony in *Thunder Gods*, I would like to acknowledge those persons and institutions that served as my primary sources.

Data regarding the tactics used in the deployment of the Ohka planes was taken from documents that are now part of the archives of the Military History Division of the Japanese Defense Agency Research Institute. These documents were confiscated by the American armed forces following the end of World War II in 1945, but were later returned to Japan.

The story of the formation and operation of the Thunder Gods Corps is based on copious notes taken by Motoji Ichikawa, who was the leader of the Konoike fracas and a key figure in the corps. I met Ichikawa shortly before his death in 1980. This was also just before the aerial survey company which he had been managing in Tokyo went bankrupt. He had sent his wife back to his home province, and was living alone in a shabby room, obviously in very poor health.

Gathering his strength, Ichikawa told me that he had been intending to write the story of the Thunder Gods. He had not much time left, however, and asked me to write the story instead of him. The several volumes of notes and reference materials that Ichikawa gave me are now kept in the office of the Thunder Gods Association in Tokyo.

As for the technical aspects of the Ohka, I received full cooperation from Tadanao Miki, its chief designer. Miki had been greatly troubled by his role in the development of the notorious suicide weapon, and for years after the war refused to release his documents for publication. His justification was that he would like to see the records of the development of the Ohka erased from the nation's history, for the honor of the naval aviation technicians, as well as everyone else in the Thunder Gods Corps.

In 1955, however, Miki saw an American film called *Test Pilot*, a documentary about the U.S. Air Force's experimental X1 Series rocket. The X1 was a small craft suspended below the bomb bay of a B-29. In the film, the American test pilot was shown climbing into the X1 through a hatch in the floor of the mother craft, and then disengaging from the B-29 by pressing a detach button—exactly the same process used to get the Ohka airborne and then detach it once the mother craft was at the scheduled altitude. These X1 Series tests were of great significance, because they were the first aviation tests in history to break the sound barrier.

It occurred to Miki that the American developers of the X1 rocket plane had probably had access to the Ohka archives while they were in the U.S., an impression tacitly confirmed by an American naval commander involved in special attack weapons research. Eventually Miki reversed his position regarding the development of the Ohka suicide plane, apparently believing that shedding light on its history might be of technological value. In 1973 and 1974 he published the account of the research and work on the Ohka in an aviation magazine. I cannot overemphasize the value of Mr. Miki's cooperation.

Thanks are also due to Boye De Mente for his editing and advice, to Mayumi Ichikawa for the translation, and, last but not by any means least, to Prue Moodie and Shigeyoshi Suzuki, my editors at Kodansha International.

Index

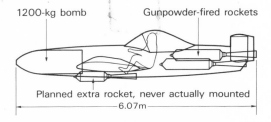

1200-kg bomb   Gunpowder-fired rockets

Planned extra rocket, never actually mounted
6.07m

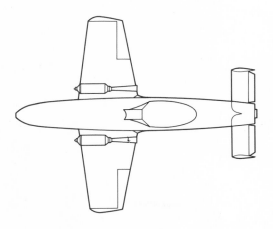

5.12m

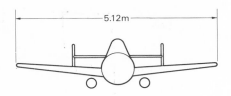

Ohka Type-11